Statements	Dialects[b]	Your System[c]	Examples	Pages
REM	1 2 3 4		REM Exam Averaging Program	18
RESTORE	1 2 3 4		RESTORE	32
RETURN	1 2 3 4		RETURN	92
STOP	1 2 3 4		STOP	93
WEND	4		See WHILE/WEND	77

WHILE/NEXT	3		WHILE J < N
			    PRINT "J = "; J
			    LET J = J + 1
			NEXT
				77

WHILE/WEND	4		WHILE J < N
			    PRINT "J = "; J
			    LET J = J + 1
			WEND
				77

WRITE #	4		WRITE #1, SCORE	181

(Use this space to add additional statements of interest for your system)

D1363633

---

[a]*Note 1:* The reserved words (keywords) in statements may not be used as variable names.
  Note 2: Statements must be appropriately delimited or separated from surrounding matter by spaces or other
  special characters allowed by the syntax; otherwise, BASIC will not recognize the reserved words.

[b]1 = Minimal BASIC
  2 = ANS BASIC or True BASIC
  3 = VAX-11 BASIC
  4 = Microsoft BASIC on the IBM PC

[c]Try to get a listing of the statements that apply to your system. Then place a check in this column for each
  statement that's the same on your system.

WADSWORTH SERIES IN COMPUTER INFORMATION SYSTEMS

Ageloff and Mojena Applied Structured BASIC
Ageloff and Mojena Essentials of Structured BASIC
Amsbury Data Structures: From Arrays to Priority Queues
Athappilly Programming and Problem Solving with VAX-11 BASIC
Brown From Pascal to C: An Introduction to the C Programming Language
Clarke and Prins Contemporary Systems Analysis and Design
Duffy Four Software Tools
Duffy Software Tool Casebook
Lombardi The Microcomputer Handbook
Molluzo Structured Cobol Programming
Rob Big Blue BASIC: Programming the IBM PC and Compatibles
Rob IBM PC BASIC
Rob Introduction to Microcomputer Programming
Rob Programming with dBASE II and dBASE III
Senn Information Systems in Management, 3rd edition
Texel Introductory Ada: Packages for Programming
Vasta Understanding Data Base Management Systems

Essentials of Structured BASIC

ROY AGELOFF
University of Rhode Island

RICHARD MOJENA
University of Rhode Island

Wadsworth Publishing Company
Belmont, California
A Division of Wadsworth, Inc.

To Hilda and Shana, with love   RA

**To Al Simone, for planting and
nurturing the text seed**   RM

Data Processing Editor: Frank Ruggirello
Editorial Assistant: Reita Kinsman
Production Editor: Harold Humphrey
Managing Designer: MaryEllen Podgorski
Print Buyer: Karen Hunt
Art Editor: Marta Kongsle
Art Production: Alan Noyes, Willa Bower, Susan Breitbard,
Joan Carol, Marilyn Krieger, Salinda Tyson
Compositor: Graphic Typesetting Service
Cover: MaryEllen Podgorski

Printed in the United States of America
3 4 5 6 7 8 9 10   91 90 89 88

ISBN 0-534-06810-3

Library of Congress Cataloging-in-Publication Data

Ageloff, Roy, 1943–
    Essentials of structured BASIC.

    (Wadsworth series in computer information systems)
    Includes index.
    1. BASIC (Computer program language) 2. Structured
programming. I. Mojena, Richard. II. Title.
III. Series.
QA76.73.B3A374 1987   005.13′3   86–9067
ISBN 0-534-06810-3

Preface

This textbook is designed for a first, short course in BASIC programming. No prerequisites are required, other than a willingness to develop problem-solving skills coupled with patience and endurance. (Learning a computer language takes time, practice, and effort.)

The combination of features described below distinguishes this book from others in the field.

Treatment of Dialects. The nonstandardization of BASIC raises major presentation problems in any textbook that is not machine/dialect specific. Yet, there are now enough similarities across machines/dialects that certain generic treatments make sense. For example, we can generically classify IF-type statements as traditional IF/THEN, enhanced IF/THEN, single-line IF/THEN/ELSE, and multiline IF/THEN/ELSE. Whenever major differences appear (as in WHILE and multiline IF/THEN/ELSE implementations), we use a table that shows the following four dialects: *Minimal BASIC* (the earlier ANS version), *ANS BASIC* (the currently proposed standard), *VAX-11 BASIC*, and *Microsoft BASIC* (on the IBM PC). ANS BASIC implementations use the *TRUE BASIC* compiler. For the most part, dialect-specific material is restricted to these clearly differentiated tables, so as to minimize student confusion. Moreover, each table has a section for the student's own dialect/machine, if different from those illustrated.

Structured Programming. Structured programming concepts are adhered to throughout the book. All programs strictly use defined control structures (sequence, selection, repetition). Both Minimal-BASIC and structured-statement versions are illustrated. GOTO-less programming is encouraged whenever it's possible in a given dialect.

Top-down Design. Stepwise refinement is introduced and motivated at a point (Chapter 3) where programs start getting more elaborate. Other top-down design procedures like top-down execution and top-down structured programming are discussed at strategic points.

Modular Programming.   Modular programs are discussed in Chapter 6 and used from that point forward when appropriate. This topic immediately follows decision and loop structures, to emphasize its place as a top-down/ structured programming tool. The traditional placement of modular programs after arrays is discarded in favor of this current design emphasis.

Design and Style.   Program design and style are emphasized throughout in keeping with the current (and future) emphases on both reducing software development/maintenance costs and improving the user interface. Each chapter ends with a *Pointers* section that includes the following two subsections: *Design and Style* and *Common Errors*.

Modular Chapters.   The five modules at the end of the text grant the instructor flexibility in choice and sequencing of topics. The earliest assignments of modular chapters are:

Module		Can be assigned anytime after Chapter
A	Running BASIC Programs	1
B	Debugging Programs	2
C	Built-In Functions	3
D	PRINT USING Statement and Formatted Output	2
E	External Data Files	5

No one module depends on any other, which adds even greater flexibility to selection and sequence.

Interactive Programming.   Design issues affecting the user interface in interactive applications are discussed throughout. Menus, screen design, and input error trapping are treated where appropriate.

Flowcharts and Pseudocode.   Both flowcharts and pseudocode (program design language) are illustrated. Flowcharts are deemphasized, however, in keeping with their reduced use within commercial environments and their misuse from a "structured" point of view. We primarily use flowcharts to teach control structures. We use pseudocode primarily as a program design and documentation tool.

Applications Programs.   Meaningful applications of the computer are emphasized in our choice of sample programs and programming assignments. Our samples have wide variety, including business, economics, mathematics, statistics, the sciences, and public-sector areas like health-care delivery and governmental administration.

Exercises.   The book has a carefully designed set of exercises, many with multiple parts. Exercises include both *follow-up exercises* (to reinforce, integrate, and extend preceding material) and *additional exercises* (for complete programming assignments at the end of chapters and modules). *Answers to most follow-up exercises (those without asterisks) are included at the end of the text.* The follow-up exercises with answers give the book a "programmed learning" flavor without the traditional regimentation of such an approach. Additionally, the follow-up exercises are an excellent basis for planning many classroom lectures.

Software Development Cycle.   A four-step software development cycle (Analysis, Design, Code, Test) is first described and illustrated in Chapter 1.

Subsequently it's used in all major applications programs throughout the text. As in commercial environments, this stepwise organization facilitates the development of programs. Students are asked to structure each end-of-chapter assignment along these four steps.

FOR/NEXT Loops.   Unlike traditional texts, FOR/NEXT loops are introduced early (Chapter 3) as the first of the loop structure implementations. We find that this loop implementation is the easiest for the students to master. Moreover, the early treatment of loops (before decision structure implementations) allows the very early illustration of realistic programs that show the power of repetitive processing (which, after all, is the *raison d'être* for computing).

String Processing.   The processing of string data is emphasized throughout the text, which reflects the enormous extent of information processing applications in practice. Certain specialized and more difficult text processing and editing applications are covered in Module C.

External Files.   The use of external data files is a must in practice, but it's a difficult topic for beginning programmers. Module E covers sequential files. Elsewhere in the text, where appropriate, we simulate data file concepts by using DATA statements as *internal data files*.

Camera-ready Programs.   All complete programs and their input/output are reproduced by camera rather than typeset. This increases the realism of the programming material and ensures the reliability of programs. Moreover, many of the programs include color shading and margin notes to enhance student understanding. The camera-ready programs and runs feature either the IBM PC, the VAX-11, or both, depending on the topic.

Other Aids.   Additional learning aids include:

- Many short, complete programs as examples and exercises. These can be used more easily by instructors for classroom demonstrations, and by students as practice exercises on the computer.

- The use of color type (for user input in the computer runs, important terms, and notes), color screens (to highlight and draw attention to the topic of interest), and arrowed margin notes.

- Important concepts and explanations set off from the rest of the text by especially marked "Note" paragraphs.

- Inside covers of the text present summary tables of statements, functions, and commands, together with applicable BASIC dialects and page references.

Text Supplements.   The text is supplemented by an *Instructor's Manual* with teaching hints, answers not given in the text to follow-up exercises, solutions to all end-of-chapter programming assignments, a set of transparency masters, and a test bank. Text examples, end-of-chapter solutions, and the test bank are available on diskettes.

Acknowledgments

We wish to express our deep appreciation to many who have contributed to this project: to Frank Ruggirello, our editor, for unique humor, support, and expert advice; to Reita Kinsman, the "Assistant Coach," for keeping us on track; to Hal Humphrey, our production editor, for production magic; to Cynthia Bassett for outstanding design; to Joy Westberg for the best ads east (and west) of Belmont; to the rest of the Wadsworth team for all the help in getting the text "out the door"; to Robert Clagett, Dean, University of Rhode Island, for administrative support; to the Computer Laboratories at the University of Rhode Island, for obvious reasons; to our reviewers, Beverly Blaylock of Grossmont College, Michael Breck of the Oregon Institute of Technology, Eugene Dolan of the University of the District of Columbia, Marilyn Meyers of Fresno Community College, Herbert Rebhun of the University of Houston Downtown Campus, Donald Davis of the University of Mississippi, David Gustafson of Kansas State University, and Richard Moller of Fresno Community College, who provided invaluable suggestions and corrections for manuscript revisions; to our students, who always teach us something about teaching; and to our immediate families, who sometimes wonder what we look like.

ROY AGELOFF
RICHARD MOJENA
Kingston, Rhode Island

Contents

C H A P T E R

4

DECISIONS 56

C H A P T E R

5

MORE LOOPS 75

M O D U L E

EXTERNAL DATA FILES 172

Essential Concepts

1

This chapter presents some essential computer concepts for a short course in programming using the BASIC language. Its primary purpose is to provide concepts and terminology that facilitate an understanding of computers and their programming. It also orients you to the specialized world of computer terminology. You need not be befuddled any longer by computerspeak like "My computer uses 7-bit ASCII codes for each byte" and "My ROM is fine but I need more RAM."

We see one major prerequisite to doing well in this course: A curiosity, or better yet, a desire to learn more about computers and computer programming. By the time this course is over we hope that we (together with your instructor) shall have helped you translate that curiosity into a continuing, productive, and rewarding experience.

1.1 ESSENTIAL ESSENTIALS

Let's start by describing the functional organization of a computer, and follow by defining other related terms that are useful in a first computer course.

What's a Computer?

We can define a **computer** as a device that rapidly processes arithmetic and logical tasks without human intervention. The typical computer that most of us use is best defined by the five components shown in Figure 1.1 and described next. First, however, let's introduce two terms that are often confused.

Instructions are specific tasks for the computer to accomplish. For example, we might instruct the computer to

- Input and store a student's name and grades
- Calculate and store the grade-point average
- Print the name and grade-point average

A **computer program** is a complete set of instructions for accomplishing a defined task.

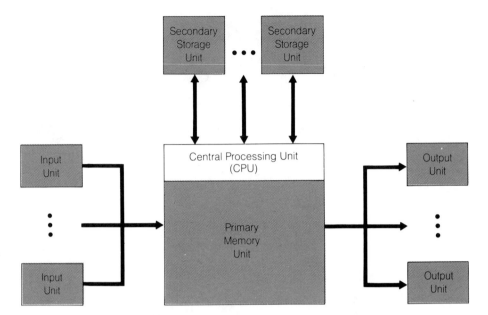

Figure 1.1 Functional organization of a computer

Data are facts or observations that the computer inputs, manipulates, and outputs. A student's name, grades, and grade-point average are all examples of data. Data are acted upon or processed by the instructions within computer programs.

Input Units. The input unit brings data and programs from the outside world to the computer's memory. For most of us this is accomplished by the typewriter-like keyboard and accompanying monitor (display screen) of a video display terminal (VDT). The keyboard and monitor of a desktop computer also serves as an input unit. Other input units include optical character readers (OCRs) for processing coded forms like exam answers, sales slips, and other handwritten or typed documents; magnetic ink character readers (MICRs) for processing bank checks; modems for receiving incoming data and instructions from another computer; mice for moving a screen pointer and selecting menu items; and voice recognition units for processing human speech. As shown in Figure 1.1, a computer can have more than one input unit.

Output Units. The function of an output unit is exactly opposite to that of an input unit: An output unit receives data from the computer in the form of electronic signals and converts these data into a form that is usable by either humans or computers. The most common output units are monitors (on VDTs and desktop computers) for output that's viewed and line printers for output that's printed on paper. Other output units include modems for sending data and instructions to another computer and voice response (synthesis) units for processing verbal output.

Primary Memory Unit. This unit temporarily stores programs and data during input, output, and processing operations. The most common primary memory unit is actually a set of tiny memory chips, each smaller than the tip of a finger. A typical memory chip stores roughly 64 thousand (or 64K) bits of data, where a **bit** is a binary digit that assumes one of two possible values: 0 or 1 from a mathematical point of view; off or on from a mechanical perspective; and low voltage or high voltage from an electronic viewpoint.[1] Computers store characters as a packet or series of bits called a **byte**. A common coding scheme abbreviated as **ASCII** (**A**merican **S**tandard **C**ode for **I**nformation **I**nterchange) uses seven bits to represent a byte or character. For example, the letter R would be coded and stored as 1010010 and the digit 8 would be coded and stored as 0111000. Most computers enhance the ASCII code to eight bits, which allows additional characters like graphics and foreign language symbols. As a result, the usual assumption is that a *byte is eight bits*. The storage capacity of primary memory is usually expressed as the number of characters (bytes) that can be stored. For example, the IBM PC has a quoted memory capacity of 640K bytes (or 640 KB), and many large computers have primary memories in excess of 15 megabytes (or 15 MB), where a megabyte is 1 million bytes. The Cray-2 supercomputer addresses 2 billion bytes (or 2 gigabytes) of primary memory. By the way, primary memory on desktop computers is usually called **random-access memory (RAM)**, to distinguish it from **read-only memory (ROM)**. Data and instructions are permanently placed in ROM at the factory. In contrast, the contents in RAM are temporary in the sense that our data and instructions reside there while we are online (connected) to the computer.

Secondary Storage Units.   Primary memory is said to be volatile because it retains our data and programs only while we are online. In contrast, secondary storage units allow us to "permanently" (Is anything permanent?) store data and instructions in external memory for later recall. Computer programs and data not currently in use are stored on media like magnetic tape and disks, and read into primary memory when needed. Common secondary storage units are tape drives and disk drives. Compared with primary storage, secondary storage has greater capacity (many gigabytes) at much less cost per byte, but the amount of time it takes to access data is greater.

Central Processing Unit (CPU).   The CPU, or simply the **processor**, directs the operation of all other units. Its function is to repetitively perform the following three steps:

1. Fetch or obtain an instruction from the program in primary memory
2. Interpret this instruction
3. Execute the instruction by transmitting directions to the appropriate computer component

The processor, together with primary memory, is what most professionals think of as *the* computer. Input, output, and secondary storage units are called **peripherals**. These are not thought of as the "computer" since they are peripheral or external to the computer. We can think of the processor, primary memory, and peripherals as forming a computer system. Current technology can place a CPU on a logic chip that's about one-quarter of an inch square. These are called **microprocessors**. The pace of technology is such that the microprocessor we can balance on the tip of our finger is more powerful than the large computers that filled a room in the early 1970s.

---

[1] Actually, 64K bits really stands for 65,536 bits (or 64 × 1024) instead of 64,000 bits. This is because computers use base 2 arithmetic instead of base 10 (decimal) arithmetic. Two raised to the tenth power gives us the magical number 1024, which is the computer equivalent of Kilo or "one thousand."

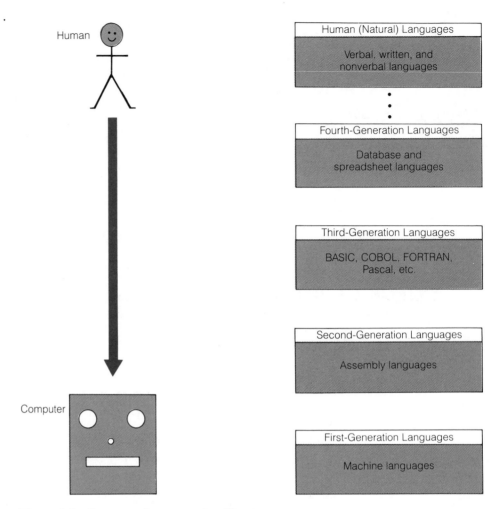

Figure 1.2   Computer language classifications

Last of the Essential Terminology

Mainframes, Minis, and Micros.   Computers are often distinguished by size, which generally translates into storage capacity, speed, and cost. **Mainframe** computers are physically large, process huge amounts of data at incredible speeds on the order of 30 mips (million instructions per second), and strain computer budgets. **Minicomputers** generally range in size from a filing cabinet to a closet. They contain less primary memory, work more slowly, and are cheaper than mainframe computers. **Microcomputers** come in sizes that fit pockets to desktops, with correspondingly lower storage capacities, processing speeds, and prices. Microcomputers are often further classified by the number of bits that their logic chips can process. For example, the Apple II is an 8-bit microcomputer, the IBM PC is a 16-bit microcomputer, and the Macintosh is (partly) a 32-bit microcomputer.

Computer Languages.   We communicate our instructions to the computer by writing programs in a computer language. Figure 1.2 indicates one way of classifying computer languages. Any language can be distinguished from any other language by its syntax; that is, by the rules for arranging a specified set of symbols into recognizable patterns. At the computer level the machine only understands **machine language**, which is in a binary syntax for compatibility with electronic circuitry. Instructions in this first-generation language can be written as a series of bits (0s and 1s), although other forms are available, including hard-wired instructions at the factory. As you can imagine, this language is tedious and difficult for us humans, and so second-generation languages were born. These are usually called **assembly languages.** Unlike machine languages, assembly languages use human-like syntax such as S for subtract. Thus, it's easier and faster to program in an assembly language than in a machine language. To a nonspecialist, however, assembly language syntax is cryptic, and is wedded or specific to the particular processor being used.

In the late 1950s the first third-generation language was invented by developers at IBM. Called FORTRAN, this language is particularly popular in scientific and engineering applications. Other third-generation languages include BASIC, the most popular language on microcomputers; COBOL, the traditional language of choice in commercial data processing environments; and Pascal, a more recent language with a wide following in computer science circles. Compared to assembly languages, the third-generation languages are easier to program and reasonably portable from computer to computer. Assembly languages, however, require less cpu time to process and have more detailed control of computer resources than do third-generation languages.

Fourth-generation languages are the latest attempt at getting closer to human language syntax. The most popular of these are database languages such as *Focus* and *dBase* for creating, maintaining, querying, and generating reports from personnel, airline reservations, student, and other databases. Spreadsheet software like *Lotus 1-2-3* is another example of fourth-generation languages. As time goes on we can expect computer languages to continue the evolution toward human language syntax, since this promotes greater use of computer technology among the masses (and more profits for the computer industry).

Interpreters and Compilers. A computer program that's written in a third-generation language like BASIC cannot be understood directly by the computer, since the computer itself only communicates in machine language. Interpreters and compilers are specialized computer programs that translate third-generation language instructions to machine-language instructions, much as a foreign language interpreter would translate from English into, say, Spanish.

An interpreter first translates a single instruction into its machine language equivalent and then immediately executes, or carries out, this instruction. Then it goes on to the next instruction and repeats the translation and execution tasks. This process continues until all instructions have been translated and executed. If any one instruction violates syntax, then a correction is requested before continuing with the next instruction.

A compiler is like an interpreter, except all instructions are first translated but not executed. If there are no syntax errors, then the translated program is executed. Interpreters facilitate the process of correcting programs, but they are slower than compilers once programs are correct. Moreover, compiled programs can be stored as separate programs (in machine language) and reexecuted without retranslation, which is cost efficient for large programs.

Computer Hardware and Software. The term computer hardware, of course, refers to the physical equipment, whereas software refers to computer programs. Software itself has two useful classifications: systems software and applications software.

Systems software is designed for tasks that facilitate the use of hardware. The **Operating System (OS)** is the most important piece of systems software. On microcomputers this is usually called the **Disk Operating System (DOS).** Among other things, operating systems supply the appropriate compiler or interpreter, allocate storage for programs and data, store and retrieve programs from secondary storage units, and display the contents of programs. We illustrate the use of operating systems in Modules A and B in the back of this text.

Applications software is programs that solve specific problems or conduct specific tasks for end users. For example, applications programs are common for problems and tasks such as engineering analysis, payroll, tracking inventories, billing, class scheduling, simulation of traffic flows, games, airline scheduling, and tax preparation. The types of programs that you will be writing as part of this course (and all programs in this book) are examples of applications programs.

Processing Environments.   There are two major approaches to computing activity: batch processing and interactive processing. There is also a process related to both of these, called distributed processing.

Batch processing periodically accumulates programs (jobs) in groups, or batches, to await execution. Each program is then run or executed according to job priorities established by computing-center personnel. It may take from a few minutes to several hours before the results of a program are available. Typical batch jobs include weekly payrolls, monthly billings, elaborate scientific analyses, and other jobs that require many computations and/or large amounts of input and output.

In **interactive processing** the user directly interacts or dialogs with the program while it executes. This type of processing is usually implemented on either a microcomputer or a time-sharing system, whereby many users working at terminals share the computer. Interactive processing is common in automated banking systems, in airline reservation and other inquiry systems, and in decision-oriented applications that implement "What if . . .?" interactive analyses. This textbook emphasizes interactive programming.

Communications networks that link various computers and automated office equipment (such as word processors, copying machines, electronic mail, and teleconferencing equipment) at scattered locations are called **distributed processing systems**. A typical system at universities includes a centralized mainframe computer linked to satellite minicomputers and microcomputers at different locations on and off campus. Distributed processing systems usually include both batch and interactive processing. For example, jobs that transmit different sets of data from a computer in San Francisco to a computer in Boston might be batched for transmission during the "graveyard" shift; a student might interactively access the university's mainframe computer first and its minicomputer next to accomplish two different tasks either from home or campus, using either a terminal or a microcomputer.

1.2 SOFTWARE DEVELOPMENT CYCLE

As you know, a computer program is an organized set of instructions written in a computer language; its purpose is to solve a problem that has been defined. This problem is solved when the computer program is correctly executed by the computer.

Writing a computer program involves the following four-step procedure:

1. Problem analysis (understanding the problem and requirements)
2. Program design (flowchart or pseudocode version)
3. Program code (BASIC version)
4. Program test (getting out the "bugs")

These four steps are the basis of the **software development cycle**. Thus the act of writing a program includes a step-by-step process, beginning with an analysis of the problem and ending with a program that executes as intended. In actual environments, the software development cycle also includes steps for implementing the newly developed software on an ongoing basis, evaluating its usefulness, and maintaining or modifying it over time.

This four-step process is not a rigid, lock-step procedure. In practice, the development of software cycles through these four steps until the program executes correctly. This means, for example, that the test in Step 4 may indicate a change in design (which takes us back to Step 2) or even a change in the analysis (which takes us to Step 1). By the way, within commercial environments, the software development cycle never really ends throughout the life cycle of a program; new bugs, changes in the environment, and additional requirements are facts of computerized life that promote continued cycling through these steps.

Step 1: Problem Analysis

First, it's essential to completely understand the structure of the problem and the requirements or needs of the user (or group of users) who will benefit from the program. A common approach is to specify:

a. The output we wish to receive as the solution to the problem

b. The data we shall provide the computer

c. The computations and/or logical processes by which the computer will convert the provided data to the output data

As an illustration, suppose that the Board of Regents, which oversees the State College System, wants to have a program for assessing the effects of various policies on the tuition revenue collected by state institutions of higher education. For example, how much is revenue affected if there is a change in enrollment? What is the effect of increasing student tuition on tuition revenue?

In our problem analysis we need to specify clearly three aspects of this problem.

a. *Data output*
Total tuition revenue received by the college

b. *Data input*
Name of college
Tuition per student
Number of students enrolled

c. *Computations*
To determine tuition revenue, multiply the tuition per student by the enrollment

NOTE When describing the data input, we need to ask ourselves: Does the input data represent the information necessary to generate the required output?

In practice (the "real world"), the requirements for output include not only *what* is to be output but also *where* (VDT, line printer, etc.), *when* (daily, weekly, on demand, etc.), and *how* (design of the display, document, or report). Similar requirements apply to the provided data.

Other considerations in the problem analysis include how the proposed program fits into the organization's computer-based goals, the projected ben-

Table 1.1 Flowcharting Symbols

Symbol	Name	Meaning
	Terminal	Indicates the start or end of the program.
	Input/output	Indicates when an input or output operation is to be performed.
	Process	Indicates calculations or data manipulation.
	Flowline	Represents the flow of logic.
	Decision	Represents a decision point or question that requires a choice of which logical path to follow.
	Connector	Connects parts of the flowchart.
	Preparation	Indicates a preparation step as in describing a FOR/ NEXT loop (Chapter 3).
	Predefined process	Indicates a predefined process or step where the details are not shown in this flowchart, as in calling a subprogram (Chapter 6).

efits and costs, the needs for additional hardware and software, and future expectations with respect to modifications, enhancements, and extensions.

For us, the analysis in Step 1 is fairly brief. In practice, however, this step is elaborate and can take many months to complete, especially for large applications programs that integrate within a complex system of programs and users.

Step 2: Program Design

It's best to design a computer program before it is actually written, much as a building is designed before it is constructed. A program design identifies the necessary processing tasks and spells out the exact sequence or logic by which these tasks are to be carried out. The description of this design is often called an algorithm. The manner in which we specify the algorithm, however, is closer to the problem-solving logic of the computer than to the type of prose statement in our preceding step. Throughout this textbook we use flowcharts and/or pseudocode to specify the algorithm.

A **flowchart** is a drawing of the algorithm. It has two primary uses: to help us write the computer program by serving as a blueprint and to document the logic of the computer program for future review.

Flowcharts use specific symbols to represent different activities and a written message within each symbol to explain each activity. Table 1.1 shows

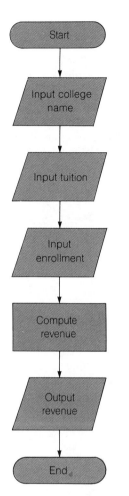

Figure 1.3 Flowchart for the tuition revenue problem

the "traditional" flowcharting symbols we use in this textbook, and Figure 1.3 illustrates the flowchart for the tuition revenue problem.

The flowchart in Figure 1.3 breaks down the problem into several steps.

1. Input the name of the college into a memory location.
2. Input the tuition into a memory location.
3. Input the enrollment into a memory location.
4. Calculate tuition revenue.
5. Print the output.
6. End processing.

Note that this flowchart uses only the first four symbols of Table 1.1. The other symbols are introduced in later chapters, as our programming becomes more sophisticated.

In general, a flowchart must indicate a *Start* and must have an *End*. The flow generally runs from top to bottom and from left to right. As an option, you can use arrowheads to indicate the direction of flow, which is our preference.

A flowchart is one way of diagramming the logic of a program. Many professional programmers and systems analysts use them regularly; others do not. One reason for not using flowcharts is the difficulty in revising them once a program has been modified.

An increasingly popular alternative to flowcharts is called **pseudocode** or **program design language**. Pseudocode expresses the logic of the algorithm using English-like phrases. A key reason for the growing acceptance of pseudocode is its compatibility with the thinking processes of the programmer. The terms and expressions in this false (pseudo) code are often defined by the person doing the programming, and as a result there are many variations in writing pseudocode. The example that follows should give you some idea of the syntax and structure of pseudocode.

Before writing the tuition revenue program, we can map out its structure by using pseudocode as follows:

```
Input college name
Input tuition
Input enrollment
Revenue = tuition × enrollment
Output revenue
End
```

A program written in pseudocode is similar to a program written in a computer language like BASIC. The major difference is the emphasis placed on content versus syntax. Pseudocode primarily concentrates on mapping out the algorithmic logic of a program, with little regard for the syntax of the actual programming language to be used. Thus we are free to concentrate on the design of the program by expressing its logic or structure in ordinary English, including abbreviations, symbols, and formulas.

Either flowcharts or pseudocode can be used to design and document programs, but the simplicity and compactness of pseudocode may tip the balance in its favor, particularly for documenting programs that are likely to undergo frequent modification.

A significant drop in the commercial sales of programs that generate flowcharts suggests the declining popularity of flowcharts as a design and documentation tool. Moreover, experimental research indicates that informal program design languages are more effective than flowcharts for program design and designer-programmer communication.[2]

We prefer pseudocode to flowcharts in designing and documenting programs but believe that flowcharts are useful tools for teaching certain programming concepts. Thus, in this textbook, we shall use either flowcharts or pseudocode, whichever is more appropriate.

Although the above example of a flowchart and pseudocode is rather simple, and you may be tempted not to use these aids for such an easy problem, we strongly suggest that you get in the habit of using either pseudocode or flowcharts now. As programs become more complex, you will find these design tools increasingly helpful.

Step 3: Program Code

Coding is the translation of our problem-solving logic from the design phase into a computer program. We use the flowchart or pseudocode as a guide for writing instructions to the computer.

The computer language that our instructions are to be written in must be decided by this step in the procedure. (Quite often the same flowchart or pseudocode can be used with any computer language.) Some languages are more suitable than others, depending on the application.

In this textbook we show several versions of the programming language called BASIC[3]. The reasons for its widespread use, particularly among microcomputer users, include the following: The relative ease of learning BASIC; its excellent mathematical and character manipulation abilities; its capabilities with sound (music), color, and graphics; its simple syntax; and its interactive orientation (it was the first interactive language).

BASIC also has its faults, as do all programming languages. For example, it's been said that "BASIC is easy to learn, easy to write, and hard to follow." We shall clear up this seeming paradox (and show what to do about it) in the chapters that follow.

The first standard for the BASIC language, approved in 1978 by the American National Standards Institute (ANSI), is called **Minimal BASIC**. This version of BASIC covers a small portion of what is considered today to be the BASIC language. Computer manufacturers and software companies have developed full-feature versions of BASIC that include commands and enhancements beyond the original standard. Unfortunately, the enhanced instructions are not exactly the same for each version. Thus many different dialects (versions) of the BASIC language evolved and exist today.

In 1984 ANSI proposed a more comprehensive standard for the BASIC language and named it **ANS BASIC**. In time, if this new standard is accepted, BASIC should become a more consistent language. In this text we cover Minimal BASIC, the new ANS BASIC, and **True BASIC**, the only implementation of ANS BASIC as of this writing. We also illustrate two widely used dialects of BASIC: **Microsoft BASIC** on the IBM PC and **VAX-11 BASIC**.

BASIC code for the tuition revenue program is shown at the top of the next page. Note the correspondence between the program and its flowchart and pseudocode predecessors.

---

[2]H. R. Ramsey, M. E. Atwood, and J. R. Van Doren, "Flowcharts Versus Program Design Languages: An Experimental Comparison," *Communications of the acm*, June 1983, pp. 445–49.

[3]BASIC (Beginners All-purpose Symbolic Instruction Code) was developed at Dartmouth College in the mid-1960s to simplify the learning of computer programming using online terminals.

BASIC	**Comments**

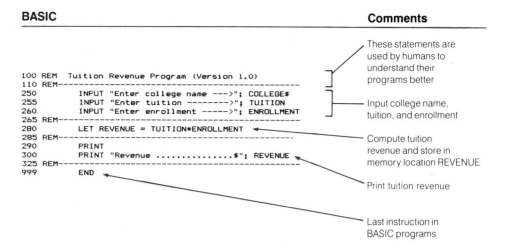

At this point you need not worry about the exact meaning of each instruction in the program, for we shall discuss them in (excruciating) detail in the next chapter. However, the program should make some sense to you.

Typically, we first design and then write our code on an ordinary sheet of paper. After we are reasonably sure that the program is correct, we enter the code through the appropriate input medium for our system, either a terminal or a microcomputer. Details on these procedures are presented in Modules A and B at the end of the text, which you should study after reading this or the next chapter; in these modules, we briefly illustrate the IBM PC and the VAX-11. You will need to fill in the details for your particular system by consulting your instructor and your User Guide.

Step 4: Program Test

The next step is to run, or execute, the program on the computer. By **run** or **execute** we mean that the instructions that make up the program code are processed (carried out) by the computer. Our purpose, in this case, is to test the program to ensure that it contains no errors. Testing involves running the program with test data to verify that the correct output is produced.

You will often write programs that fail to run or that run improperly. (It happens to all of us.) **Debugging** is the process of locating and correcting errors, or "getting out the bugs." Types of bugs and methods for correcting them are illustrated in Module B.

For the moment, let's assume that the program from Step 3 has been entered into primary memory and is currently awaiting execution. On most systems, we would execute the program by typing RUN, as the following test run indicates:

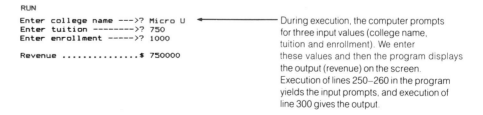

As you can see, the output of $750,000 for revenue at Micro U is correct, given a tuition of $750 per student and an enrollment of 1000 students.

ADVICE Some of you have a great aptitude for the material that follows. We hope you will get "turned on" to do fine things in this field. Others of you are less inclined to absorb this type of material readily. If you are in the latter category, then you should take the following advice seriously.

1. Pay close attention to *written detail.* The computer is not permissive. For example, if you spell PRENT instead of PRINT, the computer will not understand.

2. Pay close attention to *logical detail.* The computer is a machine. Therefore, you must tell it what to do in precise detail, which is broken down into logical steps.

3. Develop *good habits.* Work consistently (not constantly!). Try to rely on others as little as possible to sharpen your inherent problem-solving skills. Try to solve the Follow-up Exercises before looking up answers in the back of the book.

4. Take note of an interesting *paradox* in the act of programming. On one hand, good programming requires the type of "scientific method" outlined in items 1–3; on the other hand, art and creativity distinguish great programs from average programs. Look upon your programming as a written composition, and let your creative juices flow.

5. Be *patient.* Don't become frustrated by your mistakes. Don't get angry at the computer if it breaks down (after all, it also works hard). Finally, give yourself time. Our years of teaching this course have shown us that many students take several weeks before the material crystallizes.

FOLLOW-UP EXERCISES

1. Sketch the organization of a computer. Briefly describe the functions of each component.

2. Identify and briefly discuss types of computer languages.

3. Give some examples of hardware and software.

4. Briefly describe the functions of the operating system.

5. Briefly describe the functions of the compiler. How does an interpreter differ from a compiler?

6. Briefly describe and compare three processing environments.

7. Briefly describe the steps in the software development cycle.

8. How are you doing?

BASIC
Fundamentals

2

This chapter introduces certain fundamental elements of BASIC. By the end of it, you will be writing and running complete, though simple, programs of the type presented in Chapter 1 and reproduced next in Example 2.1.

E X A M P L E   2 . 1   **Tuition Revenue Program**

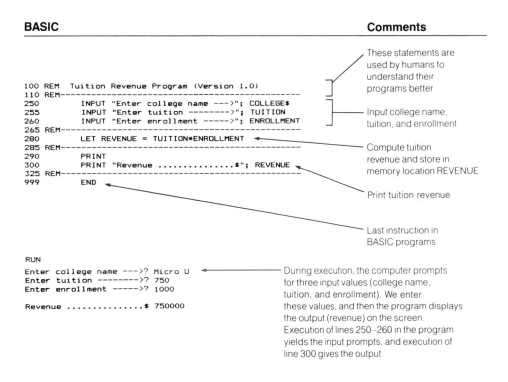

BASIC

```
100 REM   Tuition Revenue Program (Version 1.0)
110 REM------------------------------------------------
250         INPUT "Enter college name --->"; COLLEGE$
255         INPUT "Enter tuition -------->"; TUITION
260         INPUT "Enter enrollment ----->"; ENROLLMENT
265 REM------------------------------------------------
280         LET REVENUE = TUITION*ENROLLMENT
285 REM------------------------------------------------
290         PRINT
300         PRINT "Revenue ..............$"; REVENUE
325 REM------------------------------------------------
999         END
```

```
RUN
Enter college name --->? Micro U
Enter tuition -------->? 750
Enter enrollment ----->? 1000

Revenue ..............$ 750000
```

Comments

These statements are used by humans to understand their programs better

Input college name, tuition, and enrollment

Compute tuition revenue and store in memory location REVENUE

Print tuition revenue

Last instruction in BASIC programs

During execution, the computer prompts for three input values (college name, tuition, and enrollment). We enter these values, and then the program displays the output (revenue) on the screen. Execution of lines 250–260 in the program yields the input prompts, and execution of line 300 gives the output.

Let's define a **program** as a set of statements whose purpose is to solve a problem. A **statement** is an instruction that either directs the computer to perform a specific task, such as multiply two numbers and store the result, or declare information. The tuition revenue program has 12 statements (count them!). Specifically it illustrates REM, INPUT, LET, PRINT, and END statements. Briefly, these statements accomplish the following tasks:

- REM statements document programs to improve their readability
- INPUT statements request data entry
- LET statements store computational results
- PRINT statements generate computer output
- END statements define the end of programs

Each statement has a **reserved word** or **keyword**, which is a word that uniquely identifies that statement. REM, INPUT, LET, PRINT, and END are keywords in our sample program. We introduce other keywords elsewhere in the book, as summarized on the inside front and back covers. (Check this out now!)

A BASIC program is a sequence of **lines**. Each line begins with a unique **line number** on most, but not all, systems. For example, the tuition revenue program has 12 lines with the numbers 100, 110, 250, . . . , 999. Leading zeros are usually ignored, and spaces before or within the line number are not permitted.

Line numbers order the statements in a program and attach unique labels to each line. Many systems arrange the lines in ascending order (low to high) regardless of the order in which they were typed.

It's a good programming practice to number the lines in increments (steps) of 5 or 10. This practice allows us to insert new lines between old lines should we need to correct, expand, or otherwise modify the program.[1]

As illustrated above, a BASIC program is usually translated and executed by a **RUN command**. In our sample program, the interpreter translates and executes each statement in turn beginning with line 250 (the REM statements in lines 100–110 are for human consumption). As you can see, three input values are requested when lines 250–260 are translated/executed, revenue is stored in line 280, results are printed in lines 290–300, and translation/execution ends in line 999. Details for this process are given in Module A in the back of the text.

That's it in a nutshell! The excruciating details follow in the remainder of this chapter.

2.1 CONSTANTS

A **constant** is a value that does not change during the execution of a program. BASIC makes a distinction between numeric and string constants.

Numeric Constants

Numeric constants are positive or negative numbers; a constant is made up of the digits 0 to 9, an optional decimal point, and may be preceded by a plus or minus symbol. Numbers such as 175, -42, 3.14159, and $+12$ are examples of numeric constants. Commas and other special characters are *not* permitted within a numeric constant. For example, the numeric constants 6,000 and $54.50 would give syntax errors.

E-Notation.   Very small or very large numeric constants can be represented by scientific notation, or **E-notation**. For example, the constant 7,200,000,000 is written as $7.2E+09$ in E-notation, and 0.0008413 is written as $8.413E-04$. E represents "times ten to the power given by the following digits." In other words, $E+09$ in the constant $7.2E+09$ says to multiply 7.2 by 10 raised to the

---

[1] All systems limit the size of a line number. For example, line numbers cannot exceed 65529 on Microsoft Systems. ANS BASIC does not require line numbers.

power 9, or multiply 7.2 by 10^9, giving 7.2 × 1000000000 or 7200000000. In plain English, E + 09 simply means move the decimal point nine places to the *right*, and E − 04 says move the decimal point four places to the *left*.

You will most likely see E-notation when reading computer output, since systems use this convention to store and print very large and very small values. Thus an understanding of E-notation facilitates the reading of computer output. For example, if in the tuition revenue program, enrollment is 20000 instead of 1000, then revenue is $15 million. The output line appears as

```
Revenue ..............$ 1.5E+07
```

Precision and Range.   You should be aware of the following issues when working with numeric values:

1.   The maximum number of significant digits, often called **precision**, differs from system to system. ANS BASIC specifies that numeric values can be rounded to a *minimum* of six digits. Six or seven digits is common on many systems. For example, the population of the U.S. in 1980 (223,324,111) would be represented on six-digit systems as 223324000 (actually 2.23324E + 08), on seven-digit systems as 2.233241E + 08, and on nine (or more)-digit systems exactly as is. Ask your instructor about precision on your system.

2.   The range of values allowed for a number also varies from system to system. According to the ANSI standard, all conforming systems must accommodate a range of at least 1E − 38 to 1E38 (10^{-38} to 10^{38}). Thus a value such as 2.5E82 may be too large for many systems. Values that exceed the maximum limit cause an **overflow** condition; values smaller than the lower limit cause an **underflow** condition. Systems normally print an error message whenever an overflow condition is encountered, as we illustrate in Module B. An underflow condition such as 8E − 5000 typically yields a value of zero for the constant. Ask your instructor about the range on your system.

String Constants

A **string constant** is a sequence of characters that may include letters, numbers, or special characters, usually enclosed between quotation marks. For example,

"Revenue ....$"

is a string constant in line 300 of the tuition revenue program. Note that the length of the string constant is 24 characters, including the space between Revenue and the first dot. Also note that the string constant does not include the quotes. Other examples of string constants are

"$2,324.25"   "327-23-3411"   "06/03/67"   "Clark Kent"

These examples are also called quoted strings, because they are enclosed by quotation marks. Later we shall show the use of unquoted strings as well.

String constants are commonly used to print labels, report headings, messages, and other text.

2.2 VARIABLES

Programmers use symbolic names to reference unique memory locations that store data values. In BASIC this name is called a **variable**, since the value stored in that memory location can vary as the program executes; however, at any instant during the execution of a program, a variable is associated with a single value. Variables store either numeric or string values.

Numeric Variables

A variable that stores numeric values is called a **numeric variable**. (We're not usually this straightforward!) For example, the numeric value 750 stored under the numeric variable *T* might be represented as follows:

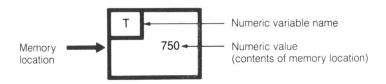

The rules for forming variable names differ depending on the version of BASIC. Minimal BASIC allows 1- or 2-character variable names; however, many versions of BASIC allow longer multicharacter names. Table 2.1 provides different rules for naming numeric variables, depending on the BASIC dialect, and illustrates some valid and invalid names for numeric variables.

Table 2.1   Rules for Naming Numeric Variables for Selected Dialects

Dialect	First Character	Other Characters	Valid Variable Names	Invalid Variable Names
Minimal BASIC	Letter	1 optional digit	T T9	TUITION NET.PAY A+ 3A
ANS BASIC True BASIC	Letter	30 optional characters (letters, digits, and underscore)	T T9 TUITION NET_PAY	NET.PAY A+ 3A
Microsoft BASIC	Letter	39 optional characters (letters, digits, and period)	T T9 TUITION NET.PAY	NET_PAY A+ 3A
VAX-11 BASIC	Letter	30 optional characters (letters, digits, underscore, and period)	T T9 TUITION NET.PAY NET_PAY	A+ 3A

Your system
(if different)

When the size of a variable name is limited in length, as it is in Minimal BASIC, digits in a variable name are often used to distinguish among related variables. For example, if three different types of costs are to be represented by simple numeric variables in a program, then it makes sense to label these C1, C2, and C3. This practice of selecting a variable name that has meaning helps us to remember the attribute that is represented by this variable.

NOTE   A good programming practice is to select variable names that have descriptive meaning within the context of the problem. For example, in the tuition revenue program, the variable names TUITION, ENROLLMENT, and REVENUE have contextual meaning.

String Variables

String variables store string values and are indicated by placing a dollar sign ($) after the variable name. For example, N$, K$, and T$ are string variables. These variables are primarily used to store names, addresses, text, and other nonnumeric data. The tuition revenue illustration stores the name of the institution being processed. For example, the string value *Micro U* is stored in the string variable COLLEGE$. The string variable COLLEGE$ and its value can be pictured in memory as follows:

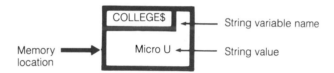

We might note the following facts and suggestions regarding string variables:

1. The rules for forming string variable names are essentially the same rules as those for naming numeric variable names, except for the trailing $ that identifies the variable as a string variable. (See Table 2.1.)

2. Select string variable names that have contextual meaning. For example, N$ is a good selection in Minimal BASIC to store the name of a college; COLLEGE$ conveys meaning in dialects that allow multicharacter names.

3. Dialects limit the maximum length of the string value that can be stored within the storage location defined by a string variable. For example, Microsoft BASIC allows up to 255 characters. Check on the limitation for your system.

NOTE 1   Don't use a variable name that's the same as a keyword (reserved word) in the BASIC dialect you're using. For example, END as a variable name is illegal for all dialects; NAME$ for storing names is illegal in Microsoft BASIC. In general, it's a good idea to have handy a list of reserved words for your dialect. Have you looked at the inside covers of this text?

NOTE 2   Our illustrative programs will generally use multicharacter variable names for variables that store descriptive items. If your system limits variable names to one or two characters, then you should be aware that these programs will not run on your system as is.

2.3 END AND REM STATEMENTS

It's important to distinguish between two classes of statements called executable and nonexecutable statements, of which END and REM statements are examples.

Executable and Nonexecutable Statements

Statements are classified as executable and nonexecutable. An **executable statement** causes activity in the CPU during execution of the program. The END, LET, PRINT, INPUT, READ, and RESTORE statements are all examples of executable statements; we introduce these statements in this chapter.

As illustrated in the tuition revenue program, programs end with the statement:

END Statement

This statement not only defines the physical end of a BASIC program but also causes execution of the program to terminate. Since the END statement is the last statement in the program, it follows that it must appear in the highest-numbered line. In our tuition revenue example, we placed it in line number 999. As a matter of programming style, we usually use the label 999 as the last line in a program with three-digit line numbers.

A **nonexecutable statement** is used to provide or declare certain information to the CPU during compilation or interpretation of the program. Nonexecutable statements are ignored during execution of the program. The REM and DATA statements introduced in this chapter are examples of nonexecutable statements.

Documentation of Programs

The statement

REM Statement

    REM *unquoted string*

is used to document programs for improved *human* readability. The next example illustrates a fully documented program.

E X A M P L E   2 . 2   Revised Tuition Revenue Program

The following version of the tuition revenue program from Example 2.1 includes more extensive documentation.

```
100 REM  * * * * * * * * * * * * * * * * * * * * * * * * * * * * * * *
105 REM  *                                                           *
110 REM  *    Tuition Revenue Program (Version 1.1)                  *
115 REM  *                                                           *
120 REM  *    I. M. Hacker                            BASIC 101      *
125 REM  *    January 1, 198x                 Professor Harvey Core  *
130 REM  *                                                           *
135 REM  * * * * * * * * * * * * * * * * * * * * * * * * * * * * * * *
140 REM  *                                                           *
145 REM  *    Interactive program that print revenue generated from  *
150 REM  *    tuition at a State College                             *
155 REM  *                                                           *
160 REM  *    Data Output:                                           *
165 REM  *      Revenue from tuition                                 *
170 REM  *                                                           *
175 REM  *    Input Data:                                            *
180 REM  *      College name, tuition per student, enrollment        *
185 REM  *                                                           *
190 REM  * * * * * * * * * * * * * * * * * * * * * * * * * * * * * * *
195 REM  *                                                           *
200 REM  *    Key:                                                   *
205 REM  *       ENROLLMENT = Enrollment at State College            *
210 REM  *       COLLEGE$   = College name                           *
215 REM  *       REVENUE    = Revenue from tuition                   *
220 REM  *       TUITION    = Tuition at State College               *
225 REM  *                                                           *
230 REM  * * * * * * * * * * * * * * * * * * * * * * * * * * * * * * *
235 REM----------------------------------------------------------------
240 REM  Input data
245 REM----------------------------------------------------------------
250          INPUT "Enter college name --->"; COLLEGE$
255          INPUT "Enter tuition -------->"; TUITION
260          INPUT "Enter enrollment ----->"; ENROLLMENT
265 REM----------------------------------------------------------------
270 REM  Calculate revenue
275 REM---------------------
280          LET REVENUE = TUITION*ENROLLMENT
285 REM----------------------------------------------------------------
290 REM  Print revenue
295 REM---------------
298          PRINT
300          PRINT "Revenue ...............$"; REVENUE
305 REM----------------------------------------------------------------
310 REM  Stop processing
315 REM-----------------
999          END
```

— Program heading with title, name, date, etc.

— Program description and other items from Step 1, Problem Analysis.

— Variable key.

— Description of segments in program's code. Essentially the same as pseudocode in Step 2.

```
RUN
Enter college name --->? Micro U
Enter tuition -------->? 750
Enter enrollment ----->? 1000

Revenue ...............$ 750000
```

NOTE 1   *Good programming style dictates that programs be well documented,* since such programs are easier to follow, modify, or otherwise update at a later time. Our documentation may seem like overkill at this time, but you will come to appreciate this point as your programs (and others you might read) increase in length and complexity. In commercial environments, extensive documentation helps to reduce software maintenance costs.

NOTE 2   The REM statement is a *nonexecutable* statement. When the program in Example 2.1 is run, the first statement executed is the INPUT in line 250. Thus REM statements are ignored during execution. They simply serve to document a program for any user who views a listing of the program (such as your instructor).

NOTE 3   Many systems allow the replacement of the keyword REM at the beginning of a line with the apostrophe or exclamation mark, which would give a cleaner look to the program in Example 2.2. Does your system allow the replacement of REM by a special character?

2.4 LET STATEMENT

A **LET statement** is used to perform and store calculations, to assign a constant to a storage location, or to copy the contents of one storage location into another. In the tuition revenue program, the statement

280 LET REVENUE = TUITION•ENROLLMENT

is an example of a LET statement. This statement multiplies tuition by enrollment and stores the numeric value 750,000 in the storage location named REVENUE.

Structure

In more general terms, the LET statement is structured as follows:

LET Statement

> **LET** *variable = expression*
>
> *LET L$ = "I love BASIC"*

On the left side of the equal sign, a single variable following the keyword LET identifies a storage location in internal computer memory.[2] The right side of the equal sign is either a string expression or a numeric expression.

LET Statement and String Expressions.   A **string expression** can be a string variable or a string constant.[3] We illustrate these next:

[2]The keyword LET can be omitted on some systems.

[3]A string expression also may include string functions and string operators, which we discuss in Module C.

E X A M P L E   2 . 3   **LETs with String Expressions**

The shaded portion in the program below illustrates two string expressions.

Program

```
100 LET L$ = "I love BASIC"          String constant
110 LET P$ = L$                      String variable
120 PRINT L$,P$
999 END
```

Output

```
I love BASIC   I love BASIC
```

After execution of lines 100 and 110, memory for these two string variables would appear as follows:

```
┌──────────┐       ┌──────────┐
│L$        │       │P$        │
│          │       │          │
│          │       │          │
│I love BASIC│     │I love BASIC│
└──────────┘       └──────────┘
```

The string expression to the right of the equal sign in line 110 is the single string variable L$. Note that the LET statement simply copies the contents of L$ into P$, leaving the contents of L$ unaffected.

LET Statement and Numeric Expressions.   A **numeric expression** may consist of a single numeric constant, a single numeric variable, or a combination of numeric constants and numeric variables separated by numeric operators and optional parentheses.[4] A **numeric operator** indicates the type of computation desired. Five symbols are used in the BASIC language to indicate the type of numeric operation, as described in Table 2.2.

Table 2.2   Numeric Operators

Numeric Operation	Numeric Operator	Example
Addition	+	$x + 2$
Subtraction	−	$x - 2$
Division	/	$x / 2$
Multiplication	☆	$x ☆ 2$
Exponentiation (raise to a power)[#]	$\wedge$	$x \wedge 2$

[#]Some systems allow the upward arrow ↑ or ☆☆ for exponentiation.

[4]A numeric expression also may include numeric functions, which we discuss in Module C.

E X A M P L E   2 . 4   **LETs with Numeric Expressions**

The shaded portion in the program below illustrates three numeric expressions.

Program
```
100 LET A = 5000
110 LET B = A
120 LET C = A + 3000
130 PRINT A,B,C
999 END
```

Output
```
5000            5000            8000
```

The relevant memory locations change as follows:

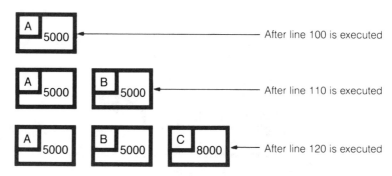

In line 100, the constant 5000 is placed in the storage location that is identified by A. In line 110, the contents of the storage location called A are copied by the storage location called B. Note, however, that this transfer is electronic; that is, whatever is in A remains there, but whatever was in B gets replaced by whatever is in A. Finally, line 120 places the computational result of the expression A + 3000 in the storage location called C. This means that the constant 3000 and the contents of A are added, and the result is stored in C.

Order of Evaluating Numeric Expressions

Computers do arithmetic on only one arithmetic operation at a time (pairwise arithmetic). Therefore, a numeric expression involving several computations must be computed in a certain sequence.

Arithmetic Hierarchy.   In BASIC, the sequence for performing pairwise numeric operations is based on the following **arithmetic hierarchy**:

- *First priority:*   All exponentiation is performed.
- *Second priority:*   All multiplication and division is completed.
- *Third priority:*   All addition and subtraction is performed.

Left-to-Right Rule.   The exact order of computation when two or more computations are at the same level of arithmetic hierarchy will be consistent with a *left-to-right scan* of the arithmetic expression, as the following example illustrates.

E X A M P L E   2 . 5   **Microeconomics Problem**

The daily cost in dollars (c) of operating a small manufacturing firm is described by the cost function

$$c = u^3 - 6u^2 + 250$$

where u represents the number of units produced by the firm per day. The following program computes this daily cost.

```
100 REM   Microeconomics Problem
110 REM
120       LET U    = 20
130       LET COST = U^3 - 6*U^2 + 250
140       PRINT COST
999       END

run
 5850
```

The LET statement is executed as follows:

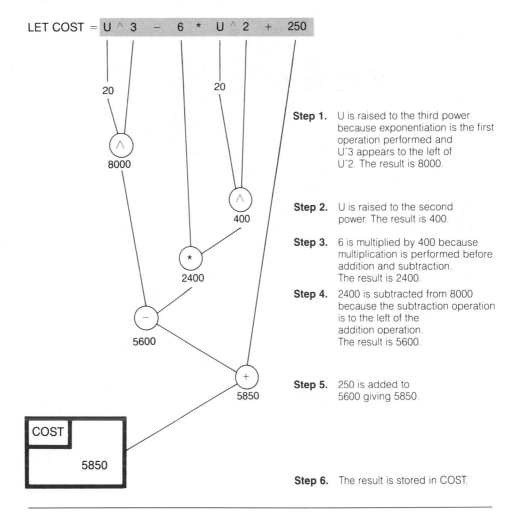

LET COST = U ^ 3 — 6 * U ^ 2 + 250

Step 1. U is raised to the third power because exponentiation is the first operation performed and U^3 appears to the left of U^2. The result is 8000.

Step 2. U is raised to the second power. The result is 400.

Step 3. 6 is multiplied by 400 because multiplication is performed before addition and subtraction. The result is 2400.

Step 4. 2400 is subtracted from 8000 because the subtraction operation is to the left of the addition operation. The result is 5600.

Step 5. 250 is added to 5600 giving 5850.

Step 6. The result is stored in COST.

Use of Parentheses.   The insertion of parentheses into arithmetic expressions changes the order of computation according to the following rules.

1. The operations inside parentheses are computed before operations that are not inside parentheses.

2. Parentheses can be embedded inside other parentheses in complicated expressions.

3. The innermost set of parentheses contains the computations done first. Note that within parentheses the hierarchy and left-to-right rules apply.

E X A M P L E   2 . 6   **Temperature Conversion**

Conversion of temperatures from Fahrenheit to Celsius is given by the formula

$$\text{Celsius} = \frac{5}{9}(\text{Fahrenheit} - 32)$$

The following program converts Fahrenheit to Celsius temperatures.

```
100 REM    Temperature Conversion
110 REM
120     LET F = 212
130     LET C = 5/9*(F - 32)
140     PRINT C
999     END

run
 100
```

The LET statement is executed as follows:

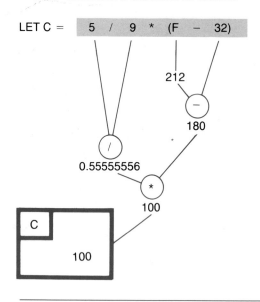

Step 1. 32 is subtracted from F because this operation is enclosed in parentheses. The result is 180.

Step 2. 5 is divided by 9 because division is to the left of multiplication.

Step 3. 0.5555556 is multiplied by 180. The result is 100.

Step 4. The result is stored in C.

NOTE   Carefully note the meaning of the equal sign (=) in BASIC; it means "place the *value* indicated by the expression to the right into the storage location indicated by the *variable* to the left." Because of this meaning, a LET statement such as

LET K = K + 1

makes sense in BASIC but not in algebra. Note that each time this statement is executed by the computer, the content (value) of K gets increased by 1. In other words, this statement instructs the computer to "add the content of K and 1, and place this result in K." This type of statement is used often in BASIC programs for the purpose of counting.

2.5 PRINT STATEMENT

The PRINT statement is used to display output values at the terminal or monitor during the execution of a program. A general form of the PRINT statement is given by

PRINT Statement

> **PRINT** *print list*
>
> PRINT "*Results*", A, B, A*B

where the print list contains one or more of the following items:

1. A constant (numeric or string)
2. A variable (numeric or string)
3. An expression (numeric or string)

Any combination of variables, constants, and expressions can be included in the PRINT statement. However, each item in the print list must be separated by either a comma or a semicolon.[5]

Printing Numeric and String Values

Study Example 2.7 and the following related points regarding the output of numeric and string values.

1. The output of a negative numeric value is preceded by the minus sign, but the output of a positive numeric value is preceded by a space to account for the missing plus sign. Output of a numeric value is usually followed by a single space. See lines 150 and 160 in Example 2.7.
2. String values are printed exactly as is, without leading or trailing blanks. See line 170 in Example 2.7.
3. A string constant in the print list must be enclosed in quotation marks. These usually serve as labels and report headings. See line 180 in Example 2.7.
4. If we omit the print list, then a blank line is "printed." This is useful for improving the readability of output. See line 190 in Example 2.7.
5. A distinct value is printed for each item in the print list. For example, line 180 in Example 2.7 prints two values; line 200 prints three values.
6. Very large and very small numeric values are printed in E-notation. See line 200 in Example 2.7.
7. Output on a print line is divided into print zones. The number of zones and the width of each varies from system to system. Five print zones of

---

[5] Some systems allow one or more blank spaces or other special characters to delimit items in the print list.

14 print columns each is common. Line 200 in Example 2.7 uses three print zones to print its three items. *How many print zones does your system use? How wide is each print zone?* (See Exercise 13.)

8. Values are printed left-justified (at the extreme left) of a print zone. See line 200 in Example 2.7.

9. When a comma in the print list precedes the item to be printed, the value is printed at the beginning of the next print zone; however, if a semicolon precedes the item, then the value is printed immediately after the last value. The use of semicolons packs the zones, which allows us to fit more output data on the print line. See lines 180, 200, and 210 in Example 2.7.

10. A trailing comma or semicolon at the end of a print list instructs the system to print the next output value on the same print line. A trailing comma moves the cursor to the next print zone on the same print line, while a trailing semicolon holds the cursor at its current location. See lines 220 and 230 in Example 2.7. Compare these to lines 150 and 160.

E X A M P L E   2 . 7   **Printing Numeric and String Values**

The following example illustrates the ten points described above.

Program	**Output**

```
100 REM   Printing Numeric and String Values
110 REM
120          LET A  = -100
130          LET B  =   15
140          LET C$ = "This begins in print column 1"
144 REM
145 REM   See points 1 and 10
150          PRINT A                              -100
160          PRINT B                               15
164 REM
165 REM   See point 2
170          PRINT C$                   This begins in print column 1
174 REM
175 REM   See points 3, 5, and 9
180          PRINT "A = "; A            A = -100
184 REM
185 REM   See point 4
190          PRINT
194 REM                         Print Zone 1   Print Zone 2   Print Zone 3
195 REM   See points 5-9
200          PRINT B, A*B, B^10         15           -1500        5.766505E+11
204 REM
205 REM   See point 9
210          PRINT B; A*B; B^10         15 -1500 5.766505E+11
214 REM
215 REM   See point 10
220          PRINT A;                   -100  15
230          PRINT B
998 REM
999          END
```

The TAB Function

Use of the comma (,) and the semicolon (;) to space output is sometimes inconvenient. The TAB function is a formatting feature that allows convenient spacing of output. This function is used only as an item within the print list of a PRINT statement. Its general form is

TAB Function

```
TAB(argument)
TAB(10)
```

where the *argument* represents a numeric constant, numeric variable, or numeric expression that is evaluated and rounded to the nearest integer value. The value of the argument determines the column in which the next character is printed.

E X A M P L E   2 . 8   **The TAB Function**

Study the following variations.

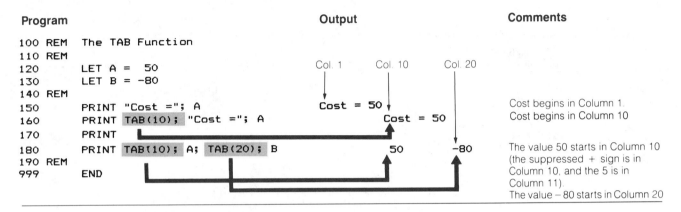

Program	Output	Comments
100 REM The TAB Function		
110 REM		
120 LET A = 50	Col. 1 Col. 10 Col. 20	
130 LET B = -80		
140 REM		
150 PRINT "Cost ="; A	Cost = 50	Cost begins in Column 1.
160 PRINT TAB(10); "Cost ="; A	Cost = 50	Cost begins in Column 10
170 PRINT		
180 PRINT TAB(10); A; TAB(20); B	50 -80	The value 50 starts in Column 10 (the suppressed + sign is in Column 10, and the 5 is in Column 11).
190 REM		The value - 80 starts in Column 20
999 END		

NOTE 1   Use the semicolon delimiter following each TAB function and item in the print list; otherwise, output may revert back to standard print zones.

NOTE 2   The PRINT USING statement discussed in Module D is the ultimate tool for the precise control of output. Try reading this module after this or the next chapter.

2.6 INPUT STATEMENT

Normally a program receives data in one or more of the following ways:

- We enter data interactively while the program is running by using INPUT statements.
- We enter data as we write the program by using READ and DATA statements.
- We enter data from data files outside the program.

We shall discuss the first two types of data entry in this chapter and wait until Module E to discuss data files.

The INPUT statement allows us to supply data to a program from the keyboard *while the program is running.* When the computer executes an INPUT statement, it prints a prompt on the screen, usually a question mark (?), and suspends execution of the program until we enter data. After the data are entered, the computer stores the data items within the variables indicated in the INPUT statement.

A simple form of the INPUT statement is

Simple INPUT Statement

> **INPUT** *input list*
> INPUT A,B,C

where the input list contains variable names (separated by commas) in the exact sequence that data items are to be entered.

A good programming practice is to print a prompting message that reminds the program user of which data are to be entered next. This is accomplished in various ways, depending on the BASIC dialect.

E X A M P L E 2 . 9 Input Approaches

Table 2.3 shows different approaches to conversational input, depending on the dialect.

Table 2.3 Input Approaches (Example 2.9)

BASIC Dialect	Code	Input/Output (I/0)
Minimal	``` 100 PRINT "Enter 3 values"; 110 INPUT A,B,C 120 PRINT A;B;C 999 END ```	Enter 3 values? 5,10,15 5 10 15

Remarks: This approach works on any system. Each INPUT statement is immediately preceded by a PRINT statement that prints the message prompt. The trailing semicolon is used in line 100 so that the system places the ? prompt on the same line as the message, thereby allowing entry of the three data values to the right of the message.

BASIC Dialect	Code	Input/Output (I/0)
ANS True	``` INPUT PROMPT "Enter 3 values? ": A,B,C PRINT A;B;C END ```	Enter 3 values? 5,10,15 5 10 15

Remarks: This approach uses a new statement called the **INPUT PROMPT statement** to serve this purpose. Note that this statement suppresses the ? prompt, so we include it as part of the message. In practice we need not use the question mark. For example, we could leave it off altogether or substitute something more appropriate such as = or ---->. Also note that the colon (:) is used to separate the message prompt from the variable input list.

BASIC Dialect	Code	Input/Output (I/0)
Microsoft VAX-11	``` 100 INPUT "Enter 3 values";A,B,C 110 PRINT A;B;C 999 END ```	Enter 3 values? 5,10,15 5 10 15

Remarks: This approach simply includes the message as a string constant within the input list. Note that the semicolon (;) is used to separate the message prompt from the input list of variables.

Your system
(if different)

Note the following:

1. The computer prints a question-mark prompt when it executes the INPUT statement and then awaits the input of three data items from the user.

2. The INPUT statement has three numeric variables in its input list; hence, the user must enter three numeric values following the prompt, each separated from the other by a comma. *Throughout the text we show what the user types in color, to distinguish it from what the computer types.*

3. The user then strikes the "Enter" or "Carriage Return" key, and the computer stores the three values 5, 10, and 15 in the respective memory locations A, B, and C. Note that the first value (5) is placed in the location corresponding to the first variable in the input list (A), the second value is matched with the second variable (10 with B), and so forth.

NOTE The type of program shown in the preceding example is called an **interactive program**, because the user enters data in response to a prompt from the program. Thus the user and program (computer) interact with one another.

E X A M P L E 2 . 10 Tuition Revenue Problem

Let's return to our tuition revenue program.

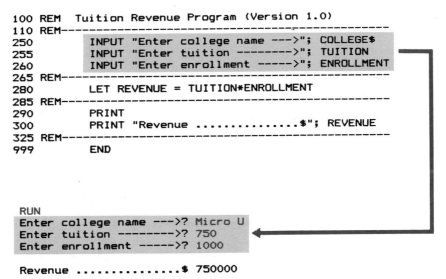

```
100 REM  Tuition Revenue Program (Version 1.0)
110 REM----------------------------------------
250       INPUT "Enter college name --->"; COLLEGE$
255       INPUT "Enter tuition -------->"; TUITION
260       INPUT "Enter enrollment ----->"; ENROLLMENT
265 REM----------------------------------------
280       LET REVENUE = TUITION*ENROLLMENT
285 REM----------------------------------------
290       PRINT
300       PRINT "Revenue ..............$"; REVENUE
325 REM----------------------------------------
999       END
```

```
RUN
Enter college name --->? Micro U
Enter tuition -------->? 750
Enter enrollment ----->? 1000

Revenue ..............$ 750000
```

Note the following:

1. We used the Microsoft and VAX-11 approach to conversational input. Is your system different?

2. The first input line illustrates how we can enter a string value. In this case we simply entered the unquoted string *Micro U* with no problem; however, suppose we were to enter as follows:

Comma delimits input

```
Enter college name --->? Micro U, Sunnyside Campus
```

This input would be interpreted as two separate values by most systems, since the comma acts as a delimiter. The typical system response is a request to reenter the data. For this situation we need to enter a quoted string:

Quotes take care
of the problem

```
Enter college name --->? "Micro U, Sunnyside Campus"
```

2.7 READ, DATA, AND RESTORE STATEMENTS

The use of READ and DATA statements is another approach to providing data. In this case, unlike the INPUT statement, data are supplied within the program prior to execution.

General Form

The READ statement assigns values to variables that are initially typed onto DATA statements. The general form of the READ statement is

> **READ Statement**
>
> **READ** *read list*
> READ CITY$,STATE$,ZIP

where the read list contains variables (separated by commas) in the same sequence as the items of data that are to be entered into memory.

The READ statement must be used with a nonexecutable statement called the DATA statement. The DATA statement contains the data items (values) that correspond to the list of variables in the READ statement. The general form of the DATA statement is

> **DATA Statement**
>
> **DATA** *data list*
> DATA "Miami","FL",33145

where each item in the data list is either a numeric constant or a string constant, separated by a comma from the preceding data item.

The READ statement, when executed, retrieves as many values from one or more DATA statements as variables in the list of the READ statement. For example, if the list of a READ statement contains five numeric variables, then execution of this READ statement processes five numeric values from one or more DATA statements. The variables in the READ statement and the values in the DATA statement are matched in an ordered fashion—that is, the first variable with the first data value, the second variable with the second value, and so on.

E X A M P L E   2 . 1 1   READ/DATA Statements

Study the following program and its run.

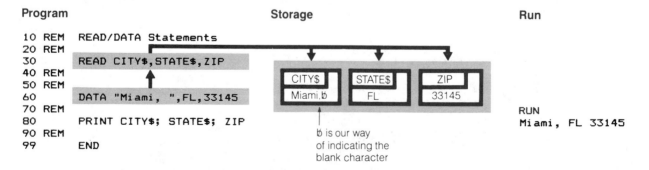

```
Program                         Storage                          Run

10 REM   READ/DATA Statements
20 REM
30       READ CITY$,STATE$,ZIP
40 REM                            CITY$      STATE$      ZIP
50 REM
60       DATA "Miami, ",FL,33145   Miami,b     FL        33145
70 REM                                                         RUN
80       PRINT CITY$; STATE$; ZIP                              Miami, FL 33145
90 REM                            b is our way
99       END                      of indicating the
                                  blank character
```

Note the following:

1. When the READ statement is executed, the three successive values in the DATA statement are entered into the three respective memory locations according to the variable list in the READ statement.

2. The portion "Miami," within the DATA statement is called a quoted string, since the string constant is within quotes. In this case, it's necessary to use quotes to store the comma (which otherwise would act as a delimiter) and trailing blank.

3. The string constant FL is an unquoted string in line 60. In this case, it's not necessary to enclose the string in quotes, since it does not contain commas, leading or trailing blanks, or other special characters that could cause problems.

4. Each item in the data list is separated from the preceding item by a comma.

5. To avoid syntax errors, make sure that items in the read list and data list correspond with respect to type; that is, match a string variable with a string constant and a numeric variable with a numeric constant.

6. The DATA statement can be placed anywhere in the program, since it's nonexecutable.

Data Blocks

The data values from *all* DATA statements in a program are combined by the BASIC compiler or interpreter into a *single* sequence of data items called a **data block**. The data values are placed into the data block in the order of their appearance in the program; that is, a data value on a lower-numbered line is placed ahead of a value on a higher-numbered line, and a data value to the left is placed ahead of a data value to the right.

The data in the DATA statements from line 60 in Example 2.11 are combined into a data block that can be visualized as follows:

Data Block

Miami, b

FL

33145

Even if the data were typed

```
60 DATA "Miami,b"
61 DATA FL
62 DATA 33145
```

the computer still would combine the data into the same data block. The only thing that counts is the sequence, or order of appearance, of data items in the data lists.

Moreover, the following READ statements could have been used:

```
30 READ CITY$
31 READ STATE$
32 READ ZIP
```

It still doesn't matter, since the only thing that counts is the order of the items, which remains CITY$, STATE$, ZIP in the READ statements and "Miami,ƀ", FL,33145 in the data block.

NOTE 1   When a program with READ/DATA statements is run, the computer maintains a *pointer* to the next item of data to be read into a memory location. When the program begins execution, this pointer indicates the first item in the block of data values. Each time a READ statement is executed, values from the data block are assigned to the variables in the READ statement based on the location of the pointer. When the execution of a READ statement is completed, the pointer is advanced to the data value immediately following the last data value read in.

NOTE 2   Take care that the number of items in the data block at least equals the number of variables processed in the read lists; otherwise, we would get an "out of data" error.

Restoring the Pointer

Sometimes it's necessary to reread the same data within the same program, which brings us to the RESTORE statement. A general form of this statement is

RESTORE Statement

> RESTORE

The RESTORE statement resets the pointer back to the beginning of the data block, so that the next READ statement executed will read data from the beginning again.

2.8 POINTERS

This chapter (and those that follow) concludes with a section called *Pointers* that reinforces and summarizes design and style suggestions and highlights common errors.

Design and Style

The following suggestions should improve the readability and reliability (and the grades!) of your programs.

1. **Variable names.**   Choose names for variables that are descriptive of the data.
2. **Use of spaces.**   Most systems ignore blank spaces except within quoted strings. In general, we should use spaces to improve the readability and visual appeal of programs.
3. **Output design.**   Pay attention to output design. Facilitate its readability and understanding by well-chosen labels, alignment, and spacing. Avoid clutter and unlabeled output. Use aids such as TAB functions and semicolons for compression, commas for blank zones, and PRINTs with no print list for blank print lines.

4. **Input design.**   Good commercial interactive programs place great emphasis on input design, since it is a key factor in ensuring correct data entry and responses.

5. **Documentation.**   Do a good job of documenting programs, as described in Section 2.3. Use proper indentation when REMs and other statements appear in the same section.

6. **Numbering lines.**   If you need to number lines on your system, then increment the line numbers by at least 10 at the outset. This gives room for inserting new lines of code.

7. **On providing data.**   Before designing and writing programs, we need to think carefully about the treatment of provided data. There are five choices:

   - As constants in an expression
   - As variables initialized through a LET statement
   - As variables through READ/DATA statements
   - As variables through INPUT statements
   - As variables through data file input statements (Module E)

   For example, consider the data items 3.141593 for *pi* and 5 for radius. The value for *pi* is best provided either as a constant in the arithmetic expression or as a variable in LET or READ/DATA statements. Since this value does not change over time, it simplifies program maintenance to treat it under one of the first three options. Data items that don't change within a computer run are usually called **parameters**. Values that are likely to change over time, however, are best treated as variables that store these values through the last three options. In particular, data input through INPUT statements is best in interactive environments where the user can experiment with different values based on a dialog with the computer. For example, we might ask a question such as "What if the radius were 6 instead of 5?" This type of what if . . .? analysis is common in practice.

Common Errors

The subsections labeled *Common Errors* describe many of the common errors made by beginning (and, sometimes, experienced) programmers. The following errors are common to the material in this chapter. (Also, see the errors described in Module B.)

1. **Naming variables.**   Confirm the syntax rules for naming variables on your system (see Table 2.1). Also, check out the keywords on your system (see the inside covers). If every line that uses a particular variable has a syntax error, then suspect a problem with the way you named that variable.

2. **REM statement.**   Don't forget to use the keyword REM (or a substitute symbol for your system) for lines that have comments or remarks.

3. **LET statement.**   Pay close attention to hierarchy, left-to-right, and parentheses rules when forming numeric expressions. Two common syntax errors are unmatched parentheses and missing numeric operators.

4. **PRINT statement.**   Don't forget to include quotes in string constants within print lists. Also, make sure each item in the print list is delimited (computer talk for separated) with a proper symbol (usually the comma or semicolon).

5. **Input errors.** Make sure to enter the exact number of values required by the input list, and that they match by type (string values paired with string variables and numeric values paired with numeric variables). For this reason, it's usually best to design INPUT statements with only one variable in the input list.

6. **READ/DATA errors.** Too few values in the data block and value/variable type mismatches are common. Also, don't place a trailing comma at the end of a data line.

FOLLOW-UP EXERCISES

1. Identify what, if anything, is wrong with each of the following constants.
   a. 1,000,000   f. 2.5E175
   b. +7.3   g. 2.5E1.5
   c. 614.25−   h. "COST
   d. −614.25   i. $500
   e. 7*5   j. 65789024517

2. Express the following constants using E-notation.
   a. -6.142×10^{15} b. 0.00007

3. Express the following constants using standard notation.
   a. 123E9   b. 4.56E−2

4. Identify each of the following as numeric variable, string variable, or unacceptable variable.
   a. 1T   e. ITEM.NAME$
   b. T1   f. PROFIT
   c. ITEM NAME$ g. $P
   d. ITEM_NAME$ h. 7

5. Modify Example 2.3 as indicated and describe the output.
   a. 115 LET L$ = "I'm not sure"
   b. 115 LET L$ = L$

6. Modify Example 2.4 as indicated and describe the output.
   a. 120 LET C = A/2
   b. 120 LET C = A*2
   c. 120 LET C = A^2

7. Consider the following sequence
   ```
   10 LET A = 37/C
   15 LET B = A + 1.6
   20 LET D = B^2
   25 LET C = C + 1
   ```
   and the current contents given below.

   Indicate the new contents after the execution of the above statements.

8. In Example 2.6, what would be stored under C if the LET statement were as follows:
   ```
   20 LET C = 5/9*F − 32
   ```

9. What values are stored in P and R after the following program segment is executed?
   ```
   100 LET E = 1000
   110 LET U = 5000
   120 LET P = E/U*100
   130 LET R = E/(U*100)
   ```

10. Indicate what would be stored in A for each of the following, given that 3 is in B and 2 is in C.
    a. 80 LET A = (4 + B^3 − C)*C^2
    b. 82 LET A = (4 + B^(3 − C))*C^2
    c. 86 LET A = 9/B*C + 5/C
    d. 92 LET A = 9/B*(C+5) /C

11. Write numeric expressions for each of the following algebraic expressions.
    a. x^{i+1}
    b. $\dfrac{s^2}{(p-1)}$
    c. $(y - 3^{x-1} + 2)^5$

12. Identify what is wrong, if anything, with each of the following LET statements.
    a. 05 LET B + C = A
    b. 10 LET D = 4.1 * −X
    c. 15 LET 5 = A
    d. 20 L = 8^K + 4

13. Run the following program on your system:
    ```
    10 PRINT "00000000011111111112222222222233333333334"
    20 PRINT "12345678901234567890123456789012345678890"
    30 LET A = −5.4
    40 PRINT A,A,A,A,A,A,A
    99 END
    ```

    How long is each print zone on your system? How many zones fit on a print line? What happens when you try to print too many items on one print line? Ask your instructor (or check your system's User Manual) if it's possible to increase or decrease the length of the print line.

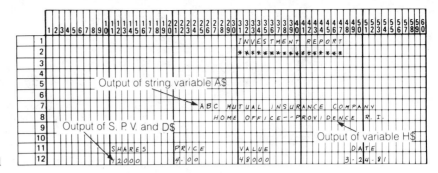

Figure 1

14. First describe the print lines for each case below. Then run these on your system. Assume −5 is stored in **X**, 10 is stored in **Y**, 15 is stored in **Z**, and AKA is stored in **N$**.
    a. 15 PRINT X,Y;Z
    b. 15 PRINT X;Y,Z
    c. 15 PRINT X;Y,
       20 PRINT Z
    d. 15 PRINT X;Y;
       20 PRINT Z
    e. 15 PRINT "X = ";X
       20 PRINT
       25 PRINT "Y = ",Y
       30 PRINT
       35 PRINT
       40 PRINT "Z = ";Z;"%"
    f. 15 PRINT "X","Y"
       20 PRINT X,Y
    g. 15 PRINT TAB(5);"X";TAB(10);"Y"
       20 PRINT TAB(5);"---------"
       25 PRINT TAB(5);X;TAB(10);Y
    h. 15 PRINT N$,N$
       20 PRINT N$;N$
       25 PRINT N$;" ";N$

*15. Supply PRINT statements that incorporate the TAB function for the output shown in Figure 1.

16. Try the program in Table 2.3 on your system. Deliberately enter too few and then too many data values to familiarize yourself with the error response on your system. What would happen if you were to omit the trailing semicolon in the Minimal BASIC version?

17. Write statements for the following conversational input:

a. Enter name, SS Number, and age (separated by commas)?
                                    Values for
                                    N$,S,A

b. Do you wish to print output (Y/N)?
                              Value for R$

*c. Enter principal ....? ◄——— Value for P
    Enter number of years ...? ◄——— Value for N
    Enter interest rate ....? ◄——— Value for I

*18. Write the segment of code that prints the following on the screen:

SAMPLE PROGRAM
A – MUSIC
B – ART
C – MORTGAGE

Enter letter of program?
                    └——— Value for C$

19. What do you expect will happen in Example 2.11 for each case below?
    a. Eliminate the quotes in line 60.
    b. Insert two spaces between FL and the comma in line 60.
    c. Reverse the read list in line 30.
    d. Use the following data list:

       "Kingston, ", RI,02881

       How would you correct the problem?
    e. Delete the portion following FL in line 60.

    Try these on your system.

20. Indicate storage contents for D$.
    a. 10 READ D$
       20 PRINT D$
       90 DATA July 21, 2001
       99 END

    b. 10 READ D$
       20 PRINT D$
       90 DATA "July 21, 2001"
       99 END

    Try running these programs.

21. Indicate the contents in A, B, C, D.

    10 READ A, B
    20 RESTORE
    30 READ C, D
    40 DATA 100, 150
    99 END

*22. Modify the tuition revenue program in Example 2.10 on page 29 by replacing INPUT statements with READ/DATA statements.

*Answers to single-starred excercises are not given in the back of the text. Ask your instructor.

A WORD OF CAUTION	Please study Modules A and B following Chapter 7 before running any of this chapter's programming exercises on your computer.

PLEASE NOTE	End-of-chapter assignments in this and other chapters generally require you to prepare and submit the following documentation of the four-step procedure:

1. *Problem Analysis.* A brief description of the problem including the required output and the provided (e.g., input) data items
2. *Program Design.* Either pseudocode or a flowchart
3. *Program Code.* A listing of your BASIC program, including program documentation
4. *Program Test.* Sample runs showing test data and results

To be sure, ask your instructor. Also, check on the procedure for your system for obtaining *hard-copy* listings and test runs.

ON THE RIGHT PERSPECTIVE	You might find it useful to take the perspective that the applications programs you develop are to be actually used by others. This will increase your awareness and appreciation of the issues that face the developers of applications software (and should improve your grade).

ADDITIONAL EXERCISES

23. Mileage Problem. Write an interactive program to compute miles per gallon and cost per mile for an automobile. For each gas stop, enter the following data:

Beginning odometer reading
Ending odometer reading
Gallons to fill tank
Cost to fill tank

After these data are entered, the program outputs the following:

miles per gallon
cost per mile

Use the following data to test your program:

	First Stop	Second Stop
Beginning odometer reading	18763	19124
Ending odometer reading	19124	19524
Gallons to fill tank	13.4	14.3
Cost to fill tank	14.85	16.15

24. Unit Pricing. Write a program that a grocery clerk can use to compute unit prices for shelf labels. The clerk enters:

Product name
Quantity in ounces
Selling price

The computer then prints the unit cost. Unit cost is determined using the following formula:

Unit cost = selling price × 100 ÷ quantity

a. Process the following data in your test runs:

Product Name	Quantity	Selling Price
Chips	8 oz	$1.29
Chore	4 lb 1 oz	1.79
Sip	67.6 oz	2.19

b. Allow the clerk to enter the quantity in pounds and ounces and then convert to ounces before unit cost is determined.

25. Mutual Funds. Investors who do not wish to buy individual stocks and bonds can invest in mutual funds, which offer a portfolio of professionally managed stocks or bonds. In so-called load funds, a sales charge is levied on the amount invested. Some funds also have a redemption fee, which levies a charge on the amount withdrawn from the fund. For example, if $10,000 is invested and the sales charge is 2%, then the amount actually invested is $10,000 \times 0.98$, or $9800. If this amount grows at an annual return of 10% per year, then after, say, five years the investment is worth $(9800) \times (1.1)^5$, or $15,783. However, if the fund charges a 1% redemption fee, then the investor can withdraw 15783×0.99, or about $15,625. The amount that can be withdrawn is computed from the formula

$$W = A(1 - s)(1 + r)^t(1 - f)$$

where W = amount that can be withdrawn after t years

A = amount originally invested
s = sales charge as a proportion
r = annual return as a proportion
t = time in years
f = redemption fee as a proportion

For our example, we have

$$W = 10000(1 - 0.02)(1 + 0.1)^5(1 - 0.01)$$
$$= 15625$$

a. Write a program that inputs A, s, r, t, and f and prints W. Use the following test data:

	A	s	r	t	f
Test 1	10000	0.020	0.10	5	0.01
Test 2	10000	0.085	0.10	5	0.00
Test 3	10000	0.020	0.10	25	0.01
Test 4	10000	0.020	0.15	25	0.01

Tests 1 and 2 represent two typical types of mutual funds: one with a low front load charge with a redemption fee and one with a high front load charge and no redemption fee. Which is best for our hypothetical investor?

b. Also output the fees (sales and redemption) that are retained by the mutual fund.

26. Bates Motel. The motel owner wants to prepare a bill for each customer at check-out time. The desk clerk is to enter the following data:

Customer name
Room number
Room charge
Restaurant charges
Bar charges

The program computes the following:

Service charge .... 5% of room and restaurant charges
Sales tax .... 6% of room, restaurant, and bar charges
Total bill .... Sum of room, restaurant, bar, service, and sales tax charges.

a. Develop a program that prepares a bill for each customer. Take some time to plan the I/O design. Use the following test data:

	First Customer	Second Customer
Customer name	Ada Lovelace	Mr. Hollerith
Room number	80	82
Room charge	$110.00	$160.00
Restaurant charges	45.15	83.50
Bar charges	0.00	15.00

b. Have the program print the following block letters across the top of the bill:

```
****        *       *****   *****   *****
*    *    *    *     *       *       *
*****    *****      *      ****    *****
*    *    *    *     *       *           *
****      *    *      *     *****   *****
```

27. Blood Bank Inventory. Decision making relating to the management of physical inventories is an established area in the management sciences, which in recent years has been applied increasingly in semi-private and public organizations.

Suppose that whenever a hospital replenishes its supply of a certain type of blood, it orders from a regional blood bank the amount indicated by the formula

$$q = \sqrt{2 \cdot c \cdot d / h}$$

where q is the number of pints of blood to order, c is the administrative and shipping cost (in dollars) of placing the order, d is the average weekly demand (usage) for this type of blood, and h is the cost (dollars per pint per week) of refrigerating the blood.

Also, it can be shown that the cost per week of this inventory policy is given by the formula

$$e = \sqrt{2 \cdot c \cdot h \cdot d}$$

where e is the expected cost (dollars) per week. Write a computer program that inputs values of c, h, and d and determines how much blood to order and the cost of such a policy.

Run your program and answer the following questions: How many units of blood should be ordered if it costs $50 to place an order, weekly demand averages 3000 pints, and it costs $0.20 per week per pint of blood to refrigerate? How much should be ordered if the refrigeration cost increases to $0.30? What is the expected cost per week for each of the above?

28. Automobile Financing. Many consumer automobile loans require the borrower to pay the same amount of money to the lending institution each month throughout the life of the loan. The monthly payment is based on the amount borrowed (purchase price − trade-in of used car − down payment), the time required for repayment, and the interest rate. A lending institution uses the following formula to determine the car buyer's monthly payment:

$$a = i \cdot (p - d - t) \cdot \left(\frac{(1 + i)^m}{(1 + i)^m - 1} \right)$$

where a = monthly payments
 p = purchase price of car
 d = down payment
 t = trade-in allowance
 i = monthly interest rate
 m = total number of monthly payments

If the interest rate is expressed on an annual basis, then i in the above formula is replaced by $i/12$. Note that $(p - d - t)$ is the amount to be borrowed.

a. Write a program that determines monthly payments, given purchase price, down payment, trade-in allowance, *annual* interest rate, and total number of monthly payments as input data. Include amount borrowed, total number of months, and annual *percent* interest rate in your output, along with the monthly payment. Also include the make and model of the automobile as part of your I/O. Process the following data:

Make	Model	Price	Down	Trade-in	Annual Interest	Months
Lotus	1	$12,000	$2,000	$1,000	0.15	60
Lotus	2	12,000	4,000	1,000	0.15	60
Lotus	3	12,000	2,000	1,000	0.15	48
Packard	Turbo	20,000	3,000	0	0.14	36

b. Design your program also to calculate and print:

total amount paid over the life of the loan
total interest paid over the life of the loan
the ratio of total interest to total amount paid

FOR/NEXT Loops

3

Looping is the ability of a programming language to repeatedly execute a set of statements. This is the most powerful feature of a programming language, as it enables the automatic processing of large amounts of similar data. For example, any realistic version of our tuition revenue program must include a loop for processing all institutions in the state system in one computer run.

3.1 FOR/NEXT LOOP MECHANICS

A **loop** is completely defined by its loop body and loop control. The **loop body** is the set of statements that is to be repeatedly executed. The **loop control** specifies either the number of times a loop is to be repeated or the test condition that determines when the loop is to be terminated.

A **FOR/NEXT loop** is defined by a **FOR statement** at the beginning of the loop and a **NEXT statement** at the end of the loop. All executable statements in between are the loop body. Loop control details are expressed in the FOR statement. See Figure 3.1 on the next page.

In the FOR statement we supply information that determines the number of **loop iterations**, that is, the number of times that the body of the loop is to be executed.

1. We specify the control variable, a simple numeric variable. In the Figure 3.1 example, *J* is the control variable.

2. We specify the initial value of the control variable as a numeric constant, numeric variable, or, generally, any numeric expression. For example, *J* is initially set to 1 in the example, since 1 is the value found in the initial-value position.

3. We specify the limit of the control variable as a numeric constant, numeric variable, or, generally, any numeric expression. The value of the control variable must exceed (when the increment is positive) or be less than (when the increment is negative) the limit before the loop is terminated. In our example, looping continues while the value of *J* is 5 or less.

4. We specify the increment as a numeric constant, numeric variable, or, generally, any numeric expression. The value of the control variable changes

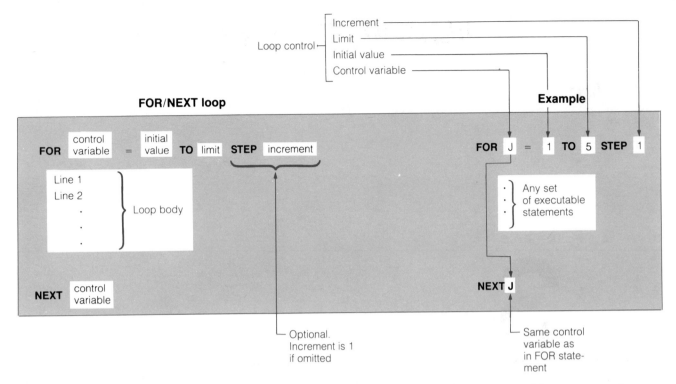

Figure 3.1   Logic of FOR/NEXT loop for positive increment (change ≤ to ≥ for negative increment). Figure continues on facing page.

by the increment at each iteration of the FOR/NEXT loop. Thus, in our example, the value of J increases by 1 each time the loop iterates.

In our simple example, the body of the loop is executed five times as J becomes 1, 2, 3, 4, and 5. By the way, the increment can be omitted, in which case BASIC assumes it has a value of 1. For example,

FOR J = 1 to 5   ◄——— STEP 1 can be omitted

is equivalent to

FOR J = 1 to 5   STEP 1

To better understand the mechanics of the FOR/NEXT loop consider Figure 3.1. When the FOR statement is executed, the FOR/NEXT loop is activated, whereby J is set to 1 (Step 1 in flowchart) and the loop-control test is made (Step 2 in flowchart). Since the current value of 1 for J does not exceed the limit of 5, the body of the loop is processed (Step 3) for the first time. Next, J is increased by its increment of 1 (Step 4) to a value of 2. Control then returns to the beginning of the loop, and the loop-control test is performed again (Step 2). J is again less than the limit; so the loop body is processed a second time. This process continues until the control variable has been incremented to 6. At this point the loop-control test yields a "No" response, which transfers control to the next executable statement (Step 5) following the FOR/NEXT loop. The FOR/NEXT loop is now *inactive*. Note that the loop iterates five times, which means that the body is sequentially processed five times.

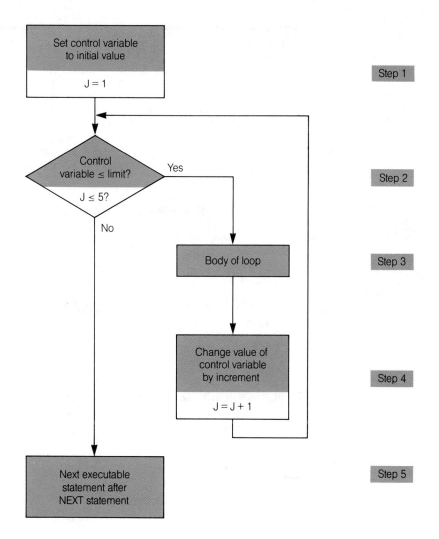

		Execution Summary	
Sample Program and Run	*J*	*Execute Body?*	*Iteration*
10 FOR J = 1 TO 5 STEP 1	1	Yes	1
20 PRINT J;	2	Yes	2
30 NEXT J			
40 PRINT "Exit"	3	Yes	3
99 END	4	Yes	4
RUN	5	Yes	5
1 2 3 4 5 Exit	6	No	Exit

NOTE 1 *The number of iterations in a FOR/NEXT loop is given by the limit when both the initial value and increment are 1.* In this case the control variable is said to be a *counter,* and the loop is called a *counter-controlled loop.* Figure 3.1 shows a counter-controlled loop that iterates five times, since both the initial value and the increment are 1 and the limit is 5.

NOTE 2 Execution of the FOR statement sets the control variable to its initial value and provides other necessary loop-control information. However, the FOR statement is never re-executed as the loop iterates; only the body gets re-executed. See the flowchart in Figure 3.1 to reinforce the fact that the

Table 3.1　FOR/NEXT Loop Mechanics

Example	K	Execute Body?	Iteration	Remark

a.　`10 FOR K = 3 TO 10 STEP 2`
　　`20   PRINT K;`
　　`30 NEXT K`
　　`40 PRINT "Exit"`
　　`99 END`
　　`RUN`
　　`3  5  7  9 Exit`
	3
	5
	7
	9
	11
		Yes
		Yes
		Yes
		Yes
		No
			1
			2
			3
			4
			Exit
				Initial values and increments need not be 1. The loop iterates 4 times.

b.　`10 FOR K = 3 TO 1 STEP -1`
　　`20   PRINT K;`
　　`30 NEXT K`
　　`40 PRINT "Exit"`
　　`99 END`
　　`RUN`
　　`3   2   1 Exit`
	3
	2
	1
	0
		Yes
		Yes
		Yes
		No
			1
			2
			3
			Exit
				The increment is negative. Note how K decreases. The loop iterates 3 times.

c.　`10 FOR K = 3 TO 1`
　　`20   PRINT K;`
　　`30 NEXT K`
　　`40 PRINT "Exit"`
　　`99 END`
　　`RUN`
　　`Exit`
	3	No	Exit	The loop never iterates (is inactive) since initial value exceeds limit and the step is $+1$.

d.　`10 FOR K = 1.5 TO 2.5 STEP .5`
　　`20   PRINT K;`
　　`30 NEXT K`
　　`40 PRINT "Exit"`
　　`99 END`
　　`RUN`
　　`1.5  2  2.5 Exit`
	1.5
	2.0
	2.5
	3.0
		Yes
		Yes
		Yes
		No
			1
			2
			3
			Exit
				The control variable is a decimal number. The loop iterates 3 times.

e.　`5 LET U = 1`
　　`10 FOR K = U TO 2*U STEP U/2`
　　`20   PRINT K;`
　　`30 NEXT K`
　　`40 PRINT "Exit"`
　　`99 END`
　　`RUN`
　　`1  1.5  2 Exit`
	1.0
	1.5
	2.0
	2.5
		Yes
		Yes
		Yes
		No
			1
			2
			3
			Exit
				FOR/NEXT parameters need not be constants. Here we show use of a variable (U) and numeric expressions. The loop iterates 3 times.

loop-back point is just above the implicit loop-control test represented by the diamond but is below the box that represents the FOR statement. To make sure you understand how loop iterations work, study the examples in Table 3.1.

3.2 INTERNAL DATA FILES

A powerful feature of loops is their ability to process large amounts of similar data. We illustrate this next by example.

E X A M P L E   3 . 1   Tuition Revenue Problem with FOR/NEXT Loop

Consider the following version of the tuition revenue problem.

Design

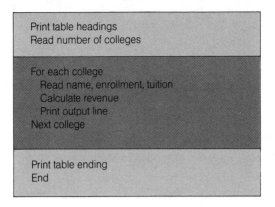

Print table headings
Read number of colleges

For each college
    Read name, enrollment, tuition
    Calculate revenue
    Print output line
Next college

Print table ending
End

Code

```
100 REM------------------------------------------------
105 REM   Tuition Revenue Program (Version 2.0)
110 REM------------------------------------------------
120      PRINT TAB(14); "TUITION REVENUE REPORT"
130      PRINT TAB(5); "-------------------------------------------"      ⎫
140      PRINT TAB(5); "College"; TAB(28); "Number of"                    ⎪ These print
150      PRINT TAB(5); "Name"; TAB(18); "Tuition"; TAB(28); "Students";   ⎬ report headings.
160      PRINT TAB(38); "Revenue"                                         ⎪ See output, Part A.
170      PRINT TAB(5); "-------------------------------------------"      ⎭
180 REM------------------------------------------------
190      READ N  ◄──────────────────────────────────────  Use of variable promotes loop generality
200 REM------------------------------------------------
210      FOR J = 1 TO N  ◄                                                ⎫
220        READ COLLEGE$,ENROLLMENT,TUITION                               ⎪
230        LET REVENUE = TUITION*ENROLLMENT                               ⎪ These print
240        PRINT TAB(5); COLLEGE$; TAB(18); TUITION; TAB(28); ENROLLMENT; ⎬ report (table) lines.
250        PRINT TAB(38); REVENUE                                         ⎪ See output, Part B.
260      NEXT J                                                          ⎭
270 REM------------------------------------------------
280      PRINT TAB(5); "-------------------------------------------"      ⎱ This prints
330 REM------------------------------------------------                   ⎰ report ending.
900      DATA 3                                                             See output Part C.
901      DATA "Micro U",1000,750
902      DATA "Mini U" ,2500,1000  ◄───────────────────────  Internal data file
903      DATA "Maxi U" ,6000,1100
998 REM------------------------------------------------
999      END
```

Test

```
         TUITION REVENUE REPORT                    ⎫
-------------------------------------------        ⎪
College              Number of                     ⎬ Part A
Name         Tuition  Students  Revenue            ⎪
-------------------------+-----------------         ⎭
Micro U       750      1000      750000            ⎫
Mini U       1000      2500     2500000            ⎬ Part B.
Maxi U       1100      6000     6600000            ⎭
-------------------------------------------        ⎱ Part C.
```

Discussion

Note the following points.

1. The number of colleges to be processed is read in under the variable *N*. Its value of 3 in the data section is consistent with the fact that three colleges are to be processed. *N* is also the limit in the FOR statement. Since this is a counter-controlled loop, the value of 3 in *N* is the number of loop iterations; that is, the loop will process three colleges.

2. The body of the loop iterates three times, which gives the successive values in memory that are shown in Table 3.2, as if a "snapshot" were taken just before the NEXT statement is executed.

Table 3.2   Successive Values in Memory

N	J	COLLEGE$	TUITION	ENROLLMENT	REVENUE
3	1	Micro U	750	1000	750000
	2	Mini U	1000	2500	2500000
	3	Maxi U	1100	6000	6600000

Note that each execution of the READ statement in line 220 processes an entire data line. Thus, when the READ statement is executed during the first iteration (*J* = 1), all data items in line 901 are read into memory; when *J* = 2, execution of line 220 processes line 902; and when *J* = 3, the READ statement processes line 903.

3. The repeated execution of the PRINT statements within the loop body (see lines 240–250) gives the output a tablelike appearance (see Part B in the output). Note that line 240 has a trailing semicolon. Thus lines 240–250 behave like a single PRINT statement. PRINT statements for labels and column headings must *precede* the loop structure (see lines 120–170), so that these are printed just before the output table (see Part A in the output). Finally, PRINT statements for post-table material, such as dashed lines and summary statistics (see line 280), are placed *after* the loop structure (see Part C in the output).

NOTE 1   Use of the variable *N* instead of the constant 3 in the FOR statement of Example 3.1 illustrates a style of programming whereby variables (symbols) are used in place of constants. *This promotes the generality of programs.* In our example, we need not make changes within the executable portion of the program (line 210) to process a different number of colleges. Instead, we simply change relevant data in the data section (line 900). This simplifies program maintenance, thereby reducing software cost in actual programming environments which may include changes to hundreds of data items dispersed throughout a large program.

NOTE 2   The data section in Example 3.1 (lines 900–903) illustrates an internal data file made up of records and fields. **A field** is a data item or attribute of some entity such as a college or person. In our example, the fields are college name, enrollment, and tuition. **A record** is a collection of related fields grouped together. In our example, the three data items for a single college define a record. Thus three records are shown in lines 901–903. **A data file**, then, is a collection of related records.

In practice (the "real world"), data files are *external* to programs and reside in secondary storage media such as magnetic disk and tape. The processing of **external data files** is an advanced topic, which we shall delay

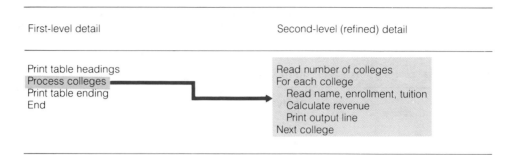

First-level detail	Second-level (refined) detail

Print table headings
Process colleges
Print table ending
End
	Read number of colleges
	For each college
	   Read name, enrollment, tuition
	   Calculate revenue
	   Print output line
	Next college

Figure 3.2   Stepwise refinement of pseudocode for tuition revenue program

until Module E. In the meantime we illustrate the principles of elementary file processing by using these data sections within programs, which we call **internal data files**.

3.3 TOP-DOWN DESIGN AND STEPWISE REFINEMENT

Top-down design is a process that simplifies and systematizes the design and development of complex programs. Strictly speaking, it is not a specific technique, but rather a philosophy that translates into a personalized process for writing programs.

Top-down design starts with an overall look at the entire problem, that is, a look from the "top." Subsequently, the problem is refined further by working "down" through successive levels of greater detail. To illustrate what we mean, consider the process of writing a textbook. First we decide the topic of the book. This is the least level of detail and the highest level of abstraction. Then we write the titles of chapters, the next level of detail. Next we specify the main headings in each chapter, a further refinement in the level of detail. Next we state the subheadings under each main heading, and finally, we provide the greatest level of detail: each word in the body of the text.

The *implementation* of top-down design at either the design or the programming stage is often carried out by a process called **stepwise refinement**, which is an iterative (stepwise) procedure that successively refines the problem at each step. In other words, stepwise refinement is a step-by-step process that continually expands or refines the flowchart, pseudocode, or program, starting at a low level of detail and working toward a high level of detail.

To illustrate stepwise refinement of pseudocode, consider Figure 3.2. In our first design pass, we specify the task "Process colleges" without giving the details of what to do with each college. Our first level of detail in the pseudocode design simply lists the major tasks in the program design. Next, we refine the "process colleges" task by providing a greater level of detail, as shown in Figure 3.2. Combining these two levels of detail gives the finalized pseudocode shown in Example 3.1.

NOTE   At this time in our programming development, stepwise refinement is of limited value. As our programs become more involved, however, we (and, hopefully, you) will use it to simplify the design process.

3.4 INITIALIZATIONS AND SUMS

Accumulating sums for one or more variables is a common computation in programming. For example, a payroll program might compute gross pay, deductions, and net pay for each employee and also compute the total gross pay, total deductions, and total net pay for all employees. To illustrate how the computer can accumulate a sum, we return to our tuition revenue problem.

E X A M P L E   3 . 2   **Tuition Revenue with Sum**

Analysis

The Board of Regents needs to know the total amount of money that will be collected from all the colleges within the state. Conceptually, we set aside a memory location (assign a variable) that represents the sum. Each time the computer calculates the amount of revenue expected from a college, the sum is increased by the revenue expected from that college. In effect, the sum can be thought of as a running total, the final value of which is not known until all the data are entered and processed.

For our test data in Example 3.1, the amounts from each college are $750,000, $2,500,000, and $6,600,000. As the program is computing, the sum is updated as follows:

- After the first college: 0 +   750,000 =   750,000
- After the second college: 750,000 + 2,500,000 = 3,250,000
- After the third college: 3,250,000 + 6,600,000 = 9,850,000

Thus a running total accumulates.

Design

```
Print table headings
Read number of colleges
Sum = 0
For each college
    Read name, enrollment, tuition
    Calculate revenue
    Print output line
    Sum = sum + revenue
Next college
Print table ending
Print sum
End
```

The highlighted portions in the pseudocode illustrate the incorporation of a sum in the version of Example 3.1. Note that the only changes are the initialization of the *summer* (sum variable) to zero before the loop, the incorporation of the summer in the loop to compute the running total, and the output of the summer following the loop.

Code

In the program, SUM is the variable that stores the accumulated revenue from all colleges. Changes from the program in Example 3.1 are shaded.

```
100 REM-------------------------------------------------------------------
105 REM   Tuition Revenue Program (Version 2.1)
110 REM-------------------------------------------------------------------
120         PRINT TAB(14); "TUITION REVENUE REPORT"
130         PRINT TAB(5); "--------------------------------------------"
140         PRINT TAB(5); "College"; TAB(28); "Number of"
150         PRINT TAB(5); "Name"; TAB(18); "Tuition"; TAB(28); "Students";
160         PRINT TAB(38); "Revenue"
170         PRINT TAB(5); "--------------------------------------------"
180 REM-------------------------------------------------------------------
190         READ N
195         LET SUM = 0          ◄──── SUM is initialized
200 REM-------------------------------------------------------------------
210         FOR J = 1 TO N
220           READ COLLEGE$,ENROLLMENT,TUITION
230           LET REVENUE = TUITION*ENROLLMENT
240           PRINT TAB(5); COLLEGE$; TAB(18); TUITION; TAB(28); ENROLLMENT;
250           PRINT TAB(38); REVENUE
255           LET SUM = SUM + REVENUE   ◄──── SUM is increased by each new
260         NEXT J                              value in REVENUE
270 REM-------------------------------------------------------------------
280         PRINT TAB(5); "--------------------------------------------"
285         PRINT TAB(5);"Total"; TAB(38); SUM  ◄──── SUM is printed following the loop
330 REM-------------------------------------------------------------------
900         DATA 3
901         DATA "Micro U",1000,750
902         DATA "Mini U" ,2500,1000
903         DATA "Maxi U" ,6000,1100
998 REM-------------------------------------------------------------------
999         END
```

Test

```
                TUITION REVENUE REPORT
    --------------------------------------------
    College              Number of
    Name      Tuition    Students   Revenue
    --------------------------------------------
    Micro U    750        1000       750000
    Mini U     1000       2500       2500000
    Maxi U     1100       6000       6600000
    --------------------------------------------
    Total                            9850000
```

Discussion

First we initialize SUM to zero in line 195. Next we place the statement

LET SUM = SUM + REVENUE

within the loop. Thus the value stored in REVENUE is added to the value stored in SUM, and the result is stored in SUM, replacing the value previously stored in SUM.

As the program executes, the contents of memory locations for REVENUE and SUM change in the following way.

After initialization:

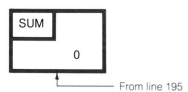

From line 195

After the first college is processed:

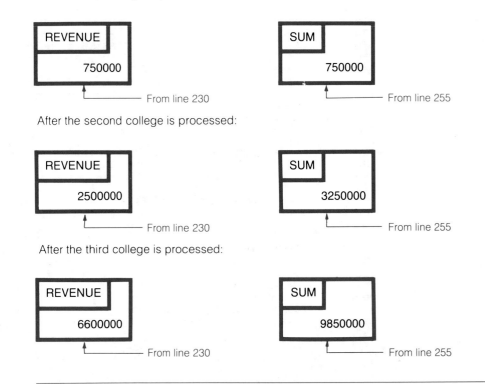

After the second college is processed:

After the third college is processed:

NOTE   Although most systems initialize all numeric variables to zero, it is good programming practice to initialize explicitly the variables that need zero initialization, as is done in line 195 of Example 3.2.

3.5 NESTED FOR/NEXT LOOPS**

As problems become more complex, solutions may require the programmer to embed one loop inside another. For every iteration of an outside loop, the inside loop iterates through a complete cycle. The inside loop is said to be **nested** within the outside loop. FOR/NEXT loops are nested when one FOR/NEXT loop lies entirely within another FOR/NEXT loop.

**This section can be skipped without loss of continuity.

E X A M P L E   3 . 3   Nested FOR/NEXT Loops

The key to understanding nested FOR/NEXT loops is careful attention to iterations and the values assigned to control variables. Consider the program and output below.

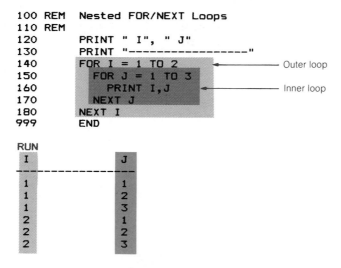

```
100 REM    Nested FOR/NEXT Loops
110 REM
120        PRINT " I", " J"
130        PRINT "------------------"
140        FOR I = 1 TO 2                          Outer loop
150            FOR J = 1 TO 3                       Inner loop
160                PRINT I,J
170            NEXT J
180        NEXT I
999        END
```

```
RUN
 I                J
----------------
 1                1
 1                2
 1                3
 2                1
 2                2
 2                3
```

The inner loop (lines 150–170) is "exhausted" for each value of the outer loop's control variable *I;* that is, *J* changes from 1 to 2 to 3 before *I* is incremented to its next value. Thus the inner loop is said to "vary the fastest." Each time the inner loop is exhausted, its control variable *J* is reset to its initial value, since the statement

FOR J = 1 TO 3

is executed for each new value of *I.* Details on the behavior of *I* and *J* are shown below.

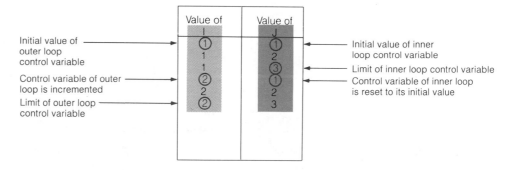

Notice that this double loop iterates a total of six times (2 × 3), or the product of the total iterations of the outer loop and the total iterations of the inner loop.

E X A M P L E   3 . 4   Student Averages

This example illustrates a problem that requires the use of nested loops.

Analysis

We wish to develop a program that calculates the average score for each student. For example, given the data

Scores

Student 1	Student 2
90	50
80	90
100	70

the program would compute and print an average of 90 for Student 1 and 70 for Student 2.

Output data

- Name of each student
- Average for each student

Read data

- Number of students
- Number of scores
- Name and scores for 1st student
- Name and scores for 2nd student
- . . .

Computations

Student average = sum of scores for student ÷ number scores for student

Design

Print table headings
Read number of students, number of scores
Process students
Print table ending
End

Refine outer loop

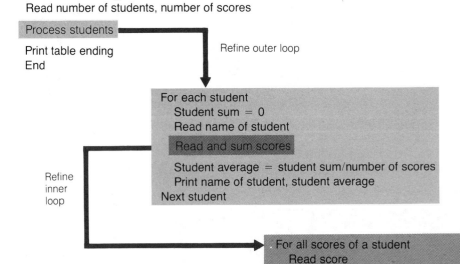

For each student
    Student sum = 0
    Read name of student
    Read and sum scores
    Student average = student sum/number of scores
    Print name of student, student average
Next student

Refine inner loop

For all scores of a student
    Read score
    Student sum = student sum + score
Next score

Code

```
100 REM------------------------------------------------
110 REM    Student Averages Program
120 REM
130 REM    Key:
140 REM      AVG      = Student's average
150 REM      M        = Number of students
160 REM      N        = Number of scores for a student
170 REM      SCORE    = Student's score
180 REM      SNAME$   = Student's name
190 REM      SUM      = Sum of scores for a student
200 REM------------------------------------------------
210       PRINT "--------------------"
220       PRINT "Name           Average"
230       PRINT "--------------------"
240 REM------------------------------------------------
250       READ M,N
260 REM------------------------------------------------
270       FOR STUDENT = 1 TO M
280         LET SUM = 0              Initializes SUM for each student
290         READ SNAME$             Outer loop
300 REM
310         FOR J = 1 TO N          Inner loop
320           READ SCORE
330           LET SUM = SUM + SCORE   Accumulates scores for a
340         NEXT J                           student
350 REM
360         LET AVG = SUM/N         SUM is used to calculate AVG
370         PRINT SNAME$,AVG        following the inner loop
380       NEXT STUDENT
390 REM------------------------------------------------
400       PRINT "--------------------"
410 REM------------------------------------------------
900       DATA 4,3
901       DATA "Smith",90,80,100
902       DATA "Jones",50,90,70
903       DATA "Ellie",85,75,65
904       DATA "Budzirk",88,72,86
998 REM------------------------------------------------
999       END
```

Test

```
RUN
--------------------
Name           Average
--------------------
Smith            90
Jones            70
Ellie            75
Budzirk          82
--------------------
```

In this example the inner loop processes the scores for a specific student, and the outer loop processes each student. In particular, note that

1. The sum *must* be reinitialized each time a new student is processed, as in line 280.

2. The scores for a student are summed within the inner loop, as in line 330.

3. The student's average is calculated and printed following the inner loop, as in lines 360–370.

3.6 POINTERS

Design and Style

1. **Indentation.**   Indent the body of the FOR/NEXT loop for better readability of the loop structure.

2. **Generalized loop parameters.**   Generalize the loop parameters within the FOR statement when these values are likely to change over time. Some examples:

Use:	Instead of:
FOR J = 1 TO N	FOR J = 1 TO 5
FOR COST = C1 TO C2 STEP C3	FOR COST = 10 TO 30 STEP 2

3. **Internal data files.**   DATA statements that represent internal data files (see Note 2, page 44) should be placed in a group that is well removed from the visual execution logic of the program.

Common Errors

1. **Control variable or loop parameters redefined within loop.**

```
FOR J = 1 TO N
    LET J = J + 1
    LET N = 2 * K
NEXT J
```
Syntax error or unexpected result when control variable or loop parameters are changed (redefined) within loop.

2. **Incomplete FOR/NEXT pair.**   Always make sure you pair a unique NEXT statement with a FOR statement.

```
10 FOR I = 1 TO N
   .
   .
90 NEXT J
```
Double syntax error; missing NEXT I and missing FOR J. Make sure control variable is identical in the paired FOR and NEXT statements.

3. **Running out of data.**   Watch out for situations in which the program attempts to read more data than are available, either through too many loop iterations or too little data. For example, the following program is missing data line 903, which gives an *out of data* error message when line 120 is executed at the third iteration.

```
100 READ N
110 FOR J = 1 TO N
120     READ  A,B,C
130     PRINT A;B;C
140 NEXT J
150                    REM
900 DATA 3
901 DATA 1,1,1
902 DATA 2,2,2
998                    REM          ──── Missing DATA line 903
999 END

RUN
  1  1  1
  2  2  2
Out of DATA in 120       ──── Execution error message when line 120
                              executes at the 3rd iteration
```

FOLLOW-UP EXERCISES

1. What values get printed for each program below? How many times does each loop iterate? Try these on your system.

   a. 10 FOR J = 1 TO 8
      20   PRINT J
      30 NEXT J
      99 END

   b. 10 FOR J = 1 TO 8
      30 NEXT J
      40 PRINT J
      99 END

   c. 10 FOR J = 6 TO 0
      20   PRINT J
      30 NEXT J
      99 END

   d. 10 FOR J = 6 TO 0 STEP −2
      20   PRINT J
      30 NEXT J
      99 END

   e. 10 FOR J = 2 TO 9 STEP 3
      20   PRINT J
      30 NEXT J
      99 END

   f. 5 LET K = 0
      10 FOR X = 5.1 TO 5.5 STEP .1
      15   LET K = K + 1
      20   PRINT X
      30 NEXT X
      40 PRINT K
      99 END

   g. 5 LET Y = 10
      10 FOR X = Y TO 2*Y − 1 STEP Y/4
      20   PRINT X
      30 NEXT X
      99 END

2. Suppose we have to process 15 institutions in Example 3.1. What changes need to be made in the program and data?

3. What would the output look like in Example 3.1 if line 170 were placed between lines 210 and 220?

4. With respect to Example 3.2,
   a. Would the output change if the summer statement in line 255 were placed just *after* the LET statement in line 230? If so, how?
   b. Would the output change if the summer statement in line 255 were placed just *before* the LET statement in line 230? If so, how?
   c. Would the output change if the initialization in line 195 were omitted? Check this out on your system.
   d. Describe the output if the statement that prints the sum were placed just before the NEXT statement.

*5. Modify the program of Example 3.2 to print total enrollment for all colleges.

*6. Modify the program of Example 3.2 to calculate and print the average revenue, AVE. Print AVE immediately under the output for sum.

7. What would be printed by the following:

   a. 10 LET K = 0
      20 FOR J = 1 TO 3
      30   LET K = K + 5
      40   PRINT J, K
      50 NEXT J
      60 PRINT J,K
      99 END

   *b. 10 LET S = 5
      20 FOR J = 1 TO 4
      30   LET S = S + J*S
      40 NEXT J
      50 PRINT S
      99 END

8. What would happen in Example 3.4 if
   a. We were to omit the initialization of SUM in line 280? Show the output.
   b. We were to place the calculation of AVG just before NEXT J?

9. Specify printed output and number of iterations for each of the following nested loops.

   a. 10 FOR J = 1 TO 4
      20   FOR K = 1 TO 4
      30   PRINT J,K
      40   NEXT K
      50 NEXT J
      99 END

   b. 10 FOR J = 1 TO 4
      20   FOR K = 1 TO 2 STEP 0.5
      30   PRINT J,K
      40   NEXT K
      50 NEXT J
      99 END

   *c. 10 LET M = 0
      15 FOR I = 1 TO 10
      20   LET J = I
      25   FOR K = 1 TO 5
      30   LET L = K
      35   LET M = M + 1
      40   NEXT K
      45 NEXT I
      50 PRINT J, L, M
      55 PRINT I, K
      99 END

10. Implement one of the following examples on your system:
    a. Example 3.1
    b. Example 3.2
    c. Example 3.3

ADDITIONAL EXERCISES

11. **Revisits.** Modify one of the following problems from Chapter 2 by including FOR/NEXT loops as indicated. Pay attention to good I/O design.

    a. **Microeconomics I.** (Example 2.5, page 23.) Use a FOR/NEXT loop to vary the units produced from an initial value to a limit by a step. Treat the initial, limit, and step values as input data. The output is a table with the columns Units and Cost. Run the program twice to print two tables: The first table varies units from 5 to 50 in 5-unit steps; the second table varies units from 5 to 15 in 1-unit steps. Use READ/DATA statements for the cost function parameters 6 and 250.

    b. **Microeconomics II.** Modify the preceding problem to print tables with the columns Units, Revenue, Cost, Profit. Revenue is given by the product of selling price and number of units sold. Profit is revenue less cost. Cost is defined by the original cost function. Treat price as an input variable. How many units should be produced and sold to maximize profit if the price is $80 per unit? If the price is $120 per unit? Answer these questions using the data in the output tables.

    c. **Microeconomics III.** Modify the preceding problem so that an outer FOR/NEXT loop varies price from an initial value to a limit by an increment. Input the initial value, limit, and increment. Try a test run that varies price from $80 to $120 in steps of $20. (Note: This test run gives three tables as output, one for each of the three prices.)

    d. **Temperature Conversion.** (Example 2.6, page 24.) Use a FOR/NEXT loop to vary Fahrenheit temperatures from an initial value to a limit by a step. Treat the initial, limit, and step values as input data. The output is a table with the columns Fahrenheit and Celsius. Run the program twice to print two tables: The first table varies degrees F from 30 to 100 in 5-degree steps; the second table varies degrees F from −30 to 32 in 2-degree steps.

    e. **Bates Motel.** (Exercise 26, page 37.) Use a counter-controlled FOR/NEXT loop to process N customers in one run. Treat N as an input variable. Print a summary report that shows a total for each of the following: room charge, restaurant charges, bar charges, service charge, sales taxes, and total bills.

    f. **Automobile Financing.** (Exercise 28, page 37.) Use a counter-controlled FOR/NEXT loop to process N car loans in one run. Treat N as an input variable.

12. **Multiplication Tables.** Consider the following multiplication table:

Multiplication Table for the Number 9

    0 times 9 =   0
    1 times 9 =   9
       .
       .
   12 times 9 = 108

    a. Develop a program that prints a multiplication table. The user enters the number used for the multiplication. The table always ranges from 0 to 12.

    b. Have your program automatically generate multiplication tables for any range of numbers entered by the user. For example, if the user enters the range 2 to 11, then the program automatically generates ten multiplication tables.

13. **Individual Retirement Account (IRA).** IRAs are an excellent means by which to build up tax-deferred retirement accounts. Essentially, a taxpayer can deduct from earned income an annual contribution to an IRA, thus reducing the federal taxes owed. The contribution is formally invested in stocks, bonds, money market account, savings account, or other approved investment vehicles. Over time, this amount increases in value (for the astute investor), with taxes still deferred. At retirement, the person can begin withdrawals, which are then taxed as if ordinary income were being earned. Develop a program that can reproduce the sample run below.

Enter current year .... ? 1986
Enter retirement year .... ? 1989
Enter annual IRA contribution .... ? 2000
Enter assumed annual % return .... ? 10

Projected IRA Accumulations

Year	Contribution	Return	Accumulation
1986	2000	200	2200
1987	2000	420	4620
1988	2000	662	7282
1989	2000	928	10210

For simplicity, assume that all contributions are made at the beginning of the year. Thus the $2000 investment at the beginning of 1986 accumulates to $2200 by the end of 1986. In 1987 the investor contributes an additional $2000, which gives an account with $4200 at the beginning of 1987. This also earns a return of 10% for the year, or $420, which gives an accumulation of $4620 by the end of 1987 ..., and so on. After 1989, the taxpayer can withdraw all or part of the accumulated $10,210. Of course, federal income taxes have to be paid at that time on any amount withdrawn. Debug your program with the above test run. Then try a second test run that changes the retirement year to 2026. Finally, try a third test run that generates a table from 1986 to 2026, but use an annual contribution of $1000. What's the effect of a change in the annual return to 15%?

14. **Form Letter.**   Write a program that prints the following personalized form letter.

Ms. Jane Budwick
10 North Road
Kingston, RI 02881

Dear Ms. Budwick,

You are indeed one of the fortunate few whom we have selected for our Gala Prize Drawing. All you need to do, Jane, is fill in the enclosed handy magazine order form, which makes you eligible for one of our many Gala Prizes. Indeed, the Budwick residence at 10 North Road may be lucky enough to receive the Most Gala Prize, a free set of encyclopedias at a maintenance cost of only 10 cents per day for 30 years.

Good luck!
Hoodwink G. Fox, Manager
Dill Comic Book Co., Inc.

In one computer run, print the letter for each of the following.

Name	Address	
Ms. Jane Budwick	10 North Road	Kingston, RI 02881
Mr. Al Bella Bitta	20 Birch St.	Cincinnati, OH 44451
Dr. H. Doolittle	10 Downing	London, UK

Make sure that each letter fits nicely within an $8\frac{1}{2}$-inch width and takes up 11 inches in length. Store all names and addresses through READ/DATA statements.

15. **Depreciation.**   The concept of depreciation plays a prominent role in the financial accounting of organizations that report profits and pay taxes. The simplest method of depreciation is called the *straight-line method*. This method uses the following formula to determine depreciation for an asset (automobile, building, machine, etc.) in any given year:

Depreciation = (cost − salvage value)/life

a. Develop a program that inputs or reads the name of the asset and its associated cost, salvage value, and life. Output should include the type of table illustrated below.

Depreciation Schedule
Asset .... Chariot
Cost $4200
Salvage .... $ 200
Life .... 4 years

Year	Depreciation Expense	Accumulated Depreciation	Book Value
1	1000	1000	3200
2	1000	2000	2200
3	1000	3000	1200
4	1000	4000	200

Process the following assets in your test runs.

Asset	Cost	Salvage	Life
Chariot	4,200	200	4
Building	200,000	0	15
Machine	75,000	5,000	5

b. Use a FOR/NEXT loop to process all assets in one computer run.

Decisions

4

Up to now we have developed programs that either strictly execute sequentially without any interruption in the flow (Chapter 2) or include looping, a repetitive execution of a group of statements (Chapter 3). This chapter presents another alteration to sequential execution: A selection or decision among two or more alternative execution flows.

4.1 THE IF-THEN-ELSE DECISION

A **decision structure** (or **selection structure**) expresses the logic by which one or more conditions are tested to determine which group of statements (from among alternatives) is to be executed next. In the two-alternative case, either a particular **block** (set of one or more executable statements) is to be executed if a condition is true, or an alternative block is to be executed if it is false. Figure 4.1a illustrates the fundamental **if-then-else structure**. Sometimes we have a situation in which, if a condition is true, we execute a particular block, otherwise we continue in the program sequence. This is called the single-choice or **if-then structure**, as illustrated in Figure 4.1b.

Study this figure, its terminology, and its execution flows. At this time, don't worry about the details of implementations in BASIC.

NOTE   The decision (selection) structure is entered by testing a *condition* or making a decision. Then, depending on the result of this test (True or False, Yes or No), a *selection* is made regarding the next segment of the program (then block or else block) that is to be executed.

4.2 SIMPLE CONDITIONS BASED ON RELATIONAL OPERATORS

Implementation of the selection structure requires the formulation of a *condition that is to be tested*. A simple condition is formulated by constructing a relational expression.

Figure 4.1 Fundamental decision structures

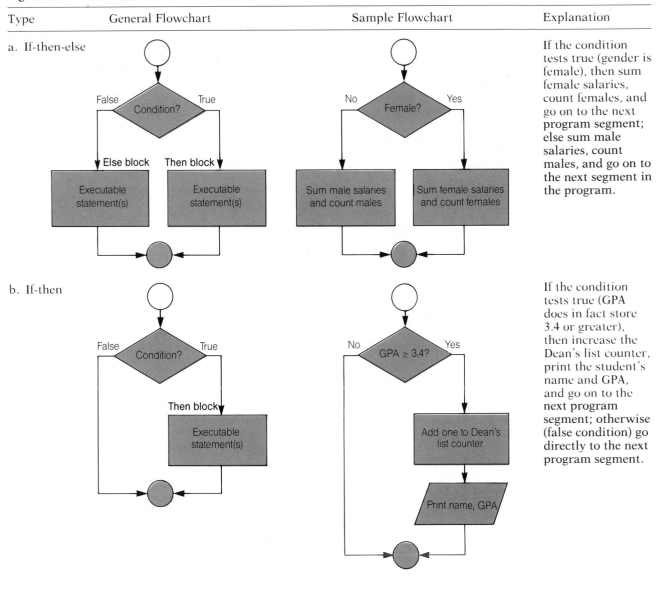

Type	General Flowchart	Sample Flowchart	Explanation
a. If-then-else			If the condition tests true (gender is female), then sum female salaries, count females, and go on to the next program segment; else sum male salaries, count males, and go on to the next segment in the program.
b. If-then			If the condition tests true (GPA does in fact store 3.4 or greater), then increase the Dean's list counter, print the student's name and GPA, and go on to the next program segment; otherwise (false condition) go directly to the next program segment.

Relational Expression

numeric expression	*relational operator*	*numeric expression*
GPA	>=	3.4

string expression	*relational operator*	*string expression*
SEX$	=	"F"

The examples above illustrate the conditions shown in Figure 4.1.

NOTE 1   The relational expression can compare either numeric values to one another or string values to one another.

Table 4.1 Relational Operators in BASIC

Mathematical Comparison	Relational Operator	Meaning
=	=	Equal to
≠	<>	Not equal to[a]
<	<	Less than
≤	<=	Less than or equal to
>	>	Greater than
≥	>=	Greater than or equal to

[a]Some systems use # in place of <>.

NOTE 2 When evaluated, a relational expression will have either the value true or the value false. This determines which group of statements (then block or else block) is executed next, as shown in Figure 4.1. For example, if the string variable SEX$ stores the value M, then the relational expression SEX$ = "F" tests false, and the else block (the one for males) is executed in Figure 4.1a.

Each of the above simple examples of relational expressions shows a variable, followed by a relational operator, followed by a constant. In general, every relational expression takes the form of an expression (numeric or string), then a relational operator, and then another numeric or string expression. A **relational operator** indicates a mathematical comparison such as less than, equal to, or greater than. BASIC uses six relational operators, as indicated in Table 4.1.

E X A M P L E   4 . 1   Relational Expressions

Condition	Relational Expression	Storage Contents	Test Result
a. Grade point average greater than or equal to 3.4?	GPA >= 3.4	GPA 2.9	False
b. Is the ratio of distance to time less than the critical velocity?	D/T < CV	D 5800 T 10 CV 650	True
c. Gender is female or equals code F?	SEX$ = "F"	SEX$ M	False

NOTE Don't forget that string constants must be enclosed in quotes, as in "F" in Example 4.1c.

4.3 SPECIFIC IMPLEMENTATIONS

The implementation of if-then-else and if-then structures depends on the particular version or dialect of BASIC that we are using. Study the common implementations in this section and focus on those that are available on your system.

Traditional One-Line IF/THEN Statement

The following statement is found in all BASIC dialects, including the *Minimal ANS BASIC dialect:*

Traditional One-Line IF/THEN Statement

IF condition   **THEN** line number
IF GPA < 3.4   THEN 45

The condition is tested, and the result is either true or false. If the result is true, then control is transferred to the line number specified immediately to the right of THEN (line 45 in our example). If the result is false, then the statement immediately following the IF/THEN is executed.

The traditional IF/THEN statement is often paired with the following GO TO statement:

GO TO Statement

GO TO line number
GO TO 230

For example, when GO TO 230 is executed, transfer of execution control goes to line 230; that is, the next statement executed is in line 230.

E X A M P L E   4 . 2   **Decision Structure Implementations Using Traditional One-Line IF/THEN and GO TO Statements**

The two decision structures first illustrated in Figure 4.1 are implemented below.

Flowchart of Decision Structure	BASIC	Explanation

a.

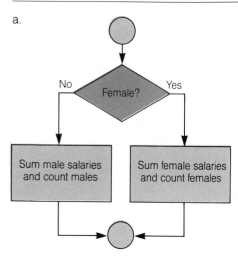

```
100 LET FSAL   = 0
110 LET MSAL   = 0
120 LET FCOUNT = 0
130 LET MCOUNT = 0
140 READ M
150 FOR J=1 TO M
160   READ SEX$,SAL
170   IF SEX$ = "F" THEN 210
180     LET MSAL   = MSAL   + SAL
190     LET MCOUNT = MCOUNT + 1      ──Else block
200   GOTO 230
210     LET FSAL   = FSAL   + SAL
220     LET FCOUNT = FCOUNT + 1      ──Then block
230 NEXT J
240 PRINT "Average female salary =";FSAL/FCOUNT
250 PRINT "Average   male   salary =";MSAL/MCOUNT
900 DATA 4
901 DATA "M",30000
902 DATA "F",35000
903 DATA "F",40000
904 DATA "M",50000
999 END
```

At line 170, if SEX$ does in fact store F, then control goes to line 210 (lines 180–200 are skipped), and lines 210–220 are executed; else control drops to line 180, and lines 180–200 are executed (lines 210–220 are skipped). Lines 170–220 implement the decision structure.

```
RUN
Average female salary = 37500
Average   male   salary = 40000
```

b.

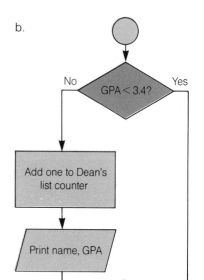

```
10 LET K = 0
15 READ M
20 FOR J=1 TO M
25   READ N$,GPA
30   IF GPA < 3.4 THEN 45
35     LET K = K + 1          ──Else block
40     PRINT N$,GPA
45 NEXT J
50 PRINT "Number on Dean's List =";  K
90 DATA 3
91 DATA "A. Smith",3.0
92 DATA "B. Smith",3.5
93 DATA "C. Smith",2.5
99 END
```

At line 30, if the value stored in GPA is in fact less than 3.4, then control immediately goes to line 45; else lines 35 and 40 are executed, followed by line 45. Lines 30–40 make up the decision structure.

```
RUN
B. Smith        3.5
Number on Dean's List = 1
```

NOTE 1   The traditional IF/THEN statement cannot directly implement the IF/THEN structure, since only a line number (not a statement) is allowed in the then block just to the right of the keyword THEN. This is why the flowchart in Example 4.2b is reversed from that in Figure 4.1b.

NOTE 2   Take care that a GO TO statement separates the else and then blocks in the traditional if-then-else structure. For example, if we were to omit line 200 in Example 4.2a then lines 210 and 220 would inadvertently be executed for false conditions.

NOTE 3 It's good style to indent else and then blocks to improve their identification, as in Example 4.2.

NOTE 4 Explicit line number transfers such as THEN 210 or GO TO 230 in Example 4.3a can be hazardous to our programming health, as they increase the likelihood of "wrong line number" logic errors. It's best to avoid this style of programming if your system includes some of the statements we discuss in the remainder of this section.

Enhanced One-Line IF/THEN Statement

Most implementations of BASIC allow the following enhanced IF/THEN statement:

Enhanced One-Line IF/THEN Statement

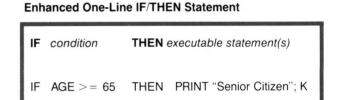

Allowed on your system?	
YES	NO

IF *condition* **THEN** *executable statement(s)*

IF AGE >= 65 THEN PRINT "Senior Citizen"; K

Thus, if the condition is true, then the executable statement to the right of THEN is executed; otherwise, execution control reverts to the first executable statement immediately below the IF/THEN statement.

E X A M P L E   4 . 3 Decision Structure Implementations Using Enhanced One-Line IF/THEN Statement

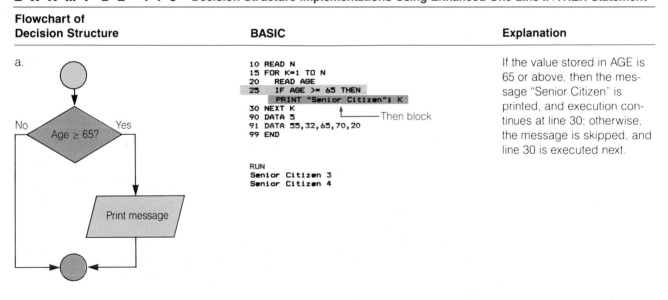

Flowchart of Decision Structure

a.

BASIC

```
10 READ N
15 FOR K=1 TO N
20    READ AGE
25    IF AGE >= 65 THEN
         PRINT "Senior Citizen"; K
30 NEXT K                    └── Then block
90 DATA 5
91 DATA 55,32,65,70,20
99 END

RUN
Senior Citizen 3
Senior Citizen 4
```

Explanation

If the value stored in AGE is 65 or above, then the message "Senior Citizen" is printed, and execution continues at line 30; otherwise, the message is skipped, and line 30 is executed next.

b.

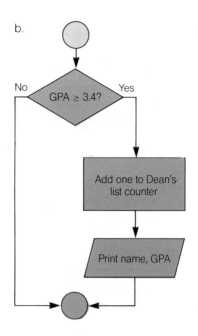

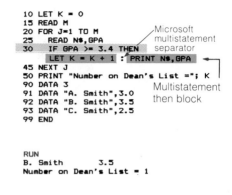

```
10 LET K = 0
15 READ M
20 FOR J=1 TO M
25   READ N$,GPA
30   IF GPA >= 3.4 THEN
         LET K = K + 1 : PRINT N$,GPA
45 NEXT J
50 PRINT "Number on Dean's List ="; K
90 DATA 3
91 DATA "A. Smith",3.0
92 DATA "B. Smith",3.5
93 DATA "C. Smith",2.5
99 END


RUN
B. Smith       3.5
Number on Dean's List = 1
```

Microsoft multistatement separator

Multistatement then block

At line 30, if GPA stores a value of 3.4 or greater, then the counter and PRINT statements are executed, followed by line 45; otherwise, line 45 is executed directly (the counter and PRINT statements are bypassed). Compare with Example 4.2b. See Note 1 regarding multistatement lines.

NOTE 1 A **multistatement line** is illustrated in Example 4.3b, which, in the example, allows us to place two statements within the then block of a single line. In the example, we used the colon as a multistatement separator, although the specific separator varies, depending on the dialect.

Dialect	Multistatement Separator
Microsoft	Colon (:)
VAX-11	Backslash (\)
Your system?	

NOTE 2 We prefer the GPA version in Example 4.3b to that in Example 4.2b, because it avoids an explicit line number transfer; that is, "THEN 45" in Example 4.2b explicitly transfers control to line 45 when the condition is true. Explicit transfers are best avoided, because they increase the likelihood of an error that transfers to the wrong line number.

One-Line IF/THEN/ELSE Statements

Many versions of BASIC include one or both of the following statements:

Older One-Line IF/THEN/ELSE Statement

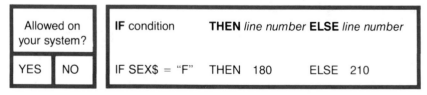

Allowed on your system?		IF condition	THEN line number ELSE line number
YES	NO	IF SEX$ = "F"	THEN 180 ELSE 210

Newer One-Line IF/THEN/ELSE Statement

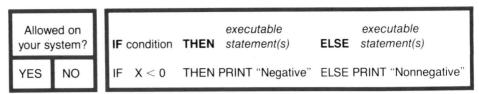

Allowed on your system?	IF condition	**THEN**	*executable statement(s)*	**ELSE**	*executable statement(s)*
YES NO	IF X < 0	THEN PRINT "Negative"		ELSE PRINT "Nonnegative"	

We illustrate these by example.

E X A M P L E   4 . 4   Decision Structure Implementations Using One-Line IF/THEN/ELSE Statements

Flowchart	BASIC	Explanation

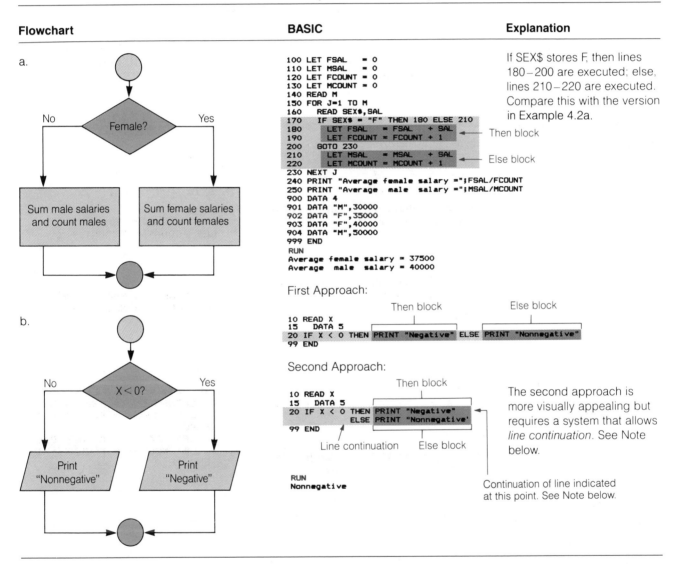

a.

If SEX$ stores F, then lines 180–200 are executed; else, lines 210–220 are executed. Compare this with the version in Example 4.2a.

```
100 LET FSAL   = 0
110 LET MSAL   = 0
120 LET FCOUNT = 0
130 LET MCOUNT = 0
140 READ M
150 FOR J=1 TO M
160   READ SEX$,SAL
170   IF SEX$ = "F" THEN 180 ELSE 210
180     LET FSAL   = FSAL   + SAL          Then block
190     LET FCOUNT = FCOUNT + 1
200   GOTO 230
210     LET MSAL   = MSAL   + SAL          Else block
220     LET MCOUNT = MCOUNT + 1
230 NEXT J
240 PRINT "Average female salary =";FSAL/FCOUNT
250 PRINT "Average  male  salary =";MSAL/MCOUNT
900 DATA 4
901 DATA "M",30000
902 DATA "F",35000
903 DATA "F",40000
904 DATA "M",50000
999 END
RUN
Average female salary = 37500
Average  male  salary = 40000
```

First Approach:

```
                        Then block          Else block
10 READ X
15    DATA 5
20 IF X < 0 THEN PRINT "Negative" ELSE PRINT "Nonnegative"
99 END
```

b.

Second Approach:

```
                        Then block
10 READ X
15    DATA 5
20 IF X < 0 THEN PRINT "Negative"
            ELSE PRINT "Nonnegative"
99 END
        Line continuation   Else block

RUN
Nonnegative
```

The second approach is more visually appealing but requires a system that allows *line continuation*. See Note below.

Continuation of line indicated at this point. See Note below.

NOTE   **Line continuation** is illustrated in the second program of Example 4.4b. Visually (at the terminal), line 20 appears as two lines, but to the system it is simply program line 20. Systems can accomplish this in different ways.

System	Method of Line Continuation
IBM PC	Simultaneously press the <Ctrl> and <Enter> keys at the end of each line that is to be continued.
VAX-11	Type an ampersand (&) at the end of each line that is to be continued.
Your system?	

Warning: Many systems limit the total length of a line to 255 characters. Check on your system's limitation.

Multiline IF/THEN/ELSE Statements

Modern BASIC dialects directly implement generalized if-then-else structures, some of which are illustrated in Table 4.2. Find or fill in the one (if any) that's appropriate to your system.

Table 4.2 Selected Multiline If-then-else Structures

Dialect	Structure	Example

ANS BASIC
True BASIC
	IF condition **THEN**
	　Group of statements executed if condition is true (then block)
	ELSE
	　Group of statements executed if condition is false (else block)
	END IF
	Note: Statements need not have line numbers.
		```IF SEX$ = "F" THEN```
		
		```LET FSAL = FSAL + SAL```
		```LET FCOUNT = FCOUNT + 1```
		
		```ELSE```
		
		```LET MSAL = MSAL + SAL```
		```LET MCOUNT = MCOUNT + 1```
		
		```END IF```

VAX-11 BASIC	line no.**IF** condition **THEN**
	　Group of statements executed if condition is true (then block)
	ELSE
	　Group of statements executed if condition is false (else block)
	END IF
	Note: The IF statement has a line number, but the other statements do not. The VAX manual calls this "a block of program code."
		```100 IF SEX$ = "F" THEN```
		``` LET FSAL = FSAL + SAL```
		``` LET FCOUNT = FCOUNT + 1```
		```ELSE```
		``` LET MSAL = MSAL + SAL```
		``` LET MCOUNT = MCOUNT + 1```
		```END IF```

Your system (if different)*		

Note: If your system doesn't have a multiline if-then-else implementation, you must use one of the approaches illustrated in Examples 4.2, 4.3, and 4.4. Microsoft does not have a multiline if-then-else implementation.

NOTE 1   Compare the if-then-else structure in Example 4.2a or Example 4.4a to the versions in Table 4.2. The if-then-else structure based on multiline IF/THEN/ELSE statements is clearly preferable to one-line implementations that use explicit line number transfers, for the following reasons:

a. The multiline version is easier to follow for us humans (it doesn't matter to the computer).

b. The multiline version completely avoids explicit line number transfers. Thus, it's more reliable (less error-prone) than versions that explicitly use line number transfers or GO TO statements.

Multiline IF/THEN/ELSE statements are consistent with good programming style, since they reflect the "GO TO less" or "block programming" orientation of modern software design.

NOTE 2   The ELSE statement and else block are optional. For example, the ANS BASIC version

```
IF GPA >= 3.4 THEN
    LET K = K + 1
    PRINT N$,GPA
END IF
```

is stylistically preferable to both the traditional version in Example 4.2b and the enhanced version in Example 4.3b.

4.4 COMPOUND CONDITIONS BASED ON LOGICAL OPERATORS

Up to now we have tested simple conditions based on a single relational expression. In many applications it's best to combine two or more simple conditions into a compound condition. This is accomplished by using one or more of the **logical operators** AND, OR, and NOT to connect simple conditions according to the following scheme:

Compound Condition

condition 1	logical operator	condition 2	logical operator	condition 3 . . .

Simple conditions based on relational expressions

As with simple conditions, the test of a compound condition yields a true or false result (logical value).

Logical Operator AND

If all simple conditions are true within a compound condition with AND logical operators, then the compound condition itself tests true. If any condition is false, however, then the compound condition is false. For example, suppose we are looking for all females who are at least 40 years old. We might write the following compound condition:

SEX$ = "F"   AND   AGE >= 40

condition 1   logical operator   condition 2

Now suppose that condition 1 is true and condition 2 is true; that is, we have a person who is female and at least 40 years old. In this case the value of the compound condition is given by

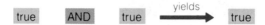

which gives the result true for the compound condition itself; however, if condition 1 is true but condition 2 is false (a female who is under 40), then we have

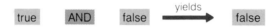

which gives the logical value false for the compound condition.

E X A M P L E   4 . 5   **Use of AND Logical Operator**

The following program prints the last name (L$), first name (F$), and age (AGE) of all female employees who are at least 40 years of age. Note how the two conditions based on gender and age are incorporated within a single IF THEN statement through the AND operator. (See Exercise 6 for the less desirable alternative.)

```
10 READ N                              Compound condition with AND operator
15 FOR J=1 TO N                                   |
20   READ F$,L$,SEX$,AGE                           ↓
25   IF SEX$ = "F"  AND  AGE >= 40 THEN PRINT L$,F$,AGE
40 NEXT J
90 DATA 3
91 DATA "Wendy","Brandon","F",29
92 DATA "Barbara","Lee","F",40
93 DATA "L. L.",  "Bean","M",100
99 END

RUN
Lee              Barbara          40
```

Logical Operator OR

If any condition is true in a compound condition with OR logical operators, then the compound condition tests true. However, if all of the simple conditions are false, then the compound condition is false.

For example, suppose an employer is interested in interviewing students with an economics (ECN) or mathematics (MTH) major. We could write the following compound condition:

MAJOR = "ECN"	OR	MAJOR = "MTH"
Condition 1	Logical Operator	Condition 2

Suppose we have an economics major (that is, MAJOR stores ECN). In this case condition 1 tests true, and condition 2 is false. Thus the compound condition given by

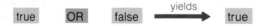

yields a true result.

E X A M P L E   4 . 6   Use of OR Logical Operator

Suppose we wish to ask the user interactively, "Do you want the forecast" and if the response is Y or YES or YEP (let's assume uppercase entries for simplicity), then we calculate and print a sales forecast.

```
100 READ S,G
110   DATA 1000,5
120 PRINT "Sales    = $"; S; "   Growth ="; G; "%"
130 PRINT TAB(35);"Do you want the forecast";
140 INPUT R$
150 IF R$="Y" OR R$="YES" OR R$="YEP" THEN PRINT "Forecast = $"; S*(1 + G/100)
999 END
```

└─ IF-THEN structure with a compound condition based on OR logical operators

```
        RUN
        Sales    = $ 1000      Growth = 5 %
                                            Do you want the forecast? Y

        Forecast = $ 1050


        RUN
        Sales    = $ 1000      Growth = 5 %
                                            Do you want the forecast? YES

        Forecast = $ 1050


        RUN
        Sales    = $ 1000      Growth = 5 %
                                            Do you want the forecast? YEP

        Forecast = $ 1050


        RUN
        Sales    = $ 1000      Growth = 5 %
                                            Do you want the forecast? N
```

In this case, the use of a compound condition replaces the inefficiency of three successive if-then structures with a single if-then structure.[1] (See Exercise 7.)

Logical Operator NOT

The logical operator NOT reverses the logical value of the condition on which it operates. For example, suppose we are looking for all persons 18 and under based on the test

    NOT   AGE > 18

Suppose AGE stores 21. Then the condition is evaluated according to

    NOT   true ──yields──▶ false
           ▲   ▲
    21 > 18 tests true   NOT changes true to false

On the other hand, if a person is 16, then the condition is evaluated as true according to the following:

    NOT   false ──yields──▶ true
           ▲   ▲
    16 > 18 tests false   NOT changes false to true

---

[1] In Module C we illustrate a much better method of processing YES/NO input responses.

4.5 MULTIPLE ALTERNATIVE DECISIONS

The solutions to many problems require that the computer choose from among several alternative courses of action the one that determines which block of statements is to be executed next. These decisions are designed and programmed as **multiple alternative decision structures**. In this section we present one of many approaches to designing and coding multiple alternative decision structures.[2]

E X A M P L E   4 . 7   **Sales Bonus Problem**

Analysis

Let's write an interactive program that determines a salesperson's weekly sales bonus based on sales and travel expenses for the week. The following schedule describes the rules for calculating the sales bonus:

Weekly Sales	Travel Expenses	Bonus
Above $5000	Below $1000	$200
Above $5000	$1000 or above	$100
$5000 or below	Any amount	$ 0

Output

Bonus

Input

Weekly sales
Travel expenses

Parameters

First bonus .... $ 200
Second bonus .... $ 100
Third bonus .... $ 0
Sales cutoff $5000
Travel cutoff $1000

The parameters in this problem are those found in the bonus schedule.

Design

We might note the following considerations in our design:

- We use INPUT statements since the program is to be interactive
- We treat the parameters in the bonus schedule as variables in the program in order to more easily update their values over time
- The rules in the bonus schedule suggest a sequence of if-then structures, whereas the sales and travel expense cutoff conditions are joined together by the AND logical operator
- We omit a loop in this program since the appropriate loop design is described in the next chapter

The following pseudocode completely describes the design of the program:

[2]For example, see Chapter 6 in *Applied Structured BASIC* by Roy Ageloff and Richard Mojena, Wadsworth Publishing Company, Belmont, CA, 1985 for a complete treatment of multiple alternative decision structures.

Initialize parameters
Print heading
Input sales and travel expenses
Calculate bonus
Print bonus
End

The bonus calculation is refined as follows:

If sales > $5000 and travel < $1000 then bonus is $200
If sales > $5000 and travel >= $1000 then bonus is $100
If sales <= $5000   then bonus is $0

The refined pseudocode describes a sequence of three distinct if-then structures. Each structure is one of the rules from the bonus schedule. Within each rule the two conditions on sales and travel expenses are joined together by the logical operator "and."

Code

```
100 REM * * * * * * * * * * * * * * * * * * * * * * * * * * * * * * * * * * *
110 REM *                                                                   *
120 REM *                   Sales Bonus Program                             *
130 REM *                                                                   *
140 REM *    Key:                                                           *
150 REM *        BONUS ........ Weekly bonus in dollars                     *
160 REM *        BONUS1,2,3 ... Possible bonus amounts in dollars           *
170 REM *        SALES ........ Weekly sales in dollars                     *
180 REM *        SALES.CUT .... Sales cutoff for bonus                      *
190 REM *        TRAVEL ....... Weekly travel expenses in dollars           *
200 REM *        TRAVEL.CUT ... Travel expenses cutoff for bonus            *
210 REM *                                                                   *
220 REM * * * * * * * * * * * * * * * * * * * * * * * * * * * * * * * * * * *
230 REM -------------------------------------------------------------------
240     LET BONUS1     = 200
250     LET BONUS2     = 100
260     LET BONUS3     = 0
270     LET SALES.CUT  = 5000
280     LET TRAVEL.CUT = 1000
290 REM -------------------------------------------------------------------
300     PRINT
310     PRINT TAB(7);"Sales Bonus Calculation"
320     PRINT
330     INPUT "Enter weekly sales =============>";SALES
340     INPUT "Enter weekly travel expenses ===>";TRAVEL
350     PRINT
360 REM -------------------------------------------------------------------
370     IF SALES >  SALES.CUT AND TRAVEL <  TRAVEL.CUT THEN LET BONUS = BONUS1
380     IF SALES >  SALES.CUT AND TRAVEL >= TRAVEL.CUT THEN LET BONUS = BONUS2
390     IF SALES <= SALES.CUT                          THEN LET BONUS = BONUS3
400 REM -------------------------------------------------------------------
410     PRINT TAB(7);"Bonus ............$";BONUS
998 REM -------------------------------------------------------------------
999     END
```

Note how all parameters are assigned values in a clearly defined section of program. This simplifies program maintenance.

Bonus is determined by a sequence of if-then structures.

Test

```
RUN

        Sales Bonus Calculation

Enter weekly sales =============>? 8000
Enter weekly travel expenses ===>? 2000

        Bonus ............$ 100


RUN

        Sales Bonus Calculation

Enter weekly sales =============>? 3000
Enter weekly travel expenses ===>? 1000

        Bonus ............$ 0


RUN

        Sales Bonus Calculation

Enter weekly sales =============>? 6000
Enter weekly travel expenses ===>? 800

        Bonus ............$ 200
```

NOTE   A sequence of if-then structures that include logical operators can be used to model any multiple alternative decision structure. See Example 4.7 and Exercises 11 and 12.

4.6 POINTERS

Design and Style

1. **Keep on spacing.**   Indent statements within then and else blocks. It helps to identify them and improves readability.

2. **Avoid explicit line number transfers.**   For example, try not to use statements such as

   100 IF A < B THEN 150 ELSE 200

   or

   175 GO TO 300

   Explicit line number transfers make programs more difficult to follow, more costly to modify, and error prone with respect to unintended line number transfers. Practice GOTOless programming if possible on your system.

3. **Write structured programs.**   Any program can be written as a set of the following building blocks:

   - *Sequence structure.* A sequence of statements that occur one after the other without any transfer of execution control. Every program in Chapter 2 is a single sequence structure.

   - *Loop structure.* The logic by which a set of statements is repeatedly executed. The repeatedly executed set of statements is called the loop body and the logic by which looping ends is called loop control. The programs in Chapter 3 were made up entirely of sequence and loop structures. Chapter 5 concludes the treatment of loop structures.

   - *Decision structure.* The logic by which one or more conditions are tested to determine which group of statements, from among alternatives, is to be executed next. The **if-then-else structure** is the most fundamental decision structure. All other decision structures are either special cases (**if-then structure**) or combinations (**multiple alternative structure**) of the if-then-else structure.

   These three types of building blocks are called **control structures**. Programs that are strictly written as sets of control structures are called **structured programs**. Try to visualize the makeup of a program as these fundamental building blocks, whereby execution control always enters the control structure at the top and exits at the bottom. Within the building block itself, the execution behavior is strictly defined (see Figure 4.1 and Figure 3.1). Thus, the execution flow in a structured program is well-defined and from top to bottom, with no surprises. GOTOless programming is often associated with structured programming precisely because the incorrect (unstructured) use of GOTO statements can wreak havoc with the execution flow. In practice, structured programs are easier to design, code, debug, and modify than unstructured programs.

Common Errors

1. **Explicit line number transfer errors.**   If you have to use a GOTO statement, then watch out for references to nonexistent line numbers as in

   200 GO TO 250

   and line 250 is missing. This would cause an "undefined line number" syntax error. Also, take care that you don't transfer to the wrong line number. This logic error is common whenever we frequently change line numbers.

2. **Incomplete relational expressions.**   Consider the following:

   IF   K > J AND   < L THEN ...
                                 └──── Missing K

   The relational expression on the right is incomplete. We tend to make this error because of the way we would state this decision verbally: "If K is greater than J and less than L." To avoid a syntax error it must be written as follows.

   IF   K > J AND   K < L THEN ...
                             └──K must be repeated

3. **Test data selection.**   When debugging, deliberately select test data that ensure execution flows through all decision blocks (then and else blocks) in your program. For example, see our test run in Example 4.7. This guarantees that all segments in your program are tested. The test data that we give in the programming exercises at the end of the chapter are designed to push you in this debugging direction. Also, always confirm the correctness of computer output by parallel hand calculations.

FOLLOW-UP EXERCISES

1. Give a true or false result (when valid) for each of the following relational expressions. Use the following storage contents.

   A 10   B 5

   P$ YES   Q$ NO

   a. A <>B
   b. A*B <= A^2
   c. P$ = "yes"
   d. Q$ = "N"
   e. A = 10
   f. A = "10"

2. Construct a relational expression for each of the following conditions.
   a. Do sales exceed $10,000?
   b. Is the last name Smith?
   c. Is the last name not Smith?
   d. Is b^2 greater than $4 \cdot a \cdot c$?

3. Indicate output from each program.
   a. 10 LET A$ = "123"
       20 LET B$ = "LOTUS"
       30 IF A$ < B$ THEN PRINT A$ ELSE PRINT B$
       99 END
   b. 10 LET X = 10
       20 LET Y = 5
       30 IF (X + Y/2) > 10 THEN PRINT "O.K."
       40 PRINT "BY ME"
       99 END

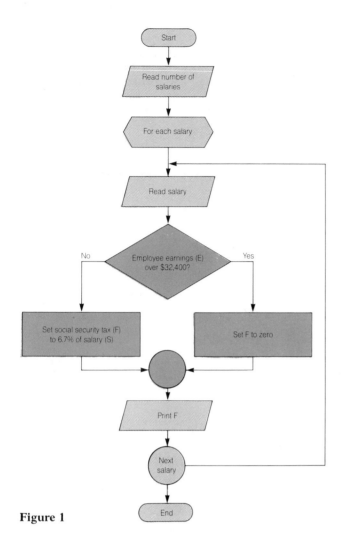

Figure 1

4. Code the given flowchart in Figure 1 into a BASIC program using the following approaches:
   a. Traditional one-line IF/THEN statement
   b. Enhanced one-line IF/THEN statement
   c. One-line IF/THEN/ELSE statement
   d. Multiline IF/THEN/ELSE statements

   Run each version on your system (if possible) using the following earnings data: 25,900; 40,000; 20,000. Which approach is preferable and why?

5. Write BASIC code for each of the pseudocode-like descriptions below. Use statements on your system that best represent good programming style.
   a. If sales for the week are above $10,000, add $150 to pay for the week; otherwise, go on to the next statement.
   b. If credits taken are 12 or more, then tuition is $1200; else, tuition is $100 times the number of credits.
   c. If part name equals "WRENCH", output the quantity on hand; otherwise, go on to the next statement.

d. If fixed costs plus variable costs are less than sales revenue, then compute profit as sales revenue minus (fixed costs plus variable costs) and output the message PROFIT = · · ·; otherwise, compute loss as fixed plus variable costs minus sales revenue and output the message LOSS = · · ·.
   e. If M = N, then add 3 to I, 2 to J, and 1 to K; otherwise, go on to the next statement in the program.
   *f. If the balance owed is under $50, the customer pays the full balance owed; else, the customer pays according to the formula $50 + 10% × (balance owed − $50). Compute and print the payment.
   *g. If the response is Y, then conversationally input the date and flight number; else, continue with the next segment in the program.

   Sample:

Flight information (Y/N)	? Y
Enter date (month,day)	? 10,25
Enter flight number	? 751

*6. Rewrite the program in Example 4.5 without using the logical operator AND. Need we ask which approach is preferable?

*7. Rewrite the program in Example 4.6 without using the logical operator OR. Need we ask which approach is preferable?

8. Given the stored values

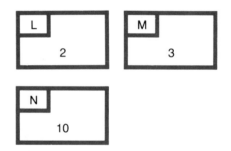

indicate whether or not the then block is executed for each of the following.
   a. IF NOT (L < M) THEN . . .
   b. IF L > M AND M = N
         OR L <= N AND M < 4 THEN . . .
   c. IF L > M AND (M = N
         OR L <= N) AND M < 4 THEN . . .

9. Develop BASIC code, given the following pseudocode. Use only compound conditions.
   a. If 0 < grade < 100 then print grade
                              else print "Grade out of range"
   b. If gender is not equal to F or M
         then print "Error in gender data"
   *c. If the response is not Y or y or YES or yes
         or N or n or NO or no
            then print "Incorrect response. Try again."

10. Consider the following bonus rules for Example 4.7:

If sales > $5000 and travel cost < $300,
   bonus is $150.
If sales > $5000 and travel cost ≥ $300 but < $600,
   bonus is $100.
If sales ≤ $5000, bonus is $0.
If travel cost ≥ $600, bonus is $0.

a. Modify the program in Example 4.7 to incorporate these new rules.

b. Implement the revised program on your system.

11. Write BASIC code for the following pseudocode.

If test score is 90 or above
   then the grade is A
If test score is 80 or above and less than 90
   then the grade is B
If test score is 70 or above and less than 80
   then the grade is C
If test score is 60 or above and less than 70
   then the grade is D
If test score is less than 60
   then the grade is F

12. **Case Structure.** Many structured BASIC dialects implement certain multiple alternative decisions using the case structure. Check your dialect for SELECT and/or CASE statements. If present, try implementing the case structure for one of the following.

a. Exercise 11.

b. Exercise 19 with marital codes D, M, S, W.

c. Exercise 19 with marital codes 1, 2, 3, 4.

13. Implement one of the following examples on your system.

a. Example 4.2
b. Example 4.3
c. Example 4.4
d. Example 4.5
e. Example 4.6
f. Example 4.7

ADDITIONAL EXERCISES

14. **Revisits.** Modify one of the problems from Chapter 3 as indicated below.

a. **Individual Retirement Account.** (Exercise 13.) Have the program check that the contribution does not exceed a maximum of $2000. If it does, print an error message to that effect and set the contribution to $2000.

b. **Depreciation.** (Exercise 15.) Have the program check that the salvage value does not exceed the cost of the asset. If it does, print an error message to that effect and set the salvage value equal to the cost.

15. **Minimum Value.** Code and test a complete program that finds the minimum quantity ordered based on the analysis and design given below.

Analysis
The following sales order data are given:

Customer Name	Quantity Ordered
Test 1	700
Test 2	500
Test 3	900
Test 4	200
Test 5	600

Output
Minimum quantity ordered
Associated name

Read
Number of customers
Customer name
Quantity ordered

Design
In our design we plan to use a FOR/NEXT loop to process the customer data: the body of the loop will include an if-then structure for recording a new minimum quantity and the corresponding customer's name.

```
Initialize minimum quantity to a large number
Read number of customers
For each customer
    Read name, quantity
    If quantity < minimum then record new minimum
       and note the associated name
Next customer
Print minimum and associated name
End
```

16. **Parking Garage.** A parking garage has the following fees schedule:

Under 3 hours $2.75
Additional hours $ .75 per hour

a. Develop an interactive program whereby the parking attendant inputs the number of hours parked, and the computer outputs the charge. Process the following hourly data: 2, 3, 3.5, 5, and 36. Note: Any part of an hour counts as an entire hour. Hint: Look up the INT function in Module C.

b. Build in a maximum charge of $9.00 per day.

17. **Personnel Analysis.** Consider the following personnel data:

Income	Sex
$ 9,000	F
12,000	M
15,000	F
25,000	F
10,000	F

   a. Design, code, and debug a program that prints the number of females who earn $10,000 or more.
   b. Include an output report that compares the average salaries of males and females.

18. **Assistance Analysis.** Consider the following data:

Income	Age	ID
$25,000	25	1
10,000	70	2
4,000	67	3
4,500	60	4
5,000	62	5

   a. Design, code, and debug a program that prints the IDs of those who either earn below $5000 or are at least 65 years old.
   b. Include an output report that compares the average salaries of those aged 65 and above to those below 65.

19. **Marital Analysis.** Consider the following data:

Name	Marital Code
Test 1	S
Test 2	M
Test 3	D
Test 4	W
Test 5	D
Test 6	M
Test 7	M
Test 8	S
Test 9	S
Test 10	M

   a. Design, code, and debug a program that prints the name and marital status (for example, single) of each person. The marital codes are defined as follows:

   D   Divorced
   M   Married
   S   Single
   W   Widowed

   b. Include an output report that summarizes how many people are in each marital category.

20. **Payroll.** Consider the calculation of gross pay for hourly workers. The following test data for three workers is collected.

Name	ID	Hourly Rate	Hours Worked
Lila	101	5.50	35
Max	102	3.75	45
Pat	103	4.65	20

Gross pay is the product of hours worked and hourly pay rate. When an employee has worked over 40 hours, however, overtime is computed at time-and-a-half for all hours above 40.

   a. Develop a program that processes the employee data as an internal data file and prints a report table with the following column headings: Employee Name, ID, Regular Pay, Overtime Pay, and Gross Pay. Also print individual totals for regular pay, overtime pay, and gross pay.
   b. Include the following deductions:
   ▪ Social security is 6.85% of gross pay.
   ▪ If gross pay is less than $100, union dues are $2.00 per week; otherwise $4.00 per week.
   Thus, add three columns to the table in part **a**: SS Deduction, Union Dues, and Net Pay.

21. **Alumni File Query.** The director of an MBA program wants to compute average salaries of alumni to include in a brochure of past graduates. The director collected the following data on students: name, year graduated, salary on first job after graduation, and prior work experience (y or n).

Alumni File

Name	Year of Graduation	Salary	Work Experience
Dewey	84	29000	y
Epcot	85	43000	y
Farmer	85	0	n
Garner	84	24500	n
Hu	85	30000	n
Jackson	85	34000	y
Kelley	84	32500	y
Moon	85	23000	n
Richards	85	0	y
Silver	85	26000	n
Teller	85	27500	y

   a. Develop an interactive query program that computes and prints the average salary for all MBA alumni in a specified graduating year. (Note: Not all MBAs have submitted salary data; to be part of the average salary computation the salary amount must be greater than 0.) Process the alumni data as an internal data file. The only input variable is the specified graduating year. Use 84 and 85 as input test data.
   b. For graduates of the specified year, also compute and print separate average salaries by work experience vs. no work experience.
   c. If salary data are unavailable for a given year, print a message to that effect. Use 83 as test input.

More Loops

5

We now complete our treatment of the repetition, or loop, structure by illustrating implementations of pre-test loops. We also cover the common data processing concept of a pre-test loop that checks for end-of-data conditions, or end-of-file loops.

5.1 PRE-TEST LOOPS

The **loop (repetition) structure** allows the repeated execution of a **loop body** based on a **loop control** test. Figure 5.1 illustrates the most fundamental loop structure variation, called a **pre-test loop structure** because the first action on entering the loop structure is to test an exit condition. The result of this test is either "execute the loop body" or "exit the loop structure." If the body is to be executed, then control passes to the set of statements that make up the loop body. In general, the loop body can be any set of executable statements. Each time the statements within the body have been executed, control returns to the exit-condition test that precedes the loop body. And so the process continues: The loop body is repeatedly executed so long as the test indicates that the body is to be executed. When the test indicates that looping is finished, control passes to the first executable statement following the loop structure.

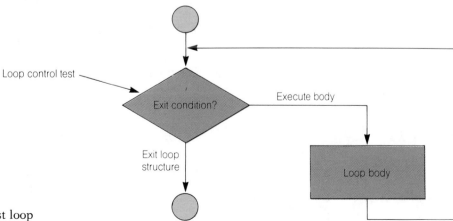

Figure 5.1   Flowchart of pre-test loop

NOTE 1   As is true in all "proper" control structures (those that reflect top-down structured programming), the flow of execution enters the loop structure through a single entry point at the "top" and exits "down" at the bottom through a single exit point.

NOTE 2   In general, the test result "execute body" is based on either a "true" or "false" logical value, depending on how the exit condition is formulated. The most common pre-test loop, called a **while structure**, executes the body *while* the exit condition tests true. In words, we tell the computer to "keep looping while the condition tests true."

Table 5.1 illustrates various pre-test loop implementations, depending on the BASIC dialect. The Minimal BASIC implementation is common to all BASIC dialects. The more modern while structure varies from dialect to dialect. Check out the implementation on your system and try running the given counter-controlled looping example to make sure you understand the implementation.

NOTE 3   Counter-controlled looping is implemented more simply by FOR/NEXT loops. In our example, we would use

```
10 FOR J = 1 TO 5
20    PRINT J;
30 NEXT J
99 END
```

In fact, the FOR/NEXT loop is itself a pre-test loop (see Figure 3.1, page 41): The body is executed *while* the control variable (J in this case) is less than or equal to the terminal value. The main examples in this chapter, however, will illustrate problems that are best implemented by other than FOR/NEXT loops.

NOTE 4   The Minimal BASIC implementation is weaker than the alternative implementations, because explicit line number transfers (THEN 99, GO TO 20) are required. *While implementations directly reflect the GO-TO-less spirit of structured programming.* Also note that while implementations repeatedly execute the body while the condition $J <= 5$ in the example tests true. The Minimal BASIC pre-test loop implementation executes the body while the condition $J > 5$ in the example is false.

E X A M P L E 5 . 1   The Inflation Curse

Analysis

High rates of inflation in a free-market economy can have devastating effects. For individuals, particularly those (such as retirees) who live on fixed incomes, purchasing power (the ability to buy goods and services) can erode dramatically over time. For the economy as a whole, it can lead to recession and unemployment as a result of such factors as uncertainty and high interest rates.

To illustrate, suppose an item currently costs $100 and increases in cost at a 10% rate of inflation per year. The future cost of this item one year from now would be $110, determined as follows:

$$100 + (100) \cdot (0.1)$$

or

$$100 \cdot (1 + 0.1)$$

Table 5.1 Selected Pre-test Loop Implementations

Allowed on Your System? (Yes/No)	Dialect	Pre-test Loop	Counter-controlled Loop Example
Yes	Minimal BASIC	**IF** *condition* **THEN** *line number* . Loop body . **GO TO** *line number*	— Exit condition 10 LET J = 1 20 IF J > 5 THEN 99 30 PRINT J; 40 LET J = J + 1 50 GOTO 20 99 END RUN 1 2 3 4 5

	ANS BASIC True BASIC	**DO WHILE** *condition*
		 .
		   Loop body
		 .
		 LOOP
			— Exit condition
			 LET J = 1
			 DO WHILE J <= 5
			   PRINT J;
			   LET J = J + 1
			 LOOP
			 END
			
			 RUN
			 1 2 3 4 5

	VAX-11 BASIC	**WHILE** *condition* . Loop body . **NEXT**	— Exit condition 10 LET J = 1 20 WHILE J <= 5 30 PRINT J; 40 LET J = J + 1 50 NEXT 99 END RUN 1 2 3 4 5
	Microsoft BASIC	**WHILE** *condition* . Loop body . **WEND**	— Exit condition 10 LET J = 1 20 WHILE J <= 5 30 PRINT J; 40 LET J = J + 1 50 WEND 99 END RUN 1 2 3 4 5
	Your system (if different)*		

*Note: *If your system lacks a specific while implementation, you must use the Minimal BASIC approach.*

Two years from now it would cost \$110 plus an additional 10% for the price increase in the second year, or

110·(1 + 0.1)

which is \$121. Thus if we define

C = current cost of item
R = rate of inflation
F = future cost of item one year from now

then we have

$F = C·(1 + R)$

for the cost at the end of one year and

$F = $ (previous year's F)·$(1 + R)$

for future costs in subsequent years.
Let's define the following data requirements.

Output

1. Years into future ⎤
2. Future cost   ⎦ In table form

Input

1. Cost multiple (ratio of future cost to current cost)
2. Current cost
3. Percent inflation rate

Design

The following design illustrates a conversational program that prints successive future costs by years *while* the future cost is less than a multiple of the current cost.

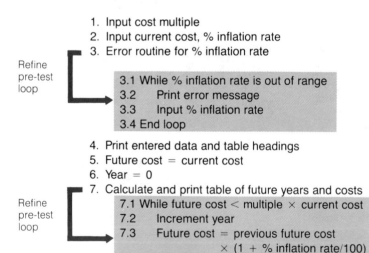

1. Input cost multiple
2. Input current cost, % inflation rate
3. Error routine for % inflation rate

Refine
pre-test
loop

   3.1 While % inflation rate is out of range
   3.2   Print error message
   3.3   Input % inflation rate
   3.4 End loop

4. Print entered data and table headings
5. Future cost = current cost
6. Year = 0
7. Calculate and print table of future years and costs

Refine
pre-test
loop

   7.1 While future cost < multiple × current cost
   7.2   Increment year
   7.3   Future cost = previous future cost
                 × (1 + % inflation rate/100)
   7.4   Print year, future cost
   7.5 End loop

8. Print table summary
9. End

Code

The code and run below were implemented in Microsoft BASIC on an IBM Personal Computer. (See Exercise 1.)

```
100 REM * * * * * * * * * * * * * * * * * * * * * * * * * * * * * * * * * * * *
110 REM *                                                                     *
120 REM *     Inflation Curse Program:   Interactive WHILE Version            *
130 REM *                                                                     *
140 REM *    Key:                                                             *
150 REM *      CCOST    = Current cost                                        *
170 REM *      FCOST    = Future cost                                         *
180 REM *      MULTIPLE = Cost multiple                                       *
190 REM *      PIRATE   = Percent inflation rate                             *
200 REM *      YEAR     = Year into future                                   *
210 REM *                                                                     *
220 REM * * * * * * * * * * * * * * * * * * * * * * * * * * * * * * * * * * * *
230 REM------------------------------------------------------------------------
240      INPUT "Enter cost multiple------------>"; MULTIPLE
250      INPUT "Enter current cost------------->"; CCOST
260      INPUT "Enter % inflation rate--------->"; PIRATE
270 REM------------------------------------------------------------------------
280      WHILE PIRATE < 1  OR  PIRATE > 100
290        PRINT: PRINT "*** Percent inflation rate must be in range 1 to 100."
295        PRINT: INPUT "Enter % inflation rate--------->"; PIRATE
300      WEND
310 REM------------------------------------------------------------------------
320      PRINT "---------------------------------------------------------------"
330      PRINT "Current Cost: $"; CCOST
340      PRINT "Inflation Rate:"; PIRATE; "%"
350      PRINT "---------------------------------------------------------------"
360      PRINT "Future Years","Future Costs"
370      PRINT "---------------------------------------------------------------"
380 REM------------------------------------------------------------------------
390      LET FCOST = CCOST
400      LET YEAR  = 0
410 REM------------------------------------------------------------------------
420      WHILE FCOST < MULTIPLE*CCOST
430        LET YEAR  = YEAR + 1
440        LET FCOST = FCOST*(1 + PIRATE/100)
450        PRINT TAB(5);YEAR,INT(FCOST)
460      WEND
470 REM------------------------------------------------------------------------
480      PRINT "---------------------------------------------------------------"
490      PRINT "Cost increased by a factor of"; MULTIPLE; "in year"; YEAR
500 REM------------------------------------------------------------------------
999      END
```

— Interactive error routine as pre-test loop (lines 280–300)

— Pre-test loop for output table (lines 420–460)

Test

```
RUN
Enter cost multiple------------>? 2
Enter current cost------------->? 90000
Enter % inflation rate--------->? .1     ← Incorrect entry

*** Percent inflation rate must be in range 1 to 100.

Enter % inflation rate--------->? 10
-----------------------------------------------------------------
Current Cost: $ 90000
Inflation Rate: 10 %

Future Years  Future Costs
-----------------------------------------------------------------
       1        99000
       2        108900
       3        119790
       4        131769
       5        144945
       6        159440
       7        175384
       8        192923
-----------------------------------------------------------------
Cost increased by a factor of 2 in year 8
```

Error routine "traps" the error and requests re-entry. See pre-test loop in lines 280–300.

— Correct entry

— Output from pre-test loop in lines 420–460

Discussion

Look at the while structure in lines 420–460 of the program. FCOST is the loop-control variable, the value of which is tested in the WHILE statement to determine whether the loop body should or should not be executed. As long as the condition "future cost less than twice current cost" is true, the body of the loop is executed. However, the first time the condition is false, the loop body is skipped, and control is transferred to the first executable statement after the WEND statement (the PRINT in line 480). In the eighth year, the future cost exceeds double the initial cost ($192,923 > $180,000); so looping terminates, based on a false value for the relational expression in the WHILE statement.

NOTE 1   Incorrect entry of data is a major reason computer programs produce incorrect results. **Data validation** is the process of checking data to be sure it is correct or valid. To do this, an **error routine** is often included as part of the program to detect errors and print appropriate error messages. The error routine in lines 280–300 of the program illustrates the usual "defensive" programming procedure of checking the data for common errors. Note that the error routine, for an interactive program, is designed with a while loop that repeatedly asks for the correct input response while the response is incorrect. In this case, the program requires entry of the inflation rate as a percent in the range 1 to 100 instead of a proportion in the range 0 to 1. Because we entered the proportion 0.1 (purposely, of course!) the error routine detects the error, prints an error message, and requests the user to reenter the inflation rate. This new entry is checked again (line 280), and control is transferred to the report headings (line 320) once the inflation rate is entered correctly.

NOTE 2   Remember that the WHILE/WEND statements in Example 5.1 are dialect-specific (Microsoft BASIC in Table 5.1). See Exercise 2 for this and other possible implementation differences for your system.

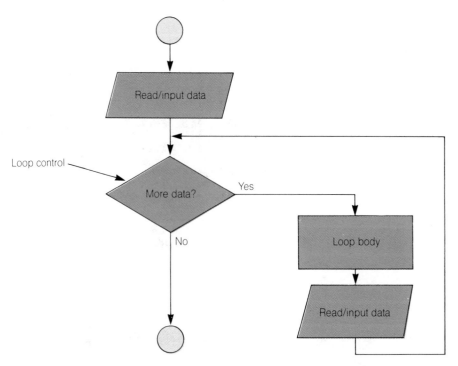

Figure 5.2   Flowchart of eof loop.

5.2 END-OF-FILE (EOF) LOOPS

FOR/NEXT loops are convenient when we know the number of desired loop iterations beforehand; while loops are useful when exit from the loop is based on a computational result within the loop. If we don't wish to specify in advance (or if we don't know) the exact number of times the loop is to be repeated, then the **end-of-file (eof) loop** may be appropriate.

The eof loop is best implemented as a pre-test loop structure, as illustrated in Figure 5.2 and by the various implementations in Table 5.2. Take a moment now to study the eof loop structure that applies to you in the table, and trace through the execution of its corresponding example.

As you can see, the first action actually precedes the loop: a READ (or INPUT) statement is executed. Next, the loop is entered, and an **end-of-file (eof) condition** is tested. This means that a test is performed to determine whether or not the end of the data has been reached. The test, therefore, requires a special data item at the end of the data called a **trailer number**, or **sentinel**. To be special, this numeric (or string) value must never be part of

Table 5.2   Selected Eof Loop Implementations

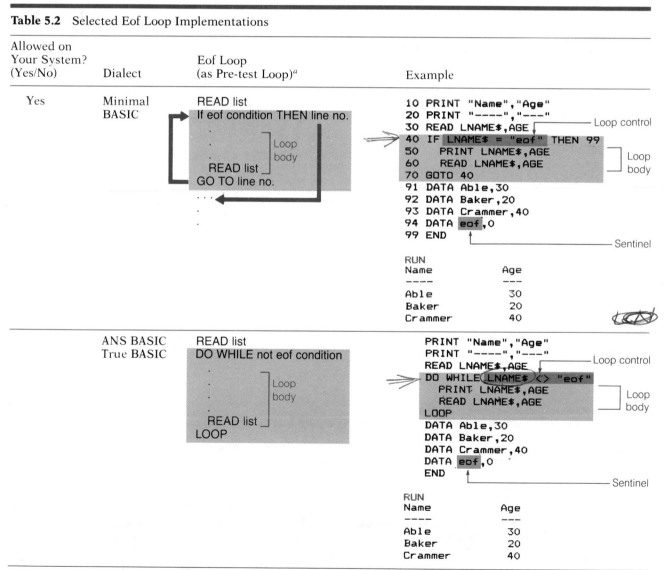

continued

Table 5.2 continued

Allowed on Your System? (Yes/No)	Dialect	Eof Loop (as Pre-test Loop)[a]	Example
	VAX-11 BASIC	READ list WHILE not eof condition . . READ list ⌐ Loop body NEXT	10 PRINT "Name","Age" 20 PRINT "----","---" 30 READ LNAME$,AGE — Loop control 40 WHILE LNAME$ <> "eof" 50 PRINT LNAME$,AGE — Loop body 60 READ LNAME$,AGE 70 NEXT 91 DATA Able,30 92 DATA Baker,20 93 DATA Crammer,40 94 DATA eof,0 99 END — Sentinel RUN Name Age ---- --- Able 30 Baker 20 Crammer 40
	Microsoft BASIC	READ list WHILE not eof condition . . READ list ⌐ Loop body WEND	10 PRINT "Name","Age" 20 PRINT "----","---" 30 READ LNAME$,AGE — Loop control 40 WHILE LNAME$ <> "eof" 50 PRINT LNAME$,AGE — Loop body 60 READ LNAME$,AGE 70 WEND 91 DATA Able,30 92 DATA Baker,20 93 DATA Crammer,40 94 DATA eof,0 99 END — Sentinel RUN Name Age ---- --- Able 30 Baker 20 Crammer 40
	Your system (if different)[b]		

[a]INPUT can be substituted for READ.
[b]**Note:** *If your system lacks the while eof implementation, you must use the Minimal BASIC eof implementation.*

the regularly provided data for the particular application. Lines 91–94 in the example show three legitimate data lines and the sentinel eof. In effect, we're telling the computer to process the values Able, Baker, and Crammer through the loop; however, when LNAME$ stores eof we wish a loop exit, since eof is the signal that all data have been processed.

Table 5.3 shows the flow of execution as we roleplay the example.

Table 5.3 Roleplay of Example in Table 5.2

Line Executed	Comment	Action	Result
30	READ before loop	Read name, age	LNAME$ = Able AGE = 30
40	1st loop iteration	Test for eof	False (Min BASIC); True (other dialects)
50		Print name, age	Able 30 is printed
60		Read name, age	LNAME$ = Baker AGE = 20
70		Loop back to line 40	Line 40 is executed next
40	2nd loop iteration	Test for eof	False (Min BASIC); True (other dialects)
50		Print name, age	Baker 20 is printed
60		Read name, age	LNAME$ = Crammer AGE = 40
70		Loop back to line 40	Line 40 is executed next
40	3rd loop iteration	Test for eof	False (Min BASIC); True (other dialects)
50		Print name, age	Crammer 40 is printed
60		Read name, age	LNAME$ = eof AGE = 0
70		Loop back to line 40	Line 40 is executed next
40	Exit loop	Test for eof	True (Min BASIC); False (other dialects)
99		END executed	Execution ends

NOTE 1 The eof loop processes data *while* data remain to be processed; thus, it's an example of a while structure.

NOTE 2 Did it occur to you that the following approach might be simpler?

```
10 PRINT "Name","Age"
20 PRINT "----","---"
30 READ N                          ┐ Loop control
40 FOR J = 1 TO N
50    READ LNAME$,AGE              ┐ Loop body
60    PRINT LNAME$,AGE
70 NEXT J
90 DATA 3
91 DATA Able,30
92 DATA Baker,20
93 DATA Crammer,40
99 END

RUN
Name        Age
----        ---
Able         30
Baker        20
Crammer      40
```

True. However, many applications (especially in data processing) require the processing of large amounts of data. The FOR/NEXT approach requires an exact count of the number of data items, which introduces the likelihood of error in this count. The eof approach more simply requires a sentinel at the very end of the data. Primarily for this reason, the eof loop is the most common loop design in commercial applications that process sequential (disk and tape) data files. Module E looks at this in some detail.

NOTE 3   Carefully note that the eof pre-test loop structure requires a READ (or INPUT) statement just before the loop and a second READ (or INPUT) statement at the very end of the loop body. Thus the eof loop itself performs all READ (or INPUT) operations except the first. This may seem strange at first, so we give you another shot to think about this in Exercise 9.

NOTE 4   As usual, the test condition in the Minimal BASIC version (LNAME$ = "eof") is the complement of the test condition in the while versions (LNAME$<>"eof"). Alternatively, we could restate the while versions as NOT (LNAME$ = "eof").

5.3 POINTERS

Design and Style

1.   **Indentation.**   Improve the readability of a loop (for us humans) by clearly indenting the loop body and identifying the *beginning* and *end* of the loop.

2.   **Structure of loop.**   Be conscious of the correct loop structure in structured programming. Use a single entry point at the top and a single exit point at the bottom. The incorrect use of GO TO statements is one means to violate this top-down principle. It's best to use the pre-test (or post-test, as in Exercise 7) design exclusively, since it simplifies the identification of the loop (its control and body).

3.   **Eof vs. FOR/NEXT loops.**   In general we should use an eof loop whenever a loop is to process many lines of data (records in an internal data file), the number of which is likely to change from run to run. This approach is convenient and reliable, since it avoids the error-prone activity of having to specify beforehand the exact number of loop iterations, as in using a FOR/NEXT loop. This is a key reason why the eof approach is the method of choice in commercial data processing applications such as payrolls, billings, and inventory control.

4.   **Error messages.**   The design of error messages takes on rather rich dimensions in interactive user-friendly minicomputer and microcomputer environments. For example, the error routine in lines 280–300 of Example 5.1 can be designed to alert the user to a problem by using a combination of sound, color, blinking, and reverse video (hopefully, not all at once!). At a minimum we should print clearly distinguishable error messages that alert users to the exact nature of the problem.

5.   **Screen design.**   The input/output design of interactive programs takes special care. Input requests should be stated concisely and clearly, without clutter. Likewise, output should be designed to enhance readability. It's also best to segregate input from output visually. For example, input can appear in one part of the screen and output in another. Better yet, many dialects have a special statement for clearing the screen. For example, the Microsoft BASIC statement **CLS** clears the screen and places the cursor in the *home* position (the upper-left corner). It's an especially useful statement to place at the beginning of a program so that dated or unrelated material doesn't clutter the screen.

Another common problem is the scrolling of output on a screen. For example consider a screen that fits 24 lines and a loop that prints a 30-

line table. In this case, the first six lines of the table would be scrolled off the top of the screen. To view the top 24 lines of the table on the screen, we could press the proper "pause" key, or combination of keys, to freeze the output as it's scrolling. Then we can usually continue by pressing another key. Do you know how to pause output to your screen? Better yet, programs can be designed to pause execution at certain strategic points. For example, the VAX-11 BASIC statement

```
SLEEP 120
```

would suspend execution for 120 seconds. Ask your instructor how this might be done on your system.

Common Errors

1. **Loop iterations.**   Programming an incorrect number of loop iterations is a very common mistake. One cause of this error is an incorrect description of a boundary in the construction of the loop-control condition. In particular, pay attention to $>=$ versus $>$ and $<=$ versus $<$ operators. For example, do we want $A > 5$ or $A >= 5$? Also note, for example, that $J >= K+1$ and $J > K$ are equivalent when J and K store integer values exclusively.

2. **Infinite loop.**   In designing loop structures, take care that the loop control satisfies the condition sometime during the processing of the loop. If the loop exit condition is never met, then we have committed a logic error called an **infinite loop**. In this case, the body of the loop is continually processed until execution is stopped by outside intervention (the user hits the "break" key or turns off the machine).

3. **Incomplete sentinel data line.**   Make sure that the sentinel data line for an eof loop is complete with respect to the expected number of data items:

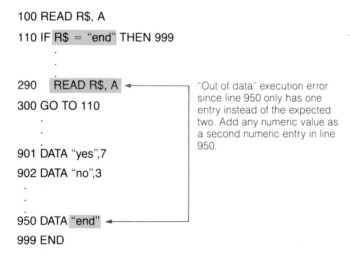

```
100 READ R$, A
110 IF R$ = "end" THEN 999
      .
      .
      .
290    READ R$, A
300 GO TO 110
      .
      .
      .
901 DATA "yes",7
902 DATA "no",3
      .
      .
      .
950 DATA "end"
999 END
```

"Out of data" execution error since line 950 only has one entry instead of the expected two. Add any numeric value as a second numeric entry in line 950.

4. **Data validation.**   If we can't find fault with our algorithm, yet computer output does not validate our hand-calculated results, then (assuming that our hand-calculated results are correct) we should look for the possibility of faulty input data.

In general, we should program defensively by testing all parts of our program and by training ourselves to anticipate potential errors that can be overcome by good program design.

FOLLOW-UP EXERCISES

1. Implement the example in Table 5.1 on your system. Use a while structure if it's available.

2. Implement Example 5.1 on your system. Be careful with any implementation differences regarding:
   i. While structure in lines 280–300 and lines 420–460.
   ii. Multistatement lines in lines 290–295.
   iii. INPUT with prompt in lines 240–260, 295.

3. Confirm the output in Example 5.1 by roleplaying the computer. As you do this, fill in the contents of the indicated storage locations below as if a "snapshot" of memory were taken just before execution of the WEND statement.

CCOST	PIRATE	YEAR	FCOST

4. In Example 5.1
   a. What would happen if the statement

      390 LET FCOST = CCOST

      were omitted?
   b. What would happen if line 440 were changed to

      440 LET FCOST = CCOST * (1 + PIRATE/100)

   c. What would happen if YEAR were initialized to 1? Modify the program to obtain the same output if the year is initialized to 1.
   d. If we were to enter 0.2 as the inflation rate, what inflation rate would be used to calculate future cost?
   e. Can you think of a way of improving the computational efficiency within the body of the loop?
   f. Why would it be unwise to use the loop-control test

      FCOST<> MULTIPLE * CCOST

*5. Modify the program in Example 5.1 to terminate looping either when future cost equals or exceeds the multiple of current cost or when ten years have passed.

*6. **Nested Loops.** Consider the following changes in Example 5.1.
   a. Modify the program to incorporate an outer while loop that processes multiple sets of input data. Prompt the user with the question

      Do you wish to process more data (Y/N)?

   It's not necessary to ask this question at the beginning of the run.

   b. Run the program for the following sets of values.

CCOST	PIRATE
90000	5
90000	10
90000	15
180000	10

*7. **Post-test Loops.** The while or, more generally, the pre-test loop structure is the fundamental loop structure, but it is not necessarily preferred for all types of looping. Some problems are best solved by the **post-test loop structure** illustrated in Figure 1. The term *post-test loop* means that the loop-control test now follows the loop body. The first action on entering the post-test loop is to execute the loop body, which is any set of executable statements. After the statements within the loop body have been executed, the exit condition is tested. The result of this test is either "execute the body" or "exit the loop." If the body is to be executed, then control passes once again to the set of executable statements that make up the body; otherwise, loop exit is achieved. The minimal BASIC implementation of the post-test loop is as follows.

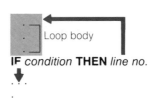

IF *condition* **THEN** *line no.*

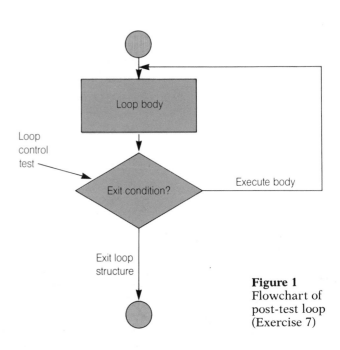

Figure 1
Flowchart of post-test loop (Exercise 7)

a. Rewrite the program in Table 5.1 using the post-test loop. Either use the minimal BASIC implementation or your system's implementation based on the keyword UNTIL. Run the revised program on your system.

b. Rewrite the pre-test loop in lines 420–460 of Example 5.1 as a post-test loop. Either use the Minimal BASIC implementation or your system's implementation based on the keyword UNTIL. Run the revised program on your system.

8. Implement the example in Table 5.2 on your system. Use a while structure if it's available.

9. What would happen in the example of Table 5.2 if
   a. We were to delete the READ in line 30 and move the READ in line 60 to line 45?

*b. We were to use the following post-test design?

   (Delete lines 30 and 70)
   40   READ LNAME$, AGE
   50   PRINT LNAME$, AGE
   60 IF LNAME$ <>"eof" THEN 40

10. What would happen in the run of Table 5.2 if line 94 had been written as
    a. 94 DATA "eof," 9
    b. 94 DATA "eof"
    c. 94 DATA "end,"0
    d. How could you change line 40 to process the DATA line given in part c?

ADDITIONAL EXERCISES

11. **Revisits.** Modify one of the problems from Chapter 4 as indicated below.
    a. **Parking Garage.** (Exercise 16, page 73.) Use a loop design that keeps processing until zero is input for hours.
    b. **Personnel Analysis.** (Exercise 17, page 74.) Use an eof loop to process the data file.
    c. **Assistance Analysis.** (Exercise 18, page 74.) Use an eof loop to process the data file.
    d. **Marital Analysis.** (Exercise 19, page 74.) Use an eof loop to process the data file.
    e. **Payroll.** (Exercise 20, page 74.) Use an eof loop to process the employee file.
    f. **Alumni File.** (Exercise 21, page 74.) Use an eof loop to process the alumni file. Use a yes/no loop control to process queries from the MBA Director.

12. **Student Grades.** A student is assigned a grade A, B, C, D, or F according to the following rule.

test score $\geq$ 90	grade is A
80 $\leq$ test score < 90	grade is B
70 $\leq$ test score < 80	grade is C
60 $\leq$ test score < 70	grade is D
test score < 60	grade is F

    A program is to use the following read/output:

    Output
      1. Student name
      2. Letter grade

    Read
      1. Student name
      2. Test score

    a. Design a program (flowchart or pseudocode) that uses an eof loop to process students. Use parameters to store the grade class ranges (100, 90, 80, 70, and 60). Include an error routine that prints name and error message for grades outside the range 0–100.

    b. Write a BASIC program that can be implemented on your system.

    c. Test the program for the following data:

       Test 1,80
       Test 2,75
       Test 3,110
       Test 4,50
       Test 5,95
       Test 6,64

13. **Property Tax Assessment.** The property tax rate in a town is set at an increasing rate according to the following table.

    Annual Property Tax Schedule

Value of Property	Tax Rate
Less than $10,000	3%
$10,000 or more but under $30,000	4%
$30,000 or more but under $60,000	5%
$60,000 and over	6%

    a. Run a program to read in the value of the property, then determine and print the tax charge. Process the following test data as an internal data file. Use an eof loop.

Lot Number	Owner's Name	Property Value
613	A. Smith	$ 8,900
975	A. B. Smith	25,000
152	B. C. Smith	42,000
1642	C. B. Smith	37,000
1785	Deaf Smith	75,000

Sample Output

Lot Number	Owner	Property Value	Tax Charge
613	A. Smith	8900	267
975	A. B. Smith	25000	1000
152	B. C. Smith	42000	2100
1642	C. B. Smith	37000	1850
1785	Deaf Smith	75000	3750

b. Modify the program in part **a** so that it prints the sum of property values, the total tax charge, the average property value, and the average tax charge.

c. Check the entered data for errors by ensuring that lot numbers are greater than zero and less than 5000 and property values are greater than $1 and less than $5 million. If an error is found, print an appropriate error message, bypass the tax charge calculation, and go on to the next property. Add new data to test each of these possible errors.

14. **Optimal Cost per Credit.** Suppose that the cost per credit charged by a college directly affects student enrollment according to the following *demand* curve.

$$S = D1 - D2 \cdot C$$

where

S = number of students enrolled
C = cost ($) per credit
$D1$ = first parameter in demand curve
$D2$ = second parameter in demand curve

For example, if the tuition charge is $80 per credit, $D1$ is 14,000, and $D2$ is 100, then the number of students that will enroll is estimated by

$$S = 14000 - (100) \cdot (80)$$
$$= 6000$$

If the cost per credit is increased to $90, then the estimated enrollment drops to

$$S = 14000 - (100) \cdot (90)$$
$$= 5000$$

The average balance due the college is given by

$$B = A \cdot C + F$$

where

B = average balance due the college
A = average number of credit hours for the college
C = cost per credit
F = average fee for the college

For example, if the average number of credit hours taken by students is 14, the cost per credit is $80, and average fees are $250, then the average bill per student is

$$B = (14) \cdot (80) + 250$$
$$= \$1370$$

Since projected enrollment is 6000 students when the per-credit charge is $80, it follows that the col-

lege would realize a projected revenue of ($1370 per student) · (6000 students), or $8,220,000.

a. Develop a program that uses a FOR/NEXT loop to vary C from an initial value ($C1$) to a limit ($C2$) in increments of $C3$. Process the following data:

$D1$	$D2$	A	F	$C1$	$C2$	$C3$
14000	100	14	250	50	80	5

Store $D1, D2, A$, and F through READ statements and interactively input $C1, C2$, and $C3$.

Print an output table headed by four columns: Cost per Credit, Average Bill, Expected Enrollment, and Expected Revenue. On the basis of this output, what cost per credit maximizes expected revenue for the college?

b. Add a yes/no pre-test loop that's outer to the loop in part **a**. (See Exercise 6.) Use this loop to better "zoom in" on the desired cost per credit. For example, the user may wish to change the values of $C1, C2$, and $C3$. In this case, the program should ask "Do you wish to change the cost per credit range?" and should respond accordingly. Try a new range of 55 to 65 in steps of 1. Now what's the best cost per credit?

c. Add an outer eof loop that processes all colleges in a state-wide system. Run the following test data.

College Name	$D1$	$D2$	A	F	$C1$	$C2$	$C3$
Test 1	14000	100	14	250	50	80	5
Test 2	14000	25	14	250	200	300	5
Test 3	30000	250	13.5	500	10	60	1

Just before each output table print the name of the college, $D1, D2, A$, and F.

What tuition (cost per credit) should be charged at each college to maximize revenue? Would you say there's a flaw in the algorithmic logic if students freely change colleges within the system on the basis of tuition?

15. **Forecasting Population Growth.** In recent years, the prediction of world population levels into the next century has been a concern of many political, environmental, and agricultural planners. The following equation can be used to predict future levels of world population:

$$p = c \cdot [1 + (b - d)]^n$$

where

p = predicted level of future population
b = birth rate
c = current level of population
d = death rate
n = number of years into the future

For example, estimated data for the year 1976 show $c = 4$ (billions), $b = 0.025$ (2.5%), and $d = 0.009$ (0.9%). If b and d essentially remain constant over a

10-year period ($n = 10$), then we can predict the world population in 1986 as

$$p = 4[1 + (0.025 - 0.009)]^{10}$$
$$= 4 (1.016)^{10}$$
$$= 4(1.1720)$$
$$= 4.688 \text{ billions}$$

a. Develop a program that processes input data for c, b, d, and n using a yes/no pre-test loop. (See Exercise 6.) Calculate and print the predicted level of future population. Use the following test data:

c	b	d	n
4	0.025	0.009	10
4	0.025	0.009	20
4	0.025	0.009	30
4	0.020	0.009	30

Does a drop in the birthrate to 0.020 make much difference?

Repeatedly change the value of n to determine the number of years it would take for the population to double. Try different values for n and observe the output values for p. Answer this question for both the 0.025 and the 0.020 birthrates.

b. Let N be a counter for "years into future" in an "inner" loop that lies entirely within the outer loop in part **a**. This inner loop increments N by 1, calculates predicted population, and prints N, corresponding year, and predicted population. Initialize N by defining an input variable called $N1$. Exit from the loop when the ratio of predicted population to current population exceeds a desired ratio (R). Run the program for the following three sets of input values.

Current Population	Base Year	b	d	$N1$	R
4	1976	0.025	0.009	10	2
4	1976	0.025	0.009	25	3
4	1976	0.020	0.009	30	3

For example, your output for the first run should look like this.

Years into Future	Corresponding Year	Predicted Population
10	1986	4.688
11	1987	4.763
.	.	.
.	.	.
.	.	.
43	2019	7.915
44	2020	8.042

Note that the counter is initialized by $N1$ and that this loop terminates when the predicted population *exceeds* (not equals) double (R has a value of 2) the current population. Comment on

the number of years it takes the current world population to double and triple relative to changes in the birthrate.

16. Personnel Benefits Budget. A budget officer for the State Agency of Education is in the process of preparing the personnel budget for the next fiscal year. One phase of this process is to prepare a budget of personnel expenditures paid by the state in addition to salaries. The additional expenditures include the following.

1. *Social Security.* The state contributes 6.7% of an employee's salary up to \$32,400. No deduction is made for earnings above that amount.
2. *Retirement.* The state contributes 9.6% of total salary if the employee belongs to the state retirement plan; 9% is contributed by the state if the employee elects a private plan; and nothing is contributed by the state if the employee is not eligible for a retirement plan (for example, employees under 30 years of age are not eligible for a retirement plan).
3. *Group Life Insurance.* The state contributes \$1.30 for every \$1000 of salary paid to the employee. For purposes of calculation, round every salary to the next highest \$1000. For example, a yearly salary of \$11,150 results in a \$15.60 contribution (12×1.30).

The data for each employee consist of
1. Name
2. Social Security number
3. Annual salary
4. Code for retirement: NE = not eligible; SP = state plan; PP = private plan

a. Run a program that outputs each employee's name, Social Security number, salary, Social Security contribution, retirement contribution, group life contribution, and total contribution. After all employees have been processed, print the totals of each budget category (the four contribution columns) for all employees. Use the test data below to debug your program.

Employee File

Name	Social Security Number	Salary (\$)	Retirement Code
TEST 1	111-11-1111	17,000	SP
TEST 2	222-22-2222	19,500	PP
TEST 3	333-33-3333	21,300	SP
TEST 4	444-44-4444	35,000	NE
TEST 5	555-55-5555	32,400	SP
TEST 6	666-66-6666	10,750	NE
TEST 7	777-77-7777	24,375	SP
TEST 8	888-88-8888	15,600	PP

b. Design your program to check for errors in the retirement code. If a code is in error, print an appropriate error message and bypass the employee. Add a new employee to test this logic.

Modular Programming

6

This chapter introduces, motivates, and implements a style of programming called modular programming. As we will see, this approach to programming is especially useful in designing and developing long, complex programs of the type encountered in commercial applications.

6.1 THE MODULAR CONCEPT

Behavioral research, not to mention our own experiences, clearly shows that the human brain best solves elaborate problems by a "divide and conquer" strategy. That is, we divide a large problem into distinct and manageable major portions, or tasks. Then we separately work on each task, generally completing one before going on to the next. Finally, when all major tasks are complete, we have a solution to the overall problem. Table 6.1 illustrates the breakdown of specific problems into major tasks.

Similarly, as programs increase in length and complexity, it's best to view the major processing tasks as groups of related statements called **modules**. The act of designing and developing a program as a set of modules is called **modular programming**.

As illustrated by the third example in Table 6.1, a module represents a processing task. But exactly what is a module and how is it implemented? Unfortunately, there is no unique definition of a module, nor is there just one way to implement modules. Moreover, the division of a program into modules based on processing tasks requires study, experience, talent, and insight. So, rather than answering these questions directly, let's list some key properties of a module and then illustrate their selection and implementation through a series of examples.

The following properties characterize modules:

1. **A module has a single entry point and a single exit point.** In essence, a module is like a "black box" that is uniquely activated (entered through the top), performs some assigned function, and is uniquely deactivated (exited through the bottom).

Table 6.1 Sample Major Tasks or Modules

Problem	Major Tasks (Modules)
Write book	Front matter
	Chapter 1
	.
	.
	.
	Chapter 7
	Appendix A
	Appendix B
	Index
Build house	Excavation
	Foundation
	First floor
	Second floor
	Plumbing
	Electrical work
	Finish work
Develop telephone billing program	Data input and error routine
	Calculation of bills
	Printing of bills
	Management report

2. **A module is independent from other modules.** Essentially this means that we can design, develop, change, or modify a module without affecting other modules. In reality, absolute independence may not be achievable in many cases; however, modules should at least exhibit the type of functional independence described in the four modules of the telephone billing example in Table 6.1.

3. **A module is not too large.** The industry rule of thumb says that a module should not exceed 50 to 100 lines of code, which is one or two pages of listing. The basic idea is that the size of a module should not become so unwieldy that the programmer loses intimacy (understanding in depth) with this portion of the code. Needless to say, this property is subjective but well meaning.

6.2 SUBROUTINES AS MODULES

A **subroutine** is a uniquely identifiable group of successive statements within a program that accomplishes a specific purpose within that program. Subroutines are useful because (1) they allow a modular approach to long, complicated programs, (2) they promote shorter programs when the repeated use of a sequence of statements is needed at different points in a program, and (3) they save programming effort when a code that accomplishes a popular task can be used in more than one program.

A subroutine is called through the execution of a GOSUB statement of the following type:

GOSUB Statement

```
GOSUB line number
GOSUB 400
```

This statement transfers control to the indicated line number, which should be the first line in the subroutine. The statements within the subroutine are then executed, until a RETURN statement transfers control back to the calling module.

The last statement in a subroutine is the RETURN statement, which has the following general form:

RETURN statement

RETURN

This statement transfers control back to the statement immediately following the GOSUB statement that called the subroutine.

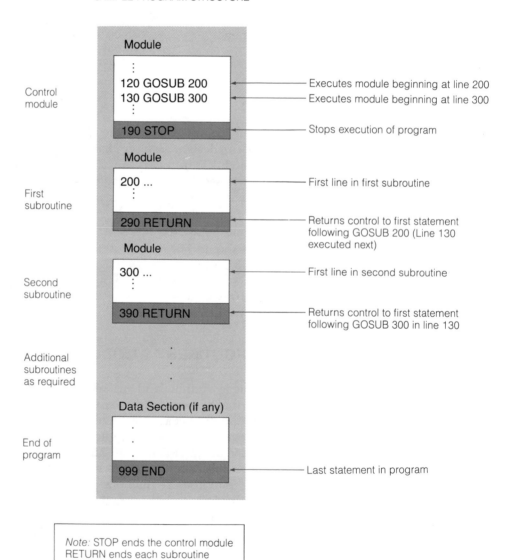

Figure 6.1   Typical structure of programs with subroutines

The STOP statement is another commonly used statement in modular programs:

Stop Statement

STOP

As you might suspect, its purpose is to stop the execution of a program. We will illustrate its use shortly.

Figure 6.1 illustrates the typical structure of a program that uses subroutines. Note that a subroutine is not used by itself; rather, it's embedded within the larger program. Also note how the scheme in Figure 6.1 effectively subdivides the program into its component modules. The first module is called the **control module**. Generally, this first module initiates the program and controls the order in which other modules within the program are executed.

The next example illustrates how we construct and execute subroutines and uses the new BASIC statements GOSUB and RETURN.

E X A M P L E   6 . 1   **Bar Chart Program**

The following steps illustrate a program with just two modules, the control module and one subroutine.

Analysis

Let's develop a noninteractive program that reads data for a frequency distribution and prints a graphical representation called a bar chart. Figure 6.2 shows a sample frequency distribution and its corresponding bar chart for final grades in an academic course.

The data requirements are as follows:

Output
Title of bar chart
Label for each bar
Bars
Length of each bar

Read
Title of bar chart
Number of bars
Label for each bar
Length of each bar

Design

The first step in the design is a top-down look at the overall modular structure. Typically, a module has either a specialized task or a set of related tasks within the overall purpose of the program. In our example, let's design a subroutine or module that prints the elements of a bar chart as in Figure 6.2b. Thus our subroutine will specialize in printing each bar in a bar chart, together with its label and length. The control module, then, must carry out the other tasks, as described below.

Control module	Reads all data.
	Prints title.
	Establishes a loop that processes a complete bar chart.
	Stops processing.
Subroutine bar print	Prints the label, bar, and length of the bar.

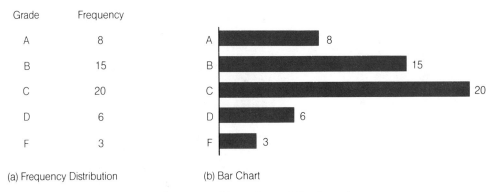

(a) Frequency Distribution   (b) Bar Chart

Figure 6.2   Frequency distribution and bar chart of final grades

The following pseudocode reflects this design.

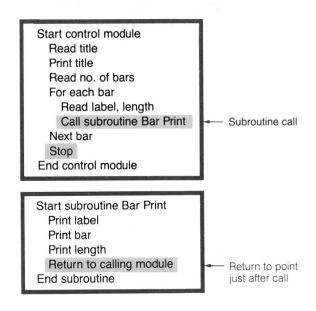

Note that the subroutine is referenced within the loop in the control module when it's time to print the label, bar, and length for any one bar. This is termed a **subroutine call.** Calling the subroutine means that we tell the computer to execute the statements within the subroutine at this time. The subroutine itself looks like any other program design we have written up to now, except that when the computer is through executing the subroutine, execution control must be "returned" to the module that called the subroutine in the first place.

Thus, from an execution point of view, the loop design in the control module works as follows:

1. Read the label and length of a bar.

2. Call the subroutine.

The subroutine prints the label, bar, and length, after which it returns control to the control module.

3. Go on to the next bar and repeat steps 1 and 2 as often as necessary.

The bar itself is printed as a set of special characters such as = , *, or + . The number of these special characters in the bar is equivalent to the length of the bar. Thus we can further refine the subroutine as follows:

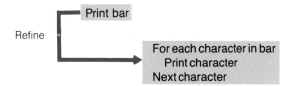

In other words, it takes a FOR/NEXT loop to print the individual characters that make up the bar.

Figure 6.3 shows equivalent flowcharts for the given pseudocode. Note that each module is a separate flowchart and that modules are "called" using the *predefined process symbol*

Code and Test

Figure 6.4 shows the program and test run for the bar chart problem. Study the program together with its output, relate it to the pseudocode design and discussion, and then go on to the text that follows the example for further explanations.

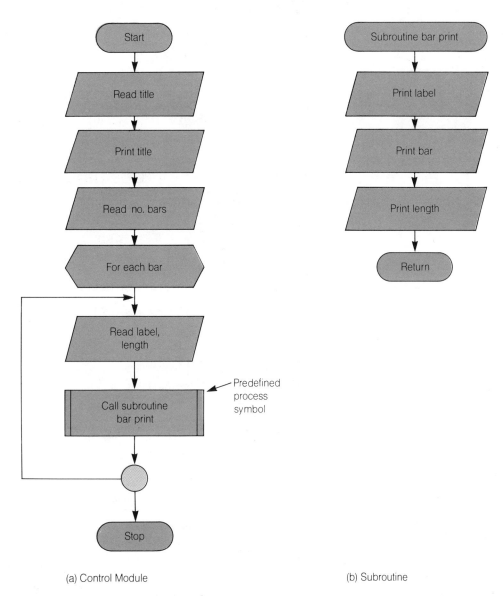

(a) Control Module   (b) Subroutine

Figure 6.3 Flowcharts for bar chart program

Discussion

The subroutine is called through the execution of the GOSUB 400 statement in line 300. Looking at the program in Figure 6.4, we see that when line 300 is executed, control is next transferred to line 400. Since lines 400 and 410 are REM statements, the next line executed is really line 420, which prints the label A for the first bar. Next, the bar is printed within the loop defined by lines 430–450, the length of the bar (8) is printed in line 460, and then the RETURN statement in line 470 is executed.

```
100 REM    * * * * * * * * * * * * * * * * * * * * * * * * * *
110 REM    * Bar Chart Program                                *
120 REM    *                                                  *
130 REM    *    Control module ... Reads data and loops for each *
140 REM    *                      bar to be printed.          *
150 REM    *                      Calls subroutine bar print. *
160 REM    *                                                  *
170 REM    *    Sub. bar print ... Prints a bar, together with  *
180 REM    *                       its label and length.      *
190 REM    * * * * * * * * * * * * * * * * * * * * * * * * * *
200 REM
210 REM--------------- Control Module -------------------------
220 REM
230      PRINT
240      READ TITLE$
250      PRINT TITLE$
260      PRINT
270      READ BARS
280      FOR J = 1 TO BARS
290        READ LABEL$,LENGTH
300        GOSUB 400                    ' Call subroutine bar print
310      NEXT J
320      PRINT
330      STOP
399 REM
400 REM--------------- Subroutine Bar Print ------------------
410 REM
420      PRINT LABEL$;" ";
430      FOR K = 1 TO LENGTH
440        PRINT "=";
450      NEXT K
460      PRINT LENGTH
470      RETURN
499 REM
900 REM--------------- Data Section --------------------------
901 REM
905      DATA "Distribution of Final Grades"
910      DATA 5
911      DATA "A",8
912      DATA "B",15
913      DATA "C",20
914      DATA "D",6
915      DATA "F",3
998 REM----------------------------------------------------------
999      END
```

```
RUN

Distribution of Final Grades

A ======== 8
B =============== 15
C ==================== 20
D ====== 6
F === 3

Break in 330
```

Figure 6.4   Bar chart program and test run

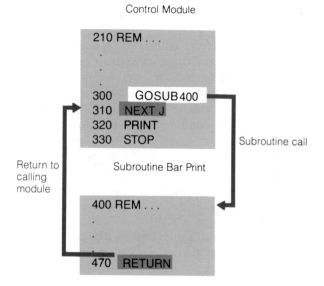

Figure 6.5   The call/return process for the bar chart program

After processing within the subroutine is completed, control is transferred back to the statement immediately following the GOSUB statement that called the subroutine. For example, execution of the RETURN statement in line 470 in Figure 6.4 transfers execution to just after the call in line 300, which means that line 310 is executed next. This call/return process is better illustrated in Figure 6.5. Note that this process is repeated five times (once for each bar) for the data given in Figure 6.4.

The STOP statement in line 330 prevents control from entering subroutine Bar Print once the program completes printing the bar chart. Thus, the program stops executing in line 330 after the FOR/NEXT loop in lines 280–310 is completed.

NOTE 1   The program in Figure 6.4 reflects the generalized modular design in Figure 6.1. In particular, note that the control module ends with a STOP statement, the bar print module ends with a RETURN statement, and the remaining portion or data section ends with an END statement. Moreover, execution of each module starts at the top of the module and exits through the bottom, which is consistent with the desirability of *top-down execution*.

NOTE 2   A subroutine does not have a unique first line, either to indicate the beginning of a subroutine or to separate it from the preceding module. Our own preference is to use a REM statement containing the name of the module as the first line of a subroutine.

NOTE 3   A subroutine can use any BASIC statement. Also, a subroutine has access to all variables in a program. In Figure 6.4, the subroutine utilized the variables LABEL$ and LENGTH, whose values were read in by the control module.

NOTE 4   Subroutines are not the only means to implementing modules in BASIC. For example, many BASIC dialects allow the "chained" execution of separate program files (modules). More recent dialects include *external modules*, whereby the module is independently stored and compiled from other modules. This feature is important in commercial environments that develop large programs. Typically, the program is written by a software team in which each team member develops one or more assigned modules.

6.3 MENUS

Interactive software is frequently designed as **menu-driven programs**. These programs present the user with a list of options (the **menu**) and then take appropriate actions based on the user's choice. Menus are very common in commercial interactive programs, since they facilitate the training of users and reduce the likelihood that users will commit errors. For example, many game programs include menus of available games, and spreadsheet programs like Lotus 1-2-3 not only have extensive main menus but also have submenus that give further options once main menu items are selected.

Figure 6.6 illustrates a sample menu for a word processing package. There are four processing options: retrieve a file, store a file, print a file, and delete a file. In addition, the user can exit the system if desired. In general, good menu design pays attention to clearly communicating the choices through text layout, meaningful choices, and use of color. Good menu design also calls for an error routine that traps incorrect choices.

Menu-driven programs usually have a separate module for implementing each menu choice. Thus, modular programming, subroutines, and the related BASIC statements (GOSUB and RETURN) are frequently used in the design and coding of menu-driven programs, as illustrated next.

```
            MENU

   R      Retrieve file
   S      Store file
   P      Print file
   D      Delete file
   X      Exit program


   Enter Choice ===>
```

Figure 6.6   Sample word processing menu

E X A M P L E   6 . 2   **Menu-Driven Student Reporting System**

Analysis

The Dean of Students at a local college needs a reporting system that will display student information in several ways. The Dean wants to access data on any student, list all students in a class, or list all students on the Dean's list. For testing purposes, the student data file contains the name, sex, class, and grade-point average (gpa) for each student. Query programs of this type are best implemented as menu-driven programs.

Output

Three separate reports based on the user's menu choice.

Choice 1: Name, class, sex, and gpa for specific student
Choice 2: Name, sex, and gpa for all students in a specific class
Choice 3: Name and class for all students on the Dean's list (those with gpa's above 3.2)
Choice 4: Farewell message

Input

Menu choice 1, 2, 3, or 4
If choice is 1 then input student's name
If choice is 2 then input class code (fr for freshman, so for sophomore, jr for junior, sr for senior)

Read (Internal data file)

For each student:

Name
Class (fr, so, jr, sr)
Sex (f, m)
gpa

Design

The primary programming tasks are divided into five modules, with pseudocode as given in Figure 6.7. Study this figure together with the following descriptions:

1. *Control module.* This module primarily sets up a processing loop that calls the other modules when the user wishes output reports. The appropriate module is called based on the user's menu choice. This task is carried out by a multiple alternative decision structure (see Figure 6.7).

2. *Menu module.* This module prints the menu and awaits the user's input choice. We don't trap incorrect choices in this version (see Figure 6.7 and Exercise 5a).

3. *Student module.* This module prints the output report for choice 1. Note that a loop processes the data file. The desired student is found using an if-then decision within the loop (see Figure 6.7). This version does not trap incorrect student names (see Exercise 5b).

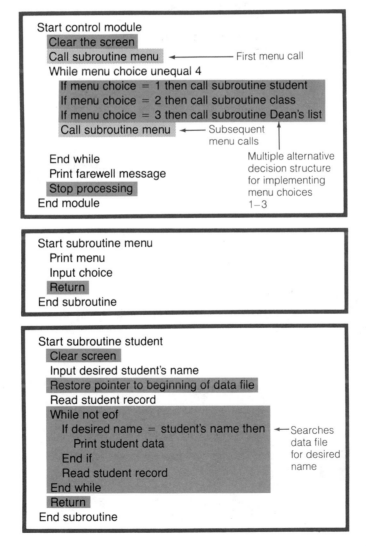

Figure 6.7 Pseudocode for student reporting system program (cont. next page)

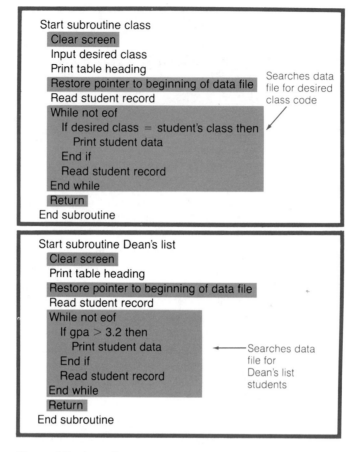

Start subroutine class
Clear screen
Input desired class
Print table heading
Restore pointer to beginning of data file   Searches data
Read student record   file for desired
While not eof   class code
   If desired class = student's class then
      Print student data
   End if
   Read student record
End while
Return
End subroutine

Start subroutine Dean's list
Clear screen
Print table heading
Restore pointer to beginning of data file
Read student record
While not eof
   If gpa > 3.2 then
      Print student data   Searches data
   End if   file for
   Read student record   Dean's list
End while   students
Return
End subroutine

Figure 6.7   (cont.)

4. *Class module.* This module prints the output report for choice 2. As in the student module, a loop processes the data file and an if-then decision finds students within the desired class (see Figure 6.7). This version does not trap incorrect class codes (see Exercise 5c).

5. *Dean's list module.* This module prints the output report for choice 3. As in the student module, a loop processes the data file and an if-then decision prints the name and class for all students who have a gpa above 3.2 (see Figure 6.7).

Code and Test

Figure 6.8 shows code in Microsoft BASIC for the IBM PC, and Figure 6.9 shows a sample run. Try studying the run in Figure 6.9 first, and then relate it to the program in Figure 6.8 and the corresponding pseudocode in Figure 6.7. In particular, note the following:

1. The control module is used to direct the execution of all the other modules in the program. Selection of the desired module is based on the user's response to the menu options. A sequence of if-then decisions determines which module is executed. Each IF statement checks for a specific menu response. In our test run, the user's choice is option 2 (see Screen 1). The if test in line 235 of the program thus tests true, and the class module is called (line 500 is executed next). At line 515 the program requests the desired class. The user enters sr and the module then prints the desired report (see Screen 2). Control now returns to the control module, and the menu is printed through the call in line 245 (see Screen 2). Other options work similarly (see Screens 3 and 4).

2. The statement **CLS** at the beginning of modules 1, 3, 4, and 5 is a Microsoft BASIC statement for clearing the screen. *How do you clear the screen on your system?* (See Exercise 4.)

3. The Dean's list module is included in the program as a **program stub** or **dummy module**. This allows for complete testing of the control module even though all the lower-level modules are not yet coded. Currently, when option 3 is chosen, control is

```
100 REM * * * * * * * * * * * * * * * * * * * * * * * * * * * * * * * * *
105 REM *                                                               *
110 REM *                   STUDENT REPORTING SYSTEM                    *
115 REM *                                                               *
120 REM *  This is a menu-driven program that displays:                *
125 REM *     . Data on any specific student                           *
130 REM *     . All students in a class                                *
135 REM *     . All students on the Dean's list                       *
140 REM *                                                               *
145 REM *  Description of modules:                                     *
150 REM *                                                               *
155 REM *     1.  Control ........... Calls menu and each report module *
160 REM *                                                               *
165 REM *     2.  Menu .............. Displays menu; enters user's choice *
170 REM *                                                               *
175 REM *     3.  Student ........... Displays data on a student        *
180 REM *                                                               *
185 REM *     4.  Class ............. Displays all students in a class  *
190 REM *                                                               *
195 REM *     5.  Dean's List ....... Displays students on Dean's list  *
200 REM *                                                               *
205 REM * * * * * * * * * * * * * * * * * * * * * * * * * * * * * * * * *
206 '
207 '================================================================
210 '          Module 1:  Control Module          Clears screen on IBM PC; see Exercise 4
212 '
215    CLS                              ' Clear screen
218 '
220    GOSUB 300                        ' Call Subroutine Menu   ←First menu
225    WHILE CHOICE <> 4                                              call
228 '
230      IF CHOICE = 1 THEN GOSUB 400   ' Call Subroutine Student
235      IF CHOICE = 2 THEN GOSUB 500   ' Call Subroutine Class
240      IF CHOICE = 3 THEN GOSUB 600   ' Call Subroutine Dean's List
242 '
245      GOSUB 300   ←——— Subsequent menu calls
250    WEND
252 '
255    PRINT
260    PRINT "Program Completed"
265    STOP   ←——Stops processing
270 '
290 '================================================================
300 '          Module 2:  Subroutine Menu
305 '
310    PRINT TAB(30);"     REPORT MENU       "
315    PRINT
320    PRINT TAB(30);"1   Specific Student   "
325    PRINT TAB(30);"2   Specific Class     "
330    PRINT TAB(30);"3   Dean's List        "
335    PRINT TAB(30);"4   Stop Processing    "
340    PRINT
345 '
350    PRINT TAB(30);"Choice is ";
355    INPUT CHOICE
360    PRINT
362 '
365    RETURN
370 '
390 '================================================================
400 '          Module 3:  Subroutine Student
405 '
410    CLS
412 '
415    INPUT "Enter name of student"; DESIRED.NAME$
420    PRINT
422 '
425    RESTORE   ←——————— Ensures that search starts at beginning of data file
430    READ FULL.NAME$,SEX$,CLASS$,GPA
435    WHILE FULL.NAME$ <> "eof"
438 '
440      IF DESIRED.NAME$ = FULL.NAME$ THEN PRINT "  Name  : "; FULL.NAME$  :
            PRINT "  Class : "; CLASS$  :  PRINT "  Sex   : "; SEX$  :
            PRINT "  GPA   :"; GPA      :  PRINT
442 '
445      READ FULL.NAME$,SEX$,CLASS$,GPA
450    WEND
452 '
455    PRINT
458 '
460    RETURN
485 '
490 '================================================================
```

Multiple alternative decision structure for implementing menu choices 1–3

Searches data file for desired name

Figure 6.8 Student reporting system program (cont. next page)

```
500 '                    Module 4:   Subroutine Class
505 '
510       CLS
512 '
515       INPUT "Enter class (fr,so,jr,sr) "; DESIRED.CLASS$
520       PRINT
525       PRINT "Class: ";DESIRED.CLASS$
530       PRINT
535       PRINT "Name","Sex"," GPA"
540       PRINT "------------------------------"
542 '
545       RESTORE
550       READ FULL.NAME$,SEX$,CLASS$,GPA
555       WHILE FULL.NAME$ <> "eof"
557 '
560          IF CLASS$ = DESIRED.CLASS$ THEN  ◄─────── Searches data file
                PRINT FULL.NAME$,SEX$,GPA              for desired class code
562 '
565          READ FULL.NAME$,SEX$,CLASS$,GPA
570       WEND
572 '
575       PRINT "------------------------------"
580       PRINT
582 '
585       RETURN
588 '
590 '=====================================================================
600 '                    Module 5:   Subroutine Dean's List
605 '
610       CLS
612 '
615       PRINT
620       PRINT "Program stub -- Dean's List module not completed"  ◄──── See
625       PRINT "See Follow-up Exercise"                                  Exercise 6
630       PRINT
635 '
640       RETURN
645 '
890 '=====================================================================
895 '                    Data Section
900 '
901       DATA D. Moore,m,fr,2.7
902       DATA G. Storm,f,sr,3.9
903       DATA M. Bono,f,sr,2.3
904       DATA S. Gilliam,m,so,3.5  ◄──── Data file
905       DATA eof, , ,0
997 '
998 '=====================================================================
999       END
```

Figure 6.8   (cont.)

transferred to the Dean's list module and a message that the module is not completed is displayed (see Screen 4). When the module for the Dean's list report is completed, it can be substituted for the program stub. The use of program stubs is common for large programs and is consistent with the spirit of stepwise refinement. (See Exercise 6.)

NOTE   The program in Example 6.2 shows two obvious advantages of modular programming:

1. The modular structure simplifies the design, coding, and understanding of the program by breaking it up into manageable segments, building blocks, or modules. This reduces the cost of developing and later modifying programs, especially those that are large and elaborate with respect to tasks.

2. Programs are shorter when the same task needs to be repeated at different points. For example, without subroutine Menu in Example 6.2, the menu logic would have to be repeated twice (at line 220 and again at line 245).

6.4 HIERARCHY CHARTS

As the number of modules and their interrelationships increases, a need for additional design and documentation tools becomes evident. One such tool is the **hierarchy chart**, **structure chart**, or **top-down chart** illustrated in Figure 6.10. This chart expresses the relationships among modules in a manner sim-

Screen 1

```
                              REPORT MENU

                        1    Specific Student
                        2    Specific Class
                        3    Dean's List
                        4    Stop Processing

Choice is ? 2
```

Screen 2

```
Enter class (fr,so,jr,sr) ? sr

Class: sr

Name            Sex           GPA
---------------------------------------
G. Storm        f             3.9
M. Bono         f             2.3
---------------------------------------

                              REPORT MENU

                        1    Specific Student
                        2    Specific Class
                        3    Dean's List
                        4    Stop Processing

Choice is ? 1
```

Screen 3

```
Enter name of student? S. Gilliam

   Name  : S. Gilliam
   Class : so
   Sex   : m
   GPA   : 3.5

                              REPORT MENU

                        1    Specific Student
                        2    Specific Class
                        3    Dean's List
                        4    Stop Processing

Choice is ? 3
```

Screen 4

```
Program stub -- Dean's List module not completed
See Follow-up Exercise

                              REPORT MENU

                        1    Specific Student
                        2    Specific Class
                        3    Dean's List
                        4    Stop Processing

Choice is ? 4


Program Completed
Break in 265
```

Figure 6.9   Test run for student reporting system program

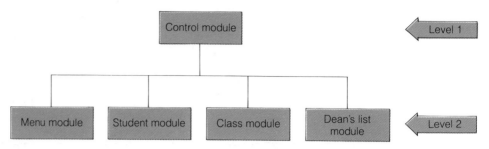

Figure 6.10   Hierarchy chart for student reporting system (Example 6.2)

ilar to that of organization charts of companies. Note that each module is represented by a box and that these boxes appear at different levels, or hierarchies. If a subroutine call is made by a particular module, then the called module is shown at the next level below the calling module. In Figure 6.10, the control module calls the menu module in addition to each report module; hence, these appear below the control module within Level 2 in the hierarchy chart.

Note that the hierarchy chart clearly shows not only the modular breakdown of the program, but also the structure or relationships among modules with respect to which modules are called and which modules do the calling.

Elaborate programs generally have three or more hierarchy levels, with many modules at each level.

6.5 POINTERS

Design and Style

1. **On using modular programming.**   The bottom line in using modular programming is lower software development and maintenance costs. Remember the following points:
    a. The assignment of sets of related tasks to modules makes large programs more manageable (the "divide-and-conquer" strategy).
    b. Tasks that need to be repeated at different points in a program are best implemented as modules, as this reduces the amount of coding.
    c. A program may use a task that has already been programmed. Assigning this task to a *utility module* makes it unnecessary to reinvent the wheel.
    d. The development of large programs requires a team of programmers. The use of modules facilitates the management of the project: one can assign specific modules to specific programmers.
    e. Modular programming is a form of *stepwise refinement* in which we need not refine a particular task at the point of call. When the module is developed, that particular task stands refined.
    f. Modular programming facilitates the debugging process, since bugs are more easily isolated in modules for diagnosis and correction.
    g. The subsequent maintenance of modular programs is easier, since tasks are more clearly defined and isolated.
2. **Program documentation.**   Modules should be visually segmented to improve their visual identification in listings. For example, we can use dashes or equal signs to separate modules. Use a REM statement to identify the name of a module, especially if the first BASIC statement within the module does not include its name (as in a subroutine). Describe the purpose of each module, either at the beginning of the module itself or within the control module.

3. Try being friendly.   It's useful to take the perspective that your program will be run by others. Commercial interactive programs pay close attention to having a "friendly" user-interface, which makes it easy for a user to learn to operate and otherwise interact with a program. (This wasn't always the case, but the widespread use of microcomputers has changed this.) For example, many commercial programs are menu-driven (as in Example 6.2), since this facilitates the selection of options and implementation of commands. Thus it pays to design the menus carefully with respect to layout, use of color, and choice of responses. It's best to avoid screen clutter by displaying a menu in isolation from preceding material or succeeding output. This is best accomplished by clearing the screen just before the menu is displayed and clearing the screen again once the menu item is selected. (See Exercise 4b.) For example, Microsoft BASIC uses the statement

CLS Statement

to clear a screen. Does your dialect have such a statement? Programs with extensive menu choices are often designed with hierarchical menus, whereby the selection of one menu item generates a submenu of other choices. Also, all incorrect user input should be trapped if possible. For example, incorrect menu choices and out-of-range data input should be detected, giving the user a chance to correct the entry. (See Exercise 5.) Many microcomputer programs effectively use sound and color to alert the user to incorrect responses. Finally, many commercial programs provide interactive *help* facilities to aid users when they are unsure of what response to make. For example, at the touch of a key a user can get a full explanation of a particular option, feature, procedure, or form of data input.

Common Errors

Two of the most common errors when using subroutines are forgetting to end the control module with a STOP statement and the subroutine with a RETURN statement. In either case, program execution inadvertently "drops" into a subroutine, thereby causing either a logic or an execution error.

FOLLOW-UP EXERCISES

1. Roleplay the execution of the FOR/NEXT loop in lines 280–310 in Figure 6.4 by indicating the line executed and the action taken. We'll get you started.

Line Executed	Action
280	Set FOR/NEXT parameters
290	Read in A for LABEL$ and 8 for LENGTH
300	Call subroutine
420	Print label A
430	Set FOR/NEXT parameters
440	
450	
440	Print 8 = signs
450	
.	
.	
.	
460	Print length 8
470	Return
310	Next bar

Fill in just for the 2nd bar

2. Is the coding of the program in Figure 6.4 general enough to handle any frequency distribution (except for changes in the data section)?
   a. Change the program in Figure 6.4 to process the following frequency distribution.

   Age Distribution of Employees

Age	Number
Under 20	5
20–29	30
30–39	50
40–49	70
50–59	40
Over 59	10

   b. Run the changed program on your system.

3. What happens in the output when the STOP statement in line 330 is executed? Can you think of alternatives to STOP that might avoid this? What's your preference?

4. In Example 6.2:
   a. What would happen in our sample run if the RESTORE statement were missing in lines 425 and 545?
   b. How would you modify the program so that each menu is printed on a fresh screen? Any problems with this? If so, can you suggest a fix-up?
   c. Implement the program on your system. If you don't have a statement for clearing the screen, then try the following generalized subroutine:

   ```
   REM Subroutine for clearing a 24-line screen
   REM
   FOR J = 1 TO 24
       PRINT
   NEXT J
   RETURN
   ```

*5. **Error Routines.** Modify Example 6.2 to include the following error routines.
   a. While a user enters a response other than 1–4, display the message "Illegal menu choice—valid entries are 1–4", and display the menu choices again.
   b. In subroutine student, if the desired student is not found in the student file, display the message "Student is not in the file" and return to the control module.
   c. In subroutine class, while a user enters a class choice other than fr, so, jr, or sr, display the message "Illegal class code. Valid entries are fr so jr sr" and reinput the desired class.
   d. Implement the revised program on your system.

*6. **Program Stub.** Modify Example 6.2 as follows.
   a. Complete the Dean's list program stub.
   b. Implement the revised program on your system.

*7. Modify Example 6.2 as follows.
   a. Write a subroutine that prints the following heading at the top of each report:

   MICRO U
   Silicon Valley, 80288
   Current date

   This subroutine is called by modules 3–5.
   b. Implement the revised program on your system.

*8. Modify Example 6.2 as follows.
   a. Include a fourth report which lists all students in the student file.
   b. Implement the revised program on your system.

*9. Draw a hierarchy chart for
   a. Example 6.1
   b. Exercise 7

ADDITIONAL EXERCISES

10. **Revisits.** Rework one of the following earlier problems according to the prescribed modular design.
    a. **Inflation Curse.** (Example 5.1, page 76.) Use two separate modules for input/error check and print heading.
    b. Modularize one of your previous assignments from Chapters 4 or 5.

11. **Population.** A staff member of the Rhode Island statewide planning division has collected population data on the five counties in the state (see Figure 1).

    Write a menu-driven, modular program that allows the planner to choose from the following options:

    1 Print population change report (see Figure 2)
    2 Print bar graph (see Figure 3)
    3 Stop processing

12. **Exam Reports.** A class of students has the following grades on four examinations taken in a **BASIC** programming course.

Name	Exam Scores			
Affrick	45	80	80	95
Bubble	60	50	70	75
Crandell	65	40	44	55
Fleck	90	85	95	100
Linus	75	60	85	70

    a. Develop a modular program that can be used by an instructor for record-keeping. The data collected for each student include name and scores on each of four exams. The program should allow the instructor to choose from the following report options:

    1 Print student names
    2 Print names and exam scores
    3 Print names and averages
    4 Print average for the class

    b. Assign letter grades to each student and include in option 3. Use the following logic to assign grades:

Grade	Range
A	Above 90
B	80–89
C	70–79
D	60–69
F	Below 60

    c. Build in a bar-chart option that plots the frequency of each letter grade.

13. **Craps Simulation.** A front line bet in a game of craps works as follows:

    First roll of dice
    1. You win what you bet if on the first toss you roll 7 or 11 (a natural).
    2. You lose what you bet if on the first toss you roll a 2, 3, or 12 (a crap).
    3. If you roll a 4, 5, 6, 8, 9, or 10 on the first toss, then this number becomes your *point* for subsequent rolls.

    Subsequent rolls of dice
    4. To win, you must roll your point again *before* you roll a 7.
    5. If you roll a 7 while trying to get your point, then you lose.
    6. If neither your point nor 7 is rolled, then roll again.
        a. Write a modular program that simulates the roll of dice. Note that you need two random numbers for each roll—one for the first die and one for the second die. *Hint:* Uniform digits between 1 and 6 can be simulated using

        INT(RND·6 + 1)

        See Module C for the functions INT and RND.

Figure 1 Population for Five RI Counties

	1970	1980
Bristol	45,900	43,200
Kent	142,400	152,000
Newport	94,200	82,700
Providence	581,500	561,300
Washington	85,700	87,600

Figure 2 Population Change

	1970	1980	% Change
Bristol	45,900	43,200	− 5.9
Kent	142,400	152,000	6.7
Newport	94,200	82,700	− 12.2
Providence	581,500	561,300	− 3.4
Washington	85,700	87,600	2.2

Figure 3 Population 1970

```
Bristol      *****  45,900
Kent         **************  142,400
Newport      *********  94,200
Providence   ***************************************************************  581,500
Washington   *********  85,700
```

b. Design a loop that simulates a single game of craps as described in items 1 through 6 above. The outcome of this loop is either "won" or "lost."

c. Add a second loop that simulates N games. Assume $1 is bet on each game. Keep track of wins and losses. Debug your program by simulating five games. In your output for each roll, print the point on the first die, the point on the second die, and the overall point (sum of the two dice). At the end of a game print "won" or "lost." At the end of the five games print the following summaries: number of games won, number of games lost, your total dollar winnings (or losses), and the percent (of the total amount bet) dollar winnings (or losses).

d. Provide an option in the program to suppress the output for each roll and the "won" or "lost" output at the end of each game. For each of the following runs just print the summary statistics:

(1) N = 100
(2) N = 500
(3) N = 1000
(4) N = 5000

Based on your output, estimate the expected (percent) loss by betting the front line in craps.

14. **Depreciation.** The concept of depreciation plays a prominent role in the financial accounting of organizations that report profits and pay taxes. The simplest method of depreciation is called the straight-line method. This method uses the following formula to determine depreciation for an asset (automobile, building, machine, etc.) in any given year:

$$\text{Depreciation} = \frac{(\text{Cost} - \text{Salvage value})}{\text{Life}}$$

A second method is the double-declining balance method (a method used to increase the amount of depreciation in early years). This method uses the formulas:

$$\begin{pmatrix} \text{Book value} \\ \text{of asset} \end{pmatrix} = \begin{pmatrix} \text{Cost of} \\ \text{asset} \end{pmatrix} - \begin{pmatrix} \text{Accumulated} \\ \text{depreciation} \\ \text{from all prior years} \end{pmatrix}$$

$$\text{Depreciation} = \begin{pmatrix} \text{Book value} \\ \text{of asset} \end{pmatrix} \cdot (2) \cdot \begin{pmatrix} \frac{1}{\text{Life of asset}} \end{pmatrix}$$

a. Develop a menu-driven, modular program that has the following options:

1 Data entry
2 Straight-line depreciation schedule
3 Double-declining balance depreciation schedule
4 Stop processing

Enter the data for each asset using the following screen design.

```
Asset type = = = = = = = =>
Cost       = = = = = = = =>
Salvage    = = = = = = = =>
Life       = = = = = = = =>
```

Sample output for menu-choice 2 might look as follows:

DEPRECIATION SCHEDULE
Method: Straight Line

Asset .... Chariot
Cost $4200
Salvage .... $ 200
Life .... 4 years

Year	Depreciation Expense	Accumulated Depreciation	Book Value
1	1000	1000	3200
2	1000	2000	2200
3	1000	3000	1200
4	1000	4000	200

Process the following assets in your test runs:

Asset	Cost	Salvage	Life
Chariot	4,200	200	4
Building	200,000	0	15
Machine	75,000	5,000	5

b. Include a third depreciation method called sum of the years digits. Check any introductory accounting text for a description of this method.

15. **Electric Bill.** Gotham City Electric Company wishes to redesign the computerized bills that it sends to commercial and residential customers. It has announced a city-wide contest to determine the best design and BASIC program for this purpose.

a. Read data include the following.

Date data

1. Month (three letters) and day (two digits) for beginning date of monthly billing cycle
2. Month and day for ending date of monthly billing cycle
3. Year (two digits)

Customer data

4. Previous meter reading in kilowatt-hours (up to seven digits)
5. New meter reading in kilowatt-hours
6. Customer rate code (one digit)
7. Past due amount (dollars and cents)
8. Payment since last bill (dollars and cents)
9. Name of customer (up to 20 characters)
10. Street address of customer (up to 20 characters)
11. City, state, and ZIP (up to 24 characters)
12. Account number of customer (up to eight digits)

Use the following sample data for the computer run.

Billing Cycle

From	To	Year
SEP 19	OCT 18	1985

Use the sample data in Figure 4.

Figure 4

Previous Reading	New Reading	Rate Code	Past Due Amount	Payment	Name	Street Address	City, State, Zip	Account Number
27648	28648	1	60.10	60.10	Make these up	....		
42615	45115	2	45.20	0.00	Make these up	....		
314625	354625	3	3110.00	3110.00	Make these up	....		
615700	695700	3	8000.00	8000.00	Make these up	....		
800500	1025500	3	3000.00	1000.00	Make these up	....		

Rate codes and their corresponding rates per kilowatt-hour (kWh) are explained by the following table.

Rate Code	Rate per kWh (cents)	Comment
1	10.25	Residential, partly electric home
2	9.85	Residential, all electric home
3	8.50	Commercial, usage under 50,000 kWh
3	7.50	Commercial, usage between 50,000 kWh and 100,000 kWh
3	6.50	Commercial, usage above 100,000 kWh

If past due amount less payment is more than zero, then a 1% per month charge on this difference is added to the customer's bill. For example, the last customer in the input data is commercial and used 225,000 kWh (1,025,500 − 800,500). Thus the customer is charged at 6.5 cents per kWh, which amounts to a current bill of $14,625.00. This customer, however, has a $3000 past due account and payments of only $1000. At an interest rate of 1% per month, the interest charge is $20, that is, (3000 − 1000) × 0.01; hence, the total now due from this customer is $16,645.00, that is, 2000 + 20 + 14,625.

Output from your program should include the following.

1. Name of customer
2. Street address of customer
3. City, state, and ZIP
4. Account number
5. Billing cycle: from (month, day) to (month, day, year)
6. Kilowatt-hours
7. Current amount owed
8. Past due amount
9. Interest charge
10. Total amount due

Label your output and design it to fit within a 3- by 5-inch image, since these statements must fit in a standard size envelope.

b. Include error detection to ensure that the rate code is 1, 2, or 3 and that the new meter reading is greater than the previous meter reading. If an error is encountered, print an appropriate error message that includes the customer's name, complete address, and account number; bypass the calculations and printout for this customer; space down to the next statement; and go on to the next customer. Add new data to test each of the possible input errors.

Use a modular design for your program. By the way, the winner of the contest gets to ride the Batmobile, which recently was retrofitted with an all-electric power plant.

Arrays

7

Most of the programs that we have written or studied have had the following structure:

1. Read in or input data
2. Process the data
3. Print the results
4. Return to Step 1 if necessary

In some problems we may want to store large quantities of related data (such as a table of numbers) before the processing step (Step 2 above). This was not practical in our earlier programs, because read-in or input of new data automatically replaced the previously stored values. The alternative was either reentry of data for interactive programs or restoration of the data pointer for programs using DATA statements as internal data files. In this chapter we offer the array alternative, which allows the storage of and access to all related data.

7.1 MOTIVATION

An **array** is a group of consecutive memory locations that have the same name. The use of arrays

1. Permits access to any data item that has been stored.
2. Provides simple yet powerful capabilities to name and manipulate a large number of related storage locations.

To help you visualize this concept, the illustration below shows three storage locations for an array named DEPOSITS.

DEPOSITS

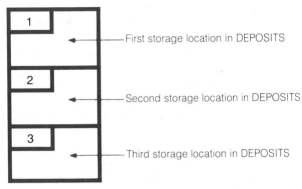

Just how we specify and manipulate arrays will become clear in the next two sections. First, however, we motivate their use by the following example.

E X A M P L E 7 . 1   Analysis of Bank Deposits

The vice-president of a bank wants to compare the percent of deposits that each branch contributes to the bank's total deposits. The number of deposits for each of the three test bank branches is given below.

Bank	Number of Deposits
1	3500
2	5000
3	4000

Let's first try to solve this problem using approaches from previous chapters. A program such as the following might be written.

```
100 REM-------------------------------------
110 REM        Bank Deposits, Version A
120 REM
130       LET TOTAL = 0
140 REM
150       READ N
160       FOR J = 1 TO N
170          READ DEPOSITS
180          LET TOTAL = TOTAL + DEPOSITS
190       NEXT J
200 REM
210       RESTORE
220 REM
230       PRINT "Bank","Deposits","Percent"
240       READ N
250       FOR J = 1 TO N
260          READ DEPOSITS
270          LET PERCENT = DEPOSITS*100/TOTAL
280          PRINT J,DEPOSITS,PERCENT
290       NEXT J
300 REM
900       DATA 3
901       DATA 3500,5000,4000
998 REM
999       END
```

```
RUN
Bank        Deposits     Percent
  1           3500        28
  2           5000        40
  3           4000        32
```

In the first loop (lines 160–190), each of the three data items is read in, and total deposits (TOTAL) are accumulated. Next, the RESTORE statement moves the data block pointer back to the beginning of the data block, which subsequently allows us to reread the data within the second loop (lines 250–290). This loop requires each data item once more in order to calculate and print the required percentages.

Note that each value stored in the variable DEPOSITS is replaced by the next value read in. Thus, never does the entire set of related data (the deposits 3500, 5000, and 4000) appear at one time in primary memory. That's why we needed to reread the data within the second loop. This approach works, but it's inefficient because the reading of data is a time-consuming machine task (by computer standards!); and this version reads the same set of data twice.

Now consider the following approach, which stores the entire set of data within primary memory.

```
100 REM----------------------------------------------
110 REM         Bank Deposits, Version B
120 REM
130         READ DEPOSITS1
140         READ DEPOSITS2
150         READ DEPOSITS3
160 REM
170         LET TOTAL = DEPOSITS1 + DEPOSITS2 + DEPOSITS3
180 REM
190         PRINT "Bank","Deposits","Percent"
200 REM
210         LET PERCENT = DEPOSITS1*100/TOTAL
220         PRINT 1,DEPOSITS1,PERCENT
230 REM
240         LET PERCENT = DEPOSITS2*100/TOTAL
250         PRINT 2,DEPOSITS2,PERCENT
260 REM
270         LET PERCENT = DEPOSITS3*100/TOTAL
280         PRINT 3,DEPOSITS3,PERCENT
290 REM
901         DATA 3500,5000,4000
998 REM
999         END
```

```
RUN
Bank          Deposits        Percent
  1            3500            28
  2            5000            40
  3            4000            32
```

This program works, but it's very rigid and inefficient. It works for three branches, but if we wish to add a fourth branch, the program will have to be rewritten extensively. Worse yet, visualize this program written for the hundreds of Chase Manhattan branch banks in New York City. What a long and tedious program it would be for such a simple problem! A simpler solution to this problem is to use an array.

```
100 REM----------------------------------------------
110 REM         Bank Deposits, Version C
120 REM
130         DIM DEPOSITS(3)
140 REM
150         LET TOTAL = 0
160 REM
170         READ N
180 REM
190         FOR J = 1 TO N
200            READ DEPOSITS(J)
210            LET TOTAL = TOTAL + DEPOSITS(J)
220         NEXT J
230 REM
240         PRINT "Bank","Deposits","Percent"
250 REM
260         FOR J = 1 TO N
270            LET PERCENT = DEPOSITS(J)*100/TOTAL
280            PRINT J,DEPOSITS(J),PERCENT
290         NEXT J
300 REM
900         DATA 3
901         DATA 3500,5000,4000
998 REM
999         END
```

```
RUN
Bank            Deposits        Percent
  1               3500            28
  2               5000            40
  3               4000            32
```

In this program the first loop reads the number of deposits for each branch bank, storing them in an array called DEPOSITS, and accumulates the total deposits for all branches in TOTAL. The second loop references, or recalls, each element in the array DEPOSITS in the expression that calculates percentages and prints the number of deposits and the relative percent of total deposits for each branch bank. At this point, don't worry about the exact nature of the array or about the DIM statement. We discuss this topic next.

You should realize, however, that after the first loop the entire set of deposit data resides within primary memory in array DEPOSITS. This is precisely why we did not need to reread the data within the second loop, as we did in Version A. Moreover, the addition of a fourth branch bank simply requires changing the 3 to a 4 in line 130 (besides the usual data line changes). If we were to use, say, 100 in line 130, then this version of the program would handle *any number* of branch banks up to 100.

7.2 ARRAY NAMES AND SUBSCRIPTS

An array is used to store a collection of related data items, as illustrated by array DEPOSITS in Example 7.1. An **array element** is the memory location within which a data item is stored.

Each array element is accessed or referenced by an **array-element name** that has two distinct parts: an array name and a subscript enclosed within parentheses.

Array-Element Name

> **Array name (subscript)**
>
> DEPOSITS (J)

The **array name** is simply the variable name that identifies the array: DEPOSITS in our example. The same rules that apply to naming simple variable names also apply to naming array variable names. The **subscript** is a *numeric expression*, within parentheses, that follows the array name. It acts as an index or pointer for locating the array element. In our example the subscript is J. If J stores the value 1, then the first array element in DEPOSITS is referenced, as illustrated below.

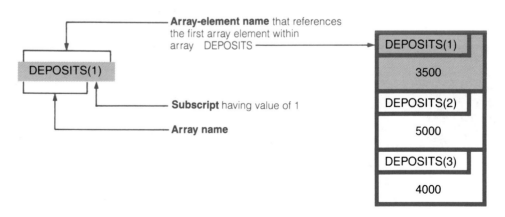

You should keep in mind the following points when working with subscripts.

1. An array-element name with a single subscript references a **one-dimensional array**. Later we will consider two-dimensional arrays.

2. Subscripts must have *non-negative values*. Usually they are either *positive integer constants* or variables that store positive (nonzero) integer values. For example,

COST(K)
— Variable as subscript

uses the *variable* K as a subscript.

When we use a variable as a subscript we can reference any element in the array on the basis of the value we assign that variable. For example, the program segment

DIM SALE(20)
.
.
.
LET K = 3
LET SALE(K) = 500

results in the storage of 500 in the third location of the array SALE.

3. Generally the subscript can be any numeric expression. The computer determines which array element is referenced by evaluating the subscript and using this result to identify the specific array element. For example, if K stores 4, then LOAD(K + 3) and LOAD(2*K + 1) are legitimate array-element names that reference the seventh and ninth elements of the array LOAD.

4. We can use the same variable name as a subscript to reference corresponding elements in different arrays. For example, the program segment

LET K = 2

LET PROFITS(K) = SALES(K) – COSTS(K)

subtracts the second array element in COSTS from the second array element in SALES and stores the result in the second array element of PROFITS.

5. Subscripts are not part of the array name; thus LAB(J) and LAB(I) both reference the array LAB. In addition, if I and J are equal, then LAB(J) and LAB(I) reference the same element in LAB.

7.3 ARRAY DECLARATION

Arrays should be *declared* for the computer to reserve a specific number of multiple memory locations. The DIM statement is used for this purpose.

DIM Statement

> DIM $\begin{array}{c}array\\name\end{array}$ (array size), $\begin{array}{c}array\\name\end{array}$ (array size), . . .
>
> DIM DEPOSITS(3)

This statement declares to the compiler or interpreter which variable names are array names and defines their size (total number of array elements). In the example, the DIM statement reserves three memory locations (array elements) for the array named DEPOSITS, which we illustrated on page 112.[1]

If we had used

DIM DEPOSITS(5)

then five memory locations would have been reserved for DEPOSITS. However, the program in Example 7.1, version C, on page 112 still would use only the first three of these locations.

More than one array can be dimensioned in a single DIM statement by using commas to separate each array specification. For example,

DIM COST(80),REV(50),PROFIT(50)

reserves 80 locations for an array named COST, 50 locations for array REV, and 50 locations for array PROFIT.

Here are some additional points to keep in mind when working with DIM statements.

1. The DIM statement is a *nonexecutable* statement that normally is placed at the beginning of a program, but it may appear anywhere in the program before the array is used.[2]

2. For compiled BASICs, the constant that specifies the size of the array *must* be an integer constant. For example,

    DIM DEPOSITS(N)
    └──── Numeric variable not allowed
          by many translators

    would yield a syntax error on the VAX-11, since a variable is *not* permitted within parentheses in the DIM statement.

    On many BASIC interpreters, however, we can reserve a variable number of array elements by placing a simple numeric variable in the DIM statement as an *array-size parameter*. For example,

    DIM DEPOSITS(N)
    └──── Numeric variable instead of numeric constant
          allowed by some translators

    is permitted in Microsoft BASIC. The actual size of the array is entered into the array-size parameter (N in our example) during the execution of the program. Arrays whose sizes change from run to run through array-

---

[1]Most versions of BASIC use a *lower bound* of zero instead of one for the value of the subscript. Thus, the statement DIM DEPOSITS(3) would actually reserve four locations: DEPOSITS(0), DEPOSITS(1), DEPOSITS(2), and DEPOSITS(3). In this case, it is best to conceptualize the integer value in the DIM statement as the *upper bound* on the value of the subscript. For our purposes, *we shall assume a lower bound of one throughout the chapter* (as does ANS BASIC).

[2]Some versions of BASIC may treat the DIM statement as an executable statement.

size parameters are called **dynamic arrays**. *Are dynamic arrays permitted on your system?*

3. Most versions of BASIC automatically initialize all numeric array elements to zero, and all string array elements to blanks.

4. We can reserve more locations for an array than are actually used in a particular program; however, if we reserve only 15 locations for an array and need 17, an error message will occur during execution of the program when the value of the subscript exceeds 15. For this reason it's a good defensive programming practice to ensure that the subscript value does not exceed the upper dimension bound.

5. What size array should we declare? In general, the size of a declared array is a trade-off between wasted storage costs and the software cost of updating the array declaration, taking into consideration actual and projected data needs. For example, if we have 75 branch banks and over the next 10 years expect at most 25 more branch banks, then it is reasonable to declare DEPOSITS as a 100-element array, since it is certain that the cost of updating the declaration in the program each time a branch bank is added far exceeds the cost of keeping 25 empty storage locations.

7.4 READ, INPUT, AND OUTPUT

In the discussions that follow, assume that we wish to read, input, or print every element in the array, beginning with the first element and moving sequentially through the array to the last element.

Read/Input

The FOR/NEXT loop is a convenient means to read in or input array values. In this case, the control variable in the FOR statement can be used as a subscript that takes on values that coincide with each element in the array. The program segment

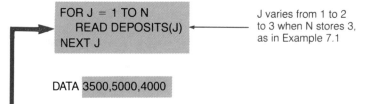

```
FOR J = 1 TO N           J varies from 1 to 2
    READ DEPOSITS(J)      to 3 when N stores 3,
NEXT J                    as in Example 7.1
```

```
DATA 3500,5000,4000
```

reads the data within the DATA statement and stores these within array DEPOSITS.

Note that a new data item is processed each time the READ statement in the FOR/NEXT loop is executed. In essence, this FOR/NEXT loop is equivalent to the following.

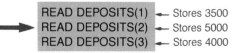

```
READ DEPOSITS(1)  ← Stores 3500
READ DEPOSITS(2)  ← Stores 5000
READ DEPOSITS(3)  ← Stores 4000
```

In other words, identical results would be obtained if the FOR/NEXT loop were replaced with the above three statements. If we were reading in deposits for 200 banks, the power of the FOR/NEXT loop approach would be apparent.

Output

This looping technique using the FOR/NEXT statements also can be used for output. For example, the statements

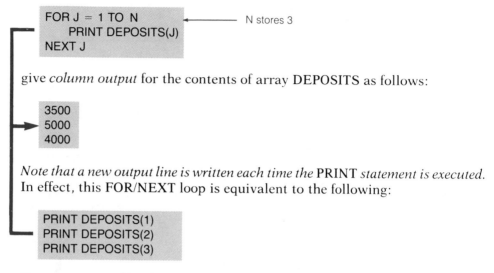

give *column output* for the contents of array DEPOSITS as follows:

```
3500
5000
4000
```

Note that a new output line is written each time the PRINT *statement is executed.* In effect, this FOR/NEXT loop is equivalent to the following:

```
PRINT DEPOSITS(1)
PRINT DEPOSITS(2)
PRINT DEPOSITS(3)
```

If *row output* rather than column output is desired, then a trailing comma or semicolon should be used in the PRINT statement, as follows:

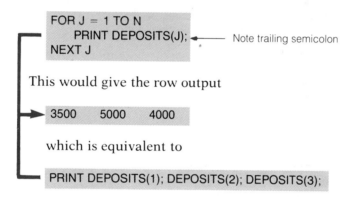

This would give the row output

```
3500     5000     4000
```

which is equivalent to

```
PRINT DEPOSITS(1); DEPOSITS(2); DEPOSITS(3);
```

NOTE For greater generality, use a variable to store the upper limit in the FOR statement. In our examples, we used N instead of 3. That way, we need not change the FOR statement should the upper limit change from 3 to, say, 50. We simply enter the proper value for N through a READ or INPUT statement.

7.5 APPLICATIONS

This section presents three examples that illustrate techniques of manipulating one-dimensional arrays.

E X A M P L E   7 . 2   **The Sum of Array Elements**

Quite often it's necessary to perform arithmetic operations on all elements in an array. The following revision of the program in Example 7.1 better highlights the common tasks of finding, using, and printing a sum.

```
100 REM------------------------------------------
110 REM            Bank Deposits, Version D
120 REM
130       DIM DEPOSITS(3)
140 REM
150       LET TOTAL = 0  ◄───── Initialize total deposits to zero
160 REM
170       READ N
180 REM
190       FOR J = 1 TO N
200          READ DEPOSITS(J)
210          LET TOTAL = TOTAL + DEPOSITS(J)  ◄───── Sum total deposits
220       NEXT J
230 REM
240       PRINT "Bank","Deposits","Percent"
250       PRINT "--------------------------------"
260 REM
270       FOR J = 1 TO N
280          LET PERCENT = DEPOSITS(J)*100/TOTAL  ◄───── Use total deposits
290          PRINT J,DEPOSITS(J),PERCENT                    to find percent
300       NEXT J
310 REM
320       PRINT "--------------------------------"
330       PRINT " Total";TAB(14); TOTAL  ◄───── Print total deposits
340 REM                                                (see run below)
900       DATA 3
901       DATA 3500,5000,4000
998 REM
999       END
```

```
RUN
Bank            Deposits        Percent
----------------------------------------
1               3500            28
2               5000            40
3               4000            32
----------------------------------------
Total           12500
```

As the value in J changes from 1 to 3, each element of array DEPOSITS is added to the summer variable TOTAL in line 210. We can describe the changes in memory as follows.

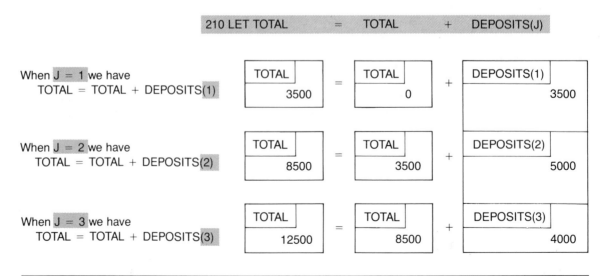

E X A M P L E   7 . 3   **Direct Access Query Program**

Sometimes we don't need to manipulate all the elements in an array. For example, a store manager can inquire about sales, costs, and profits for a specific department by using the following program.

```
100 REM-------------------------------------------------
110 REM              Departmental Query Program
120 REM
130       DIM SALES(100),COSTS(100)
140 REM
150       READ N
160 REM
170       FOR K = 1 TO N
180         READ SALES(K),COSTS(K)
190       NEXT K
200 REM
210       INPUT "Department Number"; DEPT ◄──────────────  Directly accesses or points
220 REM                                                     to desired array element.
230       IF DEPT < 1 OR DEPT > N THEN
            PRINT "Error in department number!" :
            STOP
240 REM
250       LET PROFIT = SALES(DEPT) - COSTS(DEPT)
260 REM
270       PRINT TAB(10);"Sales ......... $"; SALES(DEPT)
280       PRINT TAB(10);"Costs ......... $"; COSTS(DEPT)
290       PRINT TAB(10);"Profits ....... $"; PROFIT
300 REM
900       DATA 4
901       DATA 100,75
902       DATA 90,60
903       DATA 175,140
904       DATA 230,300
998 REM
999       END


RUN
Department Number? 3
          Sales ......... $ 175
          Costs ......... $ 140
          Profits ....... $ 35
```

The program illustrates the popular procedure of directly accessing array elements of corresponding arrays without processing any other elements in the arrays.

The sample run queries financial data for department 3 (line 210). In line 250 the third element in the array COSTS is subtracted from the third element in the array SALES, without any other array element in SALES or COSTS being processed. This effectively means that line 250 is evaluated as follows:

$$
\begin{aligned}
250 \quad \text{LET PROFIT} &= \text{SALES(DEPT)} - \text{COSTS(DEPT)} \\
&= \text{SALES(3)} \quad - \text{COSTS(3)} \\
&= 175 \quad\quad\; - 140 \\
&= 35
\end{aligned}
$$

Also note the error test in line 230, which ensures that the departmental entry does not exceed the number of departments (see Exercise 7).

E X A M P L E   7 . 4   **Table Lookup**

Table 7.1 Premium Schedule

Upper Age Limit	Annual Premium ($)
25	277
35	287
45	307
55	327
65	357

The term **table lookup** refers to procedures for accessing data that are stored in a table. These procedures satisfy a very common need across a wide variety of professional fields and occupational areas. In this example we work with one-dimensional tables; later we consider two-dimensional tables.

Analysis

Suppose that a life insurance company uses the premium schedule shown in Table 7.1 to quote insurance costs over the phone. The annual premium is based on the age of the policyholder. For example, a policyholder who is 47 years old would pay a premium of $327 per year. The required output, input, and read data are specified as follows for an interactive premium quotation program:

Output

Cost quotation for annual insurance premium

Input

Name of policyholder
Age of policyholder

Read

Premium schedule (Table 7.1) as two arrays: one for the age limits and another for the corresponding premiums

Design

The following modular design describes the program:

```
Start control module
   Call subroutine Initialize
   While more quotations
      Call subroutine Input
      Call subroutine Table Look-up
      Call subroutine Output
      Input processing flag (Another quotation?)
   End loop
   Print farewell message
   Stop
End control module
```

```
Start subroutine Initialize
   Read premium schedule into two arrays
   Initialize processing flag
   Return
End subroutine
```
← Each array is a column in Table 7.1

```
Start subroutine Input
   Input name and age
   Return
End subroutine
```

```
Start subroutine Table Lookup
   Initialize table index (row) to one
   While age > agelimit
      Increase index by one
   End loop
   Return
End subroutine
```
← This logic finds the proper row (index value) in Table 7.1

```
Start subroutine Output
   If index exceeds last row in table then
      Print uninsurable message
   Else
      Print premium
   End if
   Return
End subroutine
```
← This is printed if entered age exceeds max age limit
← This is based on the index logic in module Table Lookup

This design is self-descriptive, except perhaps for the table lookup logic. To understand this logic, consider the person aged 47 with an annual premium of $327. Confirm this premium from Table 7.1 right now. OK, how did you do this? Most likely you visually scanned down the age limit column until the age 47 showed less than the age limit of 55. This means that the fourth row is the correct row or category, with a corresponding premium of $327.

Module Table Lookup essentially does the same thing, except that we continue scanning down the column while the age is greater than the age limit. Note that the scan begins at row 1 (the index is set to 1) and continues (the index is incremented) while the age is greater than the age limit. Also note that if we scan off the table (for example, someone aged 73), then the index exceeds the last row. In this case, the print logic in Module Output would print a message to the effect that this person is uninsurable.

Code

The following code was written in Microsoft BASIC for the IBM PC.

```
100 REM * * * * * * * * * * * * * * * * * * * * * * * * * * * * * * *
110 REM *                                                           *
120 REM *     TABLE LOOK-UP: LIFE INSURANCE PREMIUM QUOTATIONS       *
130 REM *                                                           *
140 REM *    KEY:                                                    *
150 REM *       ROWS      = Number of rows in premium schedule       *
160 REM *       AGELIMIT  = Array containing upper age limits        *
170 REM *       PREMIUM   = Array containing insurance premiums      *
180 REM *       AGAIN$    = Flag to indicate whether processing is   *
190 REM *                   to continue or not                       *
200 REM *       FULLNAME$ = Name of policyholder                     *
210 REM *       AGE       = Age of policyholder                      *
220 REM *       INDEX     = Pointer to location within array         *
230 REM *                                                           *
240 REM * * * * * * * * * * * * * * * * * * * * * * * * * * * * * * *
250 '
260 '-----------------------------------------------------------------
300 '  Control Module
305 '----------------
310     GOSUB 500                                      '  Initialize
315 '
320     WHILE AGAIN$ = "y"
325 '
330        GOSUB 600                                   '  Input
340        GOSUB 700                                   '  Table Look-up
350        GOSUB 800                                   '  Output
355 '
360        INPUT "Another quotation (y/n)"; AGAIN$
370        PRINT
380        PRINT
385 '
390     WEND
395 '
400     PRINT "See you tomorrow at 8 sharp!"
405 '
410     STOP
499 '-----------------------------------------------------------------
500 '  Subroutine Initialize
505 '------------------------
508     DIM AGELIMIT(6),PREMIUM(6)
510     READ ROWS
520     FOR J = 1 TO ROWS
530        READ AGELIMIT(J),PREMIUM(J)
540     NEXT J
550     LET AGAIN$ = "y"
560     RETURN
599 '-----------------------------------------------------------------
600 '  Subroutine Input
605 '-------------------
610     INPUT "Name   :"; FULLNAME$
620     INPUT "Age    :"; AGE
630     RETURN
699 '-----------------------------------------------------------------
700 '  Subroutine Table Look-up
705 '--------------------------
710     LET INDEX = 1
720     WHILE AGE > AGELIMIT(INDEX)
730        LET INDEX = INDEX + 1
740     WEND
750     RETURN
799 '-----------------------------------------------------------------
800 '  Subroutine Output
805 '--------------------
810     IF INDEX = ROWS THEN PRINT "Uninsurable-- over";AGELIMIT(ROWS-1)
                         ELSE PRINT "Premium is:$"; PREMIUM(INDEX)
820     PRINT
830     PRINT
840     RETURN
897 '-----------------------------------------------------------------
```

— Premium schedule stored as two separate arrays (columns)

— INDEX is equivalent to the row or category being checked within the premium schedule

Stores the maximum legitimate age limit

Correct premium

```
898 '  Data Section
899 '---------------
900    DATA 6
901    DATA 25,277
902    DATA 35,287
903    DATA 45,307
904    DATA 55,327
905    DATA 65,357
906    DATA 1E30,0
998 '-----------------------------------------------------------
999    END
```

Test

The following test run represents a partial debugging of the program (see Exercise 8).

```
RUN
Name      :? Clark S. Kent
Age       :? 42
Premium is:$ 307


Another quotation (y/n)? y


Name      :? Lois S. Lane
Age       :? 28
Premium is:$ 287


Another quotation (y/n)? n


See you tomorrow at 8 sharp!
```

Discussion

First, the premium schedule is read into two one-dimensional arrays: AGELIMIT and PREMIUM. Memory locations for these arrays appear as follows *after* lines 510–540 are completed:

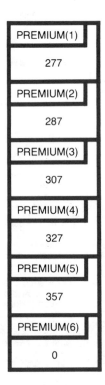

Notice that there are six array elements in each array. The sixth array element is used for the case in which the policyholder's age is greater than 65.

Next, we enter the loop that processes quotations. After the entry of name and age, the table lookup logic is implemented in lines 710–740. Starting with the first element (when INDEX = 1), the loop test sequentially evaluates each element of AGELIMIT until the proper age class is found; that is, until the age of the policyholder is less than or equal to an age limit value in array AGELIMIT. When this condition is satisfied (the while-loop test gives a false result), the appropriate premium is identified as the array element of PREMIUM that corresponds to the matching age class. For example, when 42 is stored in AGE, the while loop operates as follows.

Table Lookup Logic

INDEX	Is AGE Greater Than AGELIMIT(INDEX)?	Result
1	True; 42 is greater than 25	Continue looping
2	True; 42 is greater than 35	Continue looping
3	False; 42 is not greater than 45	Exit from loop

Thus, when loop exit is achieved, the statement

PRINT "Premium is:$"; PREMIUM(INDEX)

is executed, and the correct value of 3 in INDEX (age class) is used as the value of the subscript for PREMIUM. In this case, the contents of PREMIUM(3) are printed, which gives a premium of $307 for someone aged 42. If, however, the index value is 6, then the message that the policyholder is over 65 and uninsurable is printed.

7.6 TWO-DIMENSIONAL ARRAYS

In many situations it's convenient to store data in arrays with more than one dimension. Some computer systems allow several dimensions, but we focus here on the more common two-dimensional arrays.[3]

Motivation

Generally, it's desirable to use two-dimensional (2-D) arrays when we wish to store and manipulate data that are characterized by two attributes, as the following examples illustrate.

- Occupied beds in a hospital are tabulated by *day* of the week and by *ward*.
- Deposits for a major bank are recorded for all *branch banks* on a *monthly* basis.
- Enrollments at a college are tabulated by *major* and *class standing*.
- Five *exam scores* for a course are recorded for all *students*.
- Ten *financial ratios* from the Fortune 500 list of major U.S. corporations are recorded for all 500 *corporations*.

---

[3]For example, VAX-11 BASIC allows up to 32 dimensions and ANS BASIC includes 3-dimensional arrays.

Array Names and Subscripts

It's easier to understand a **matrix**, or **two-dimensional array** (an array with two subscripts), if we visualize a group of memory locations as a grid of boxes (table) arranged in rows and columns. An array element within a two-dimensional array is referenced by specifying two subscripts: one for row number and one for column number. For example, in the three-row by four-column array below, called DEPOSITS, the memory location that is marked with an X is found by looking at row 2, column 3; the memory location marked with XX is found in row 3, column 2.

3 × 4 Array DEPOSITS

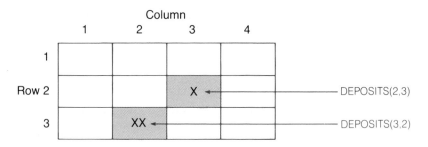

As you can see, two subscripts are needed when we use two-dimensional arrays. In BASIC, the subscripts must be enclosed in parentheses and separated by a comma. For example, in the above array named DEPOSITS, the location of the X is referenced as DEPOSITS(2,3), and the location of the XX is referenced as DEPOSITS(3,2). Notice that, in accordance with mathematical convention, the subscripts of the array-element name are always given in the following order: row subscript followed by column subscript.

Array-Element Name

> **array name (row subscript, column subscript)**
> DEPOSITS(I,J)

Except for the use of two subscripts, according to the above convention, *subscripts for two-dimensional arrays are treated in the same manner as for one-dimensional arrays.*

We can also illustrate array locations by using array-element names as follows:

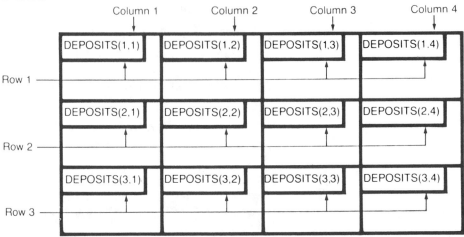

In actual practice, storage locations for two-dimensional arrays don't physically resemble a table in memory, but that need not concern us since the BASIC convention treats them like a table.

Array Declaration

Just as with one-dimensional arrays, two-dimensional arrays must be dimensioned to reserve memory locations for the array. In addition to identifying one-dimensional variables, the DIM statement can indicate which variables are two-dimensional and establishes the number of rows and columns that will be reserved in memory for the array.

The general form of the DIM statement for use with two-dimensional arrays is

DIM Statement

> **DIM** array name $\left(\begin{array}{cc} row & column \\ size, & size \end{array}\right)$ array , name $\left(\begin{array}{cc} row & column \\ size, & size \end{array}\right)$ ...
>
> DIM DEPOSITS(3,4)

For example, we might store the number of deposits for three branch banks in each of four quarters in a three-row by four-column (3 × 4) two-dimensional array named DEPOSITS, where each row stores the quarterly data for one branch. The DIM statement would be specified as

DIM DEPOSITS(3,4)

If we wanted DEPOSITS to store branch deposits for each month of the year, then we could set up an array with 3 rows and 12 columns. In this case, the DIM statement would be given by

DIM DEPOSITS(3,12)

In the first case, DEPOSITS has 12 elements in memory, whereas in the second case, 36 locations are reserved in memory.[4]

Both one- and two-dimensional arrays can be dimensioned in a single DIM statement by using commas to separate each array specification. For example,

DIM LOAD(5,10),EXP(10,8),TOT(5)

This results in the reservation of 50 locations for the 2-D array LOAD, 80 locations for the 2-D array EXP, and 5 locations for the 1-D array TOT.

Read, Input, and Output

The read, input, and output of two-dimensional arrays are best accomplished by the use of two FOR/NEXT loops, one nested within the other, as the next example illustrates.

---

[4]As in one-dimensional arrays, some versions of BASIC use a zero subscript; thus DIM D(3,12) would reserve 4 rows and 13 columns, or 52 locations, including the element D(0,0).

E X A M P L E 7 . 5 Read/Output with FOR/NEXT Loops

Let's assume that the two-dimensional array DEPOSITS stores the following data on the number of deposits by branch name and by quarter.

Bank	Quarter			
	1	2	3	4
1	1000	800	500	1200
2	500	2000	2000	500
3	1500	300	700	1500

Consider the following program which reads the bank data into the array DEPOSITS and then outputs this array. First, let's review the shaded segment of code, which reads the data into the array (lines 160–200).

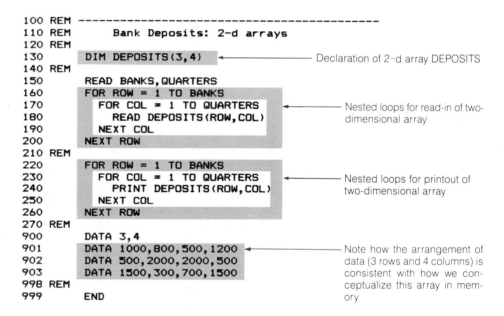

```
100 REM ---------------------------------------------
110 REM      Bank Deposits: 2-d arrays
120 REM
130         DIM DEPOSITS(3,4)              ← ——— Declaration of 2-d array DEPOSITS
140 REM
150         READ BANKS,QUARTERS
160         FOR ROW = 1 TO BANKS
170            FOR COL = 1 TO QUARTERS     ← ——— Nested loops for read-in of two-
180               READ DEPOSITS(ROW,COL)            dimensional array
190            NEXT COL
200         NEXT ROW
210 REM
220         FOR ROW = 1 TO BANKS
230            FOR COL = 1 TO QUARTERS     ← ——— Nested loops for printout of
240               PRINT DEPOSITS(ROW,COL)           two-dimensional array
250            NEXT COL
260         NEXT ROW
270 REM
900         DATA 3,4
901         DATA 1000,800,500,1200         ← ——— Note how the arrangement of
902         DATA 500,2000,2000,500                data (3 rows and 4 columns) is
903         DATA 1500,300,700,1500                consistent with how we con-
998 REM                                            ceptualize this array in mem-
999         END                                    ory
```

The flowchart in Figure 7.1 should help you visualize how the nesting of FOR/NEXT loops works. The key concept that you need to understand here is the exact manner in which the subscripts change values. Carefully look at the program and the flowchart to confirm that the subscripts of array DEPOSITS change values as follows:

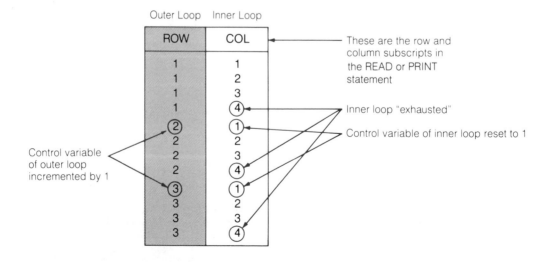

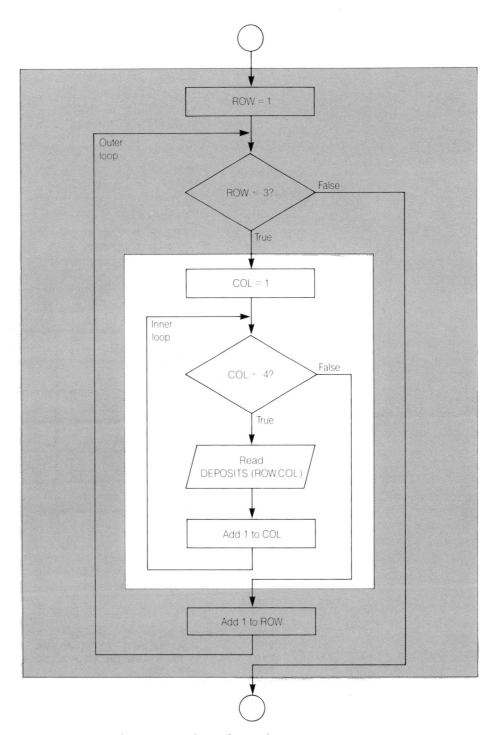

Figure 7.1 Nested FOR/NEXT loops for read-in

The first time through the loops, ROW = 1 and COL = 1, so the first data item in line 901 is read into DEPOSITS(1,1). The second time through the inner loop, ROW = 1 and COL = 2, so the second item in line 901 is read into DEPOSITS(1,2). The third time through the inner loop, ROW = 1 and COL = 3, so the third item in line 901 is read into DEPOSITS(1,3). The fourth time through the inner loop, ROW = 1 and COL = 4, so the fourth item in line 901 is read into DEPOSITS(1,4). At this point COL gets incremented to 5, and the inner loop tests false (see Figure 7.1). Then, ROW is incremented to 2 and again COL varies from 1 to 4. This results in the following sequence.

Read Operations for Second Row

ROW	COL	
2	1	READ DEPOSITS(2,1)
2	2	READ DEPOSITS(2,2)
2	3	READ DEPOSITS(2,3)
2	4	READ DEPOSITS(2,4)

Finally, ROW is set equal to 3, and COL varies from 1 to 4. This results in the sequence:

Read Operations for Third Row

ROW	COL	
3	1	READ DEPOSITS(3,1)
3	2	READ DEPOSITS(3,2)
3	3	READ DEPOSITS(3,3)
3	4	READ DEPOSITS(3,4)

At this point, read-in of the array is complete, yielding the following configuration in memory.

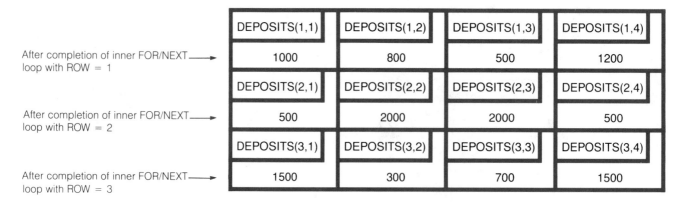

After completion of inner FOR/NEXT loop with ROW = 1

After completion of inner FOR/NEXT loop with ROW = 2

After completion of inner FOR/NEXT loop with ROW = 3

Note that the READ statement is executed exactly 12 times. *Since there is only one variable in the list of the READ statement, this means that 12 data items are required,* as given in lines 901–903 within the program on page 126.

Nested loops are likewise used to print two-dimensional arrays. For example, the statements

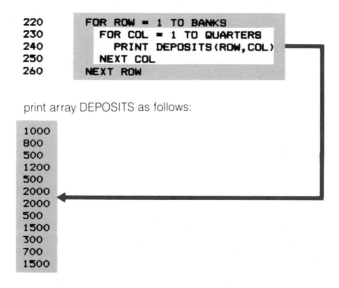

```
220    FOR ROW = 1 TO BANKS
230      FOR COL = 1 TO QUARTERS
240        PRINT DEPOSITS(ROW,COL)
250      NEXT COL
260    NEXT ROW
```

print array DEPOSITS as follows:

```
1000
800
500
1200
500
2000
2000
500
1500
300
700
1500
```

To print the two-dimensional array in the desirable table format requires a trailing comma or semicolon and a blank print line. For example,

```
220        FOR ROW = 1 TO BANKS                              Trailing semicolon holds the row
230          FOR COL = 1 TO QUARTERS
240            PRINT DEPOSITS(ROW,COL);
250          NEXT COL                        Spaces down to next row (by filling the
255        PRINT                             remainder of the current row with
260        NEXT ROW                          blanks)
```

Note how the output is consistent with the row by column table format

results in

```
1000   800   500  1200
 500  2000  2000   500
1500   300   700  1500
```

NOTE We cannot overemphasize the need for you to concentrate on the manner in which the subscripts of two-dimensional arrays in READ, INPUT, or PRINT statements change values. Again, *the inner loop must be exhausted (the control variable must exceed its limit) for each iteration (loop) of the outer loop. Once the inner loop is exhausted, then the control variable of the outer loop is incremented and the control variable of the inner loop is reset to its initial value.*

Manipulating 2-D Arrays

Processing data stored in two-dimensional arrays normally involves nesting of FOR/NEXT loops. The next example illustrates some common manipulations of two-dimensional arrays.

E X A M P L E   7 . 6   **Row Totals**

One of the more common processing tasks is finding totals of each row or column in an array. The row or column totals can be stored either in one-dimensional arrays or in an extra row or column of the two-dimensional array. For example, to find the annual bank deposits in each bank for the data given on page 126 we need to sum the entries in each row. The following revision to Example 7.5 determines row sums.

```
100 REM--------------------------------------------------------------
110 REM          Bank Deposits: Row Totals
120 REM
130        DIM DEPOSITS(3,4), SUM(3)                    Declaration
140 REM                                                 of 1-D array SUM
150        READ BANKS,QUARTERS
160        FOR ROW = 1 TO BANKS
170          FOR COL = 1 TO QUARTERS
180            READ DEPOSITS(ROW,COL)
190          NEXT COL
200        NEXT ROW
210 REM
220        FOR ROW = 1 TO BANKS
230          LET SUM(ROW) = 0
240          FOR COL = 1 TO QUARTERS
250            LET SUM(ROW) = SUM(ROW) + DEPOSITS(ROW,COL)
260          NEXT COL
270        NEXT ROW
280 REM
```

These nested loops accumulate the sum

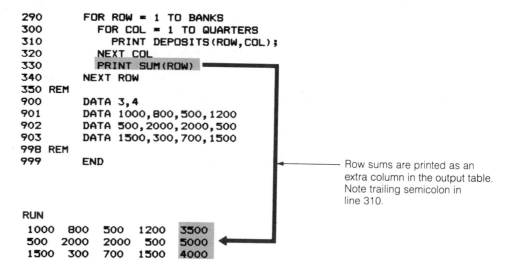

```
290         FOR ROW = 1 TO BANKS
300           FOR COL = 1 TO QUARTERS
310             PRINT DEPOSITS(ROW,COL);
320           NEXT COL
330         PRINT SUM(ROW)
340         NEXT ROW
350 REM
900         DATA 3,4
901         DATA 1000,800,500,1200
902         DATA 500,2000,2000,500
903         DATA 1500,300,700,1500
998 REM
999         END
```

Row sums are printed as an extra column in the output table. Note trailing semicolon in line 310.

```
RUN
 1000   800   500  1200  3500
  500  2000  2000   500  5000
 1500   300   700  1500  4000
```

When ROW = 1, SUM(1) is initialized to zero in line 230: the inner or column loop then sums the values in the first row given by DEPOSITS(1,1), DEPOSITS(1,2), DEPOSITS(1,3), and DEPOSITS(1,4) and stores this sum in the first element of the array SUM.

When the outer loop is incremented (ROW = 2), SUM(2) is initialized to zero, and the values in row 2 are accumulated and stored in the second element of array SUM. Finally, the outer loop iterates for the last time (ROW = 3), and the values of the third row are added to the third element in the array SUM. After execution of the nested loops in lines 220–270 is completed, memory appears as follows:

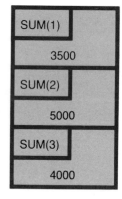

DEPOSITS(1,1)	DEPOSITS(1,2)	DEPOSITS(1,3)	DEPOSITS(1,4)	SUM(1)
1000	800	500	1200	3500
DEPOSITS(2,1)	DEPOSITS(2,2)	DEPOSITS(2,3)	DEPOSITS(2,4)	SUM(2)
500	2000	2000	500	5000
DEPOSITS(3,1)	DEPOSITS(3,2)	DEPOSITS(3,3)	DEPOSITS(3,4)	SUM(3)
1500	300	700	1500	4000

7.7 POINTERS

Design and Style

1. **Array Declarations.** Declare all arrays through DIM statements, even though most systems automatically dimension arrays if there are ten or fewer array elements. This also clearly identifies the arrays for anyone reading a listing of the program. The placement of DIM statements at the beginning of the program also facilitates the identification of arrays. It's also best to identify the arrays within the program's documentation.

2. **The Array Size/Storage Trade-off.** Make sure that the array-size parameter that defines the number of array elements is large enough to handle all normal situations. Remember, it's better to waste storage space

than to have execution-time errors resulting from a subscript value above the upper dimension bound.

3. **Defensive Programming.** Don't forget to include an error routine that catches a subscript value that exceeds its upper dimension bound. This avoids "subscript out of bound" execution errors. See Example 7.3.

4. **Generalized Programming.** Use simple variables rather than constants to define the number of repetitions in FOR/NEXT loops used to read, manipulate, and print arrays. This avoids program modification when the number of repetitions changes.

5. **Table Representations.** Apply the concept of visual tables for better readability of 2-D arrays. Specifically, set up 2-D array data in DATA statements in a row by row (a table) manner, as in Example 7.5. Print 2-D array data in table form by using a trailing semicolon, as in Example 7.5.

Common Errors

Arrays are great for giving a lot of practice in debugging. Often one small error will result in an avalanche of error messages. Pay attention to the following, and you might avoid apoplexy.

1. **Declaration of array.** Don't forget to declare your array by using the DIM statement. If you get an error message such as "Undefined array" or "Undefined function" for each line in which the subscripted variable appears, then check whether you dimensioned the array.

2. **Subscripts.** If you get an execution error message such as "Subscript out of bounds" or "Subscript out of range," then a subscript is negative, zero (in systems that don't allow this lower bound), or greater than the upper bound specified in the DIM statement. Two kinds of mistakes are possible here: either you reserved too few locations for your array, or you made a logic error in assigning values to subscripts.

3. **Array names.** A common point of confusion among beginning programmers is just what represents the array name. For example, are B(J) and B(I) one and the same array? Yes. In this case, the array name is B, not B(J) or B(I). B(J) and B(I) are called array-element names which simply reference specific elements in array B.

FOLLOW-UP EXERCISES

1. Which of the following references to array A are valid if A is dimensioned as follows:

   DIM A(500)

   a. A(-3)
   b. A(10)
   c. A(510)
   d. A(0)

2. Indicate what is wrong, if anything, with each of the following program segments.

   a. 10 READ K,X(K)
   20 DIM X(K)

   b. 10 LET M = 5
   20 LET N = 8
   30 LET A(0) = 100
   40 LET A(15) = 500
   50 LET A(M $-$ 2*N) = M*N

   *c. 10 DIM D(10),E(10)
   20 FOR J = 1 TO 26
   30   LET D(J) = J ˆ 2
   40 NEXT J
   50 FOR J = 1 TO 19
   60   LET E(J + 1) = D(J)*D(J + 1)
   70 NEXT J

   What would be stored in E(3) once the program is corrected?

3. With respect to Version C of Example 7.1:
   a. Change the program to process 100 branch banks. How many more statements would be needed in the Version B program to accomplish the same task? How about the length of the statement that calculates TOTAL? Do you now see why arrays are such a powerful means of naming and manipulating a large number of *related* storage locations?
   *b. Modify the program so that the output appears as follows:

Bank	1	2	3
Deposits	3500	5000	4000
Percentage	28	40	32

4. Consider the following program segment for the input of 50 values into an array named B:

   ```
   100 DIM B(50)
   110 INPUT B(1)
   120 INPUT B(2)
   130 INPUT B(3)
         .
         .
         .
   600 INPUT B(50)
   ```

   Rewrite this segment using the FOR/NEXT loop. In general, which approach is more efficient?

*5. Given the following data:

Cost	Sales
40	100
20	125
75	95

   a. Write an efficient program segment to read these data into the arrays C and S. What might be the most logical way of placing data on DATA statements?
   b. Write the code to output these data so they appear as presented in the above table.

6. Write a program segment to set each element in a 100-element array to 50.

7. With respect to Example 7.3.
   a. Could we have replaced lines 901–904 with

   ```
   901    DATA 100,75,90,60,175,140,230,300
   ```

   If so, why might the original approach be preferable?
   b. Roleplay the output for departmental number entries of 3 and 5.
   *c. Modify the error test so that the user can input a new departmental number if an error occurs.

8. What would the output look like in Example 7.4 if we were to process a quotation for Rip Van Winkle, aged 99? Also roleplay the output for ages 55, 63, and 20.

9. Modify the program in Example 7.4 to add a new row in the table with an age limit of 75 and a premium of $500. Do you see why we used the variable ROWS in lines 510–520 and 810?

10. Do you see anything wrong with the following table lookup logic as a replacement to lines 710–810 in Example 7.4?

    ```
    710 FOR J = 1 TO 5
    720   IF AGE < = AGELIMIT(J) GO TO 810
    730 NEXT J
    810 PRINT "Premium is:$"; PREMIUM(J)
    ```

*11. Rewrite the program in Example 7.4 to eliminate entirely the use of arrays. Try using a sequence of if/then structures to implement the table lookup logic. Which approach do you prefer and why?

12. Describe output for the following program. Any problems?

    ```
    10   DIM X(5)
    20   FOR J = 1 TO 6
    30      LET X(J) = J^2
    40      PRINT J;X(J)
    50   NEXT J
    60   END
    ```

*13. Describe output for the following program.

    ```
    100 DIM A(15)
    105 READ N
    110 FOR I = 1 TO N
    115   READ A(I)
    120 NEXT I
    125 FOR I = N TO 1 STEP − 1
    130   PRINT A(I)
    135 NEXT I
    901 DATA 4
    902 DATA 5,10,15,20
    999 END
    ```

*14. Assume that a banking program has stored the current month's total dollar deposits in array DEPA and the total dollar withdrawals in array WITA. A third array can be used to accumulate the new balance (BAL), as follows.

    ```
    300 FOR K = 1 TO N
    310   LET BAL(K) = BAL(K) + DEPA(K) − WITA(K)
    320 NEXT K
    ```

    N represents the number of customers to be processed.
    a. Suppose that before running the program segment, memory appears as follows:

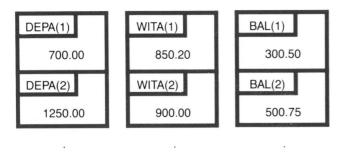

DEPA(1)		WITA(1)		BAL(1)	
700.00		850.20		300.50	
DEPA(2)		WITA(2)		BAL(2)	
1250.00		900.00		500.75	

.   .   .
.   .   .
.   .   .

160 FOR COL =
170   FOR ROW
180   READ DEH
190   NEXT ROW
200 NEXT COL

How would DEPOSITS a
DEPOSITS get filled in rov
column? How should we p
DATA statements so we st   in
DEPOSITS exactly as they app   ge 128?

*e. Modify the program to check th   ..e number of banks and number of quarters do not exceed the array boundaries. If they do, print an error message and stop processing.

What changes would occur for the first two customer accounts following execution of the given program segment?

b. Modify the loop body to print the account number, ACCNO(K), and new balance whenever the new balance is less than zero.

15. **String arrays.** Write a program segment that:
a. Reads in the days of the week (Monday, Tuesday, . . .) into the array DAY$.
b. Prints the day of the week (Monday, . . . , Sunday) based on interactive input of the day number (1, . . . , 7).

16. In Example 7.5:
a. How would the output appear if the PRINT statement in line 255 were omitted?
b. How would the output appear if the loop ROW were the inner loop and loop COL were the outer loop (that is, interchange statements 220 and 230 and 250 and 260)?
c. Suppose the following arrangement of DATA statements is used:

901 DATA 1000
902 DATA 800
903 DATA 500
904 DATA 1200
905 DATA 500
      .
      .
      .
912 DATA 1500

How does memory appear after execution of lines 160 to 200?

*d. Suppose the following program segment is executed using the DATA statements in Example 7.5.

17. Add program segments to Example 7.6 that accumulate and print the bank's total deposits for each quarter. Store these results in a one-dimensional array called TOTAL.

*18. In Example 7.6, assume that DEPOSITS has been dimensioned to four rows and five columns. Instead of using SUM as in the example and TOTAL as in Exercise 17, use the fourth row of DEPOSITS to store column totals and the fifth column to store row totals.
a. Write program segments that accomplish this. Don't forget to initialize your summers to zero.
b. Implement this program on your system.

19. Suppose an array has been dimensioned as follows:

DIM WEIGHT(100,50)

Write a program segment that initializes each element in WEIGHT to 100.

*20. Write a program segment that initializes the (4 × 4) array X in the following manner.

1 0 0 0
0 1 0 0
0 0 1 0
0 0 0 1

*21. Rewrite Example 7.4 using two-dimensional arrays to store the insurance premium schedule.

22. Implement one of the following programs on your system, after making any necessary dialect changes.
a. Example 7.1
b. Example 7.2
c. Example 7.3
d. Example 7.4
e. Example 7.5
f. Example 7.6

23. Suppose the input

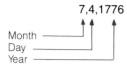

7,4,1776

Month
Day
Year

results in the output

JULY 4, 1776

Write a program to accomplish this. Terminate input if the year is zero or less. Print an error message if data input for either the month or the day is out of range.

24. **Crime Data Summary.** The data below represent the number of arrests for felony crimes in a state over a three-year period.

	Arrest Data by Year		
Felony	*1*	*2*	*3*
Homicide	1,000	1,000	1,000
Robbery	10,000	9,000	11,000
Burglary	27,000	24,000	28,000
Assault	13,000	15,000	16,000
Theft	19,000	20,000	23,000
Forgery	10,000	9,000	10,000

a. Design and write a program to read the data into several one-dimensional arrays. Print out the data in a table format that includes a new row for total arrests in each year and a new column for average arrests for each crime over the past three years. There is no need to label rows and columns here.

b. In the output of part **a**, label your columns 1, 2, 3, and AVERAGE. Label your rows according to the felony names in the above table, the last row being TOTALS. Store felony names in a one-dimensional string array.

c. Use a 2-D array instead of 1-D arrays.

25. **SAT Scores.** Every year State College prints a fact book that includes average combined (math plus verbal) SAT scores of students categorized as freshmen, sophomore, junior, and senior.

a. Write a program that reads a student data file (Figure 1) that includes student name, college code (1 = humanities, 2 = sciences), class code (1 = freshmen, 2 = sophomore, . . .), math SAT score, and verbal SAT score.

Figure 1   Student File

Student name	College code	Class code	SAT math	SAT verbal
Hicks	2	2	580	640
Garfolo	1	3	720	680
Beck	2	2	610	560
Thuki	1	2	580	420
Vasu	1	4	495	505

Figure 2 shows how the report should appear.

Figure 2   SAT Data

Code	Count	Average
Freshmen	0	0
Sophomore	3	1130
Junior	1	1400
Senior	1	1000

Use the direct access concept to calculate counts and averages for each class.

b. Modify the program to print a separate report for each college. Include a printout of the overall average for each college.

26. **Sales Forecasts.** Design and write an interactive program that calculates and prints sales forecasts by quarters for future years based on current sales and projected annual growth rate. For example, if currently we are at the end of the second quarter in the year 1985, and sales this quarter were $1.2 million with a projected growth rate of 2% per quarter, then forecasts through 1987 should appear as follows:

Sales Forecast for Ouija Board

Current Year 1985	Quarter 2	Sales $1.2 M
Year	*Quarter*	*Sales*
1985	3	1.224
1985	4	1.248
1986	1	1.273
1986	2	1.299
1986	3	1.325
1986	4	1.351
1987	1	1.378
1987	2	1.406
1987	3	1.434
1987	4	1.463

Note that the next forecast is always the last forecast increased by the growth rate.

a. Run your program for the following data.

Product Name	Current Sales	Growth Rate	Years into Future
Ouija Board	1.20	0.02	2
Star Trek Charm	0.85	0.05	4

Note that the sample output is based on the first set of data. Your program should allow input for a variable number of products.

b. Graphical Output. To the right of each sales forecast, print the asterisk character in a graph format. Do this as follows: Reserve columns 30 through 70 for graphical output. In this case, column 30 represents 0 on a graph, and column 70 represents 40 (that is, there are 40 print columns between 30 and 70). This means that all sales forecasts must be scaled to a range between 0 and 40; that is,

$$\text{Scaled forecast} = \left(\frac{\text{Forecast}}{\text{Maximum forecast}}\right) \cdot 40$$

For example, the scaled forecast for the fourth quarter in 1986 is (1.351/1.463) · 40, or 36.9. This means that we want an asterisk printed in column 66 (or 30 + 36) of the print line where 1.351 is printed for sales.

27. Stock-Portfolio Valuation. Companies, universities, banks, pension funds, and other organizations routinely invest funds in the stock market. The set of stocks in which the organization invests its funds is called a *stock portfolio*. The table below illustrates a sample stock portfolio, including the number of shares owned of each stock, the purchase price per share, and the latest price per share quoted by the stock exchange.

Stock Portfolio

Stock	Number of Shares	Purchase Price ($/share)	Current Price ($/share)
Allegh Airls	40,000	5⅞	7¼
Boeing	5,000	61½	56
EastmKo	10,000	60	64½
Hewlett P	15,000	80	100⅛
IBM	2,500	77⅛	80¾
Texaco	8,000	23½	19
Tex Inst	12,000	80	85⅞

a. Design and run a program to calculate the initial (purchase) value of the portfolio, the current value of the portfolio, and the net change in the value. Store number of shares, purchase prices, and current prices in a two-dimensional array. *Hint:* The value of the portfolio is found by multiplying shares by corresponding prices and summing.

b. Output the portfolio before printing the items in part **a**. Store the stock name in a one-dimensional string array.

c. Include a loop in the program for processing more than one portfolio. Find two copies of a newspaper that were published at least two weeks apart. Select a portfolio, make up shares owned, and use the two sets of prices for purchase and current prices. Process the given portfolio and the new portfolio in one run, and include the output of combined value of all portfolios.

28. State Taxes. The state budget office has collected the following data on state tax collections for the past year.

Tax Dollars Collected (in millions)

Tax Type	QTR 1	QTR 2	QTR 3	QTR 4
Motor vehicle	2	3	4	3
Gasoline	1	2	4	3
Cigarette	1	1	1	2
Sales	15	20	20	50
Corporate income	25	12	10	8
Personal income	25	75	12	20

Prepare a menu-driven program that has the following options:

1. *Tax Collection Report.* Report shows annual tax collected for each tax type
2. *Percentage Report 1.* Contribution of each tax's quarterly receipts in relation to the total taxes received from all sources during the quarter
3. *Percentage Report 2.* Contribution of each tax's quarterly receipts in relation to total dollars received for that tax during the year
4. *Stop Processing.*

Store the quarterly data within a two-dimensional numeric array; store the tax type description within a one-dimensional array.

Running BASIC Programs

In running BASIC programs, we assume the use of either a time-sharing or a microcomputer system. On those systems we enter our program at a terminal or keyboard directly into the computer.

On a time-sharing system, the log-in procedure includes turning on the terminal, establishing contact with the computer, and providing valid identification. Each user has a unique identification code which usually has two parts: a user name, user number, or user id (which may include letters) and a password. The user number is used by the computer center for controlling access to the computer system and for accounting purposes; the password is a means of maintaining security and privacy. *The exact log-in procedure for your system will be detailed by your instructor.*

On a microcomputer, logging in includes the act of inserting the disk operating system (DOS) diskette and turning on the computer. *The exact procedure for your system will be explained by your instructor (and User Manual).*

Once we access or log in to a computer, the process varies, depending on the computer. In the material that follows we illustrate two popular computers, but first let's define some important terms.

A.1 SYSTEM COMMANDS

We communicate with the operating system through a language that we call **system commands**, although the exact term for this language varies from system to system.[1] Among other things, system commands allow us to run (execute) the program, obtain a listing of the program code, and save the program in secondary storage for recall. Therefore, when we run programs in an interactive environment, we have to learn a set of system commands in addition to the BASIC statements that appear within the programs.

Unfortunately, system commands are not universal, which means that

---

*This module is best assigned just before, during, or just after Chapter 2.

[1]For example, the system commands are called Digital Command Language on the VAX-11 computer system and DOS commands and BASIC commands on the IBM PC. The word command is fairly common across all systems.

they differ from one system to another. *Your instructor (and User Manual), therefore, must provide you with system commands that are specific to your system.*

A.2 WORKSPACE VERSUS LIBRARY

After logging in, each user in a time-sharing system gets a separate portion of primary memory called the **workspace**. The purpose of the workspace is to store both the BASIC program and the data the program is to work with. On a microcomputer, the workspace is the portion of RAM that's available for the program and its data.

When we exit or log out from a computer system, the program in the workspace is erased. For this reason, each user on a time-sharing system has an assigned secondary storage area (on magnetic disk) called a **library** that stores programs and data for recall. Storing programs in secondary storage avoids having to retype programs. On microcomputers, diskettes are normally the secondary storage areas for programs and data.

A program within a library is often called a **program file**. We can also store data within libraries for use as input to one or more programs. A set of data stored in this manner is called a **data file**. We discuss this topic in Module E.

A.3 ILLUSTRATIONS

In this section we illustrate the process of running the program in Section 1.2 or Example 2.1 on two computer systems: Digital's VAX-11 minicomputer (Example A.1) and the IBM PC (Example A.2). *If you use a different system, then your system will not operate exactly as shown in the illustration.* In this case, just pay attention to the principles, since these are universal. *Your instructor will discuss the appropriate modifications for your system.*

In these examples, boxed segments indicate the computer run, and marginal notes describe the corresponding boxed segment.

To clearly point out the interactions between the user and the computer, all text typed by the user is in color; *text typed by the computer is in black.*

NOTE 1   As you study the examples, *keep in mind the very important distinctions between a BASIC* **statement** *and a system* **command**. This distinction seems to give beginning students much grief. System commands such as LIST and RUN are used strictly to communicate with the operating system. In our illustrations, system commands are not found *within* the BASIC programs; only BASIC statements are found within the BASIC programs.

NOTE 2   Remember that these examples are for two systems: VAX-11 and IBM PC. If you use a different system, then your system commands will differ. (See Exercise 2.) As you study the illustration, *write in the appropriate system commands for your system.* Errors that occur in this process are discussed in detail in Module B.

E X A M P L E   A . 1   Sample Session on the VAX-11 Minicomputer

1.
```
Username: ANSI
Password:

Welcome to VAX/VMS version V3.3

01:45 P.M. Monday, March 5, 1984
```

Entry of user name and password for logging in. Each time we finish typing a line, we must press the Carriage Return or Enter key on the keyboard. ANSI is the user name, but the password that was entered is not displayed by the computer for security reasons.

2.
```
$ BASIC
```

The **$** symbol is the VAX-11's Digital Command Language (DCL) prompt, which means that the operating system (OS) is waiting for us to give it a system or DCL command. **BASIC** is the DCL command for using the BASIC compiler.

3.
```
VAX-11 BASIC V2.1

Ready
```

This now takes us to the BASIC environment, which is a subset of the OS. The response **Ready** indicates that we have successfully completed the command. The BASIC environment is now waiting for us to do something.

4.
```
100 REM   Tuition Revenue Program (Version 1.0)
110 REM-----------------------------------------------
250        INPUT "Enter college name --->"; COLLEGE$
255        INPUT "Enter tuition -------->"; TUITION
260        INPUT "Enter enrollment ----->"; ENROLLMENT
265 REM-----------------------------------------------
280        LET REVENUE = TUITION*ENROLLMENT
285 REM-----------------------------------------------
290        PRINT
300        PRINT "Revenue ...............$"; REVENUE
325 REM-----------------------------------------------
999        END
```

We need to create a new program in the workspace. *These are* BASIC statements. Note that the system does not respond "Ready" after each line is typed, since these are not system commands. Also note that each line has a unique line number.

5.
```
RUN
```

Let's run the program. **RUN** is a BASIC (system) command that first compiles and then executes the program. Note that within the BASIC environment we use BASIC commands, but within the OS environment we use DCL commands. Thus two sets of commands need to be learned for working within these two environments.

6.
```
NONAME        5-MAR-1984   13:49
```

The computer first prints a header (program name, date, and time). Next it compiles the program.

7.
```
Enter college name --->? Micro U
Enter tuition -------->? 750
Enter enrollment ----->? 1000

Revenue ...............$ 750000
Ready
```

During execution, no syntax errors are found, so execution begins with line 250 in the program. The computer prompts for three input values (college name, tuition, and enrollment). We enter these values, and then the program displays the output (revenue) on the screen. Execution of lines 250–260 yields the input prompts, and execution of line 300 gives the output. Results are correct.

8.
```
SAVE REV
Ready
```

We need to save the program. **SAVE** is the BASIC command for creating in the library a copy of the program in the workspace. The program has now been saved for recall at a later date under the name REV. The response Ready indicates that we have sucessfully completed the SAVE command.

9.
```
EXIT
```

EXIT is the BASIC command for leaving the BASIC environment and returning to the operating system.

10.
```
$ LOGOFF
```

LOGOFF is the DCL command for logging out of the computer.

11.

```
OLD REV
Ready
```

Let's assume that we get back onto the computer the next day by completing Steps 1–3.
Let's retrieve the program stored previously. **OLD** is the BASIC command for retrieving a previously saved program from the library into the workspace (a copy of the program still remains in the library).

12.

```
LIST
REV            5-MAR-1984  13:53

100 REM  Tuition Revenue Program (Version 1.0)
110 REM------------------------------------------
250          INPUT "Enter college name --->"; COLLEGE$
255          INPUT "Enter tuition -------->"; TUITION
260          INPUT "Enter enrollment ----->"; ENROLLMENT
265 REM------------------------------------------
280          LET REVENUE = TUITION*ENROLLMENT
285 REM------------------------------------------
290          PRINT
300          PRINT "Revenue ..............$"; REVENUE
325 REM------------------------------------------
999          END

Ready
```

LIST is the BASIC command that displays the program currently in the workspace. This command does not execute the program; thus no results are displayed other than the listing of the program. *Note:* To obtain a hard-copy listing, use the DCL systems command **PRINT** REV.BAS; this spools the BASIC program named REV to a line printer.

13.

```
RUN
REV            5-MAR-1984  13:55


Enter college name --->? Micro U
Enter tuition -------->? 750
Enter enrollment ----->? 1000

Revenue ..............$ 750000


Ready
```

Let's run the program again. Same input/output as before.

14.

```
NEW EXAM
```

Let's key in a new program. **NEW** is the BASIC command for clearing the workspace and starting fresh with a new program. Here we gave the new program the name EXAM.

•
•
•

And so on . . .

E X A M P L E   A . 2   Sample Session on the IBM PC

1.

```
Current date is Tue 1-01-1980
Enter new date: 3/05/84
Current time is  0:00:14:66
Enter new time:


The IBM Personal Computer DOS
Version 1.10 (C) Copyright IBM Corp 1981, 1982
```

Insert the Disk Operating System (DOS) diskette in drive A and turn on the IBM PC. (*Note:* In this illustration we assume the use of two diskette drives; the DOS diskette is in drive A, and the user's file (library) diskette is in drive B.) The system prompts for the date and time, which we enter. Don't forget to press the Enter key whenever you're through typing a line.

2.

```
A>BASIC
```

The *prompt* **A**> on the screen indicates we have successfully loaded the operating system (DOS). DOS now waits for us to type a DOS command. **BASIC** or **BASICA** is the DOS command we use to load the BASIC interpreter.

3.
```
The IBM Personal Computer Basic
Version A1.10 Copyright IBM Corp. 1981, 1982
61066 Bytes free
Ok
```

This now takes us to the BASIC environment. The response **Ok** indicates that we have successfully completed the command. The BASIC environment is now waiting for us to do something.

4.
```
100 REM   Tuition Revenue Program (Version 1.0)
110 REM---------------------------------------------------
250           INPUT "Enter college name --->"; COLLEGE$
255           INPUT "Enter tuition -------->"; TUITION
260           INPUT "Enter enrollment ----->"; ENROLLMENT
265 REM---------------------------------------------------
280           LET REVENUE = TUITION*ENROLLMENT
285 REM---------------------------------------------------
290           PRINT
300           PRINT "Revenue ...............$"; REVENUE
325 REM---------------------------------------------------
999           END
```

We need to create a new program in the workspace. *These are* BASIC statements Note that the system does not respond "Ok" after each line is typed, since these are not system commands. Also note that each line has a unique line number.

5.
```
RUN
```

Let's run the program. **RUN** is the BASIC (system) command for interpreting/executing the program. Note that within the BASIC environment we use BASIC commands, but within the DOS environment we use DOS commands. Thus two sets of commands need to be learned for working within these two environments. *Note:* Instead of typing **RUN** we could press the function key **F2**.

6.

```
Enter college name --->? Micro U
Enter tuition -------->? 750
Enter enrollment ----->? 1000

Revenue ...............$ 750000
Ok
```

During execution, the computer prompts for three input values (college name, tuition, and enrollment). We enter these values, and then the program displays the output (revenue) on the screen.
Execution of lines 250–260 yields the input prompts, and execution of line 300 gives the output. Results are correct.

7.

```
SAVE"B:REV
Ok
```

We need to save the program. **SAVE** is the BASIC command that stores a copy of the program in the workspace onto the disk. The program is saved on the diskette in drive B for recall at a later date using the name REV. The Ok indicates successful completion of the SAVE command. *Note:* Instead of typing SAVE"B:REV we could press the **F4** key and type B:REV.

8.
```
SYSTEM

A>
```

SYSTEM is the BASIC command for leaving BASIC and returning to the operating system (DOS). We can carry out other housekeeping chores from DOS, such as backing up files with the **COPY** command and listing diskette directories with the **DIR** command.

•
•
•

We log out by removing the diskettes and turning off the power. Let's assume that we get back onto the microcomputer the next day.

9.
```
LOAD"B:REV
Ok
```

Let's retrieve the program stored previously. **LOAD** is the BASIC command for retrieving a previously saved program from a diskette into the workspace in RAM. In this case, we retrieve a copy of the program REV from the diskette in drive B. A copy of this program still remains on the diskette. *Note:* Instead of typing LOAD"B:REV we could press key **F3** followed by B:REV.

10.

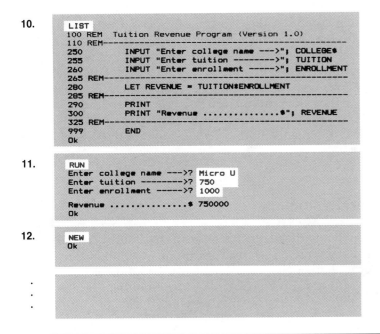

LIST is the BASIC command that displays the program currently in the workspace. This command does not execute the program; thus no results are displayed other than the listing of the program. *Note:* Instead of typing LIST we could press the function key **F1**. To obtain a hard-copy listing off the line printer, use the command **LLIST**.

11.

Let's run the program again. Same input/output as before. *Note:* To obtain a hard copy of the input/output on the screen press the **PrtSc** key.

12.

Let's key in a new program. **NEW** is the BASIC command for clearing the workspace and starting fresh with a new program.

And so on . . .

The two examples show that we generally operate within two environments: The **operating system (OS) environment** and the **BASIC environment**. Typically, the BASIC environment is a specialized subset of the OS environment and has the purpose of developing, maintaining, and running BASIC programs. Moreover, each environment has its own set of system commands: **OS commands** for the OS environment and **BASIC commands** for the BASIC environment. In our examples, the OS commands are called DCL commands on the VAX-11 and DOS commands on the IBM PC. *What are they called on your system?*

We need to be quite aware of the distinction between these two sets of commands, since they usually don't "travel" well between the two environments. For example, the OS command for listing the directory of program names in our library is most likely different from the BASIC command that accomplishes the same purpose. This is a good example of system unfriendliness.

A.4 OTHER CONSIDERATIONS

This section concludes the module by noting other items that you should be aware of.

Translation versus Execution

As you know from Chapter 1, a high-level language such as BASIC must first be translated into the machine language of the computer. If translation is by an interpreter, then each line (starting with the lowest numbered line) is first interpreted and then (if a syntax rule of the language has not been violated) executed. By executed we mean that the indicated action (input, print, etc.) is carried out.

If translation is by a compiler, then all lines in the source program are translated (starting with the lowest line number), yielding an object program. The object program is then executed, if there are no syntax errors.

In our sample program, the first executable statement is the INPUT statement in line 250 (the REMs serve only to document programs for us humans). The execution sequence thus starts at line 250 and proceeds to lines 255, 260, 280, 290, 300, and 999. The only evidence of execution we see visually is execution of the INPUT statements in lines 250–260 and of the PRINT statements in lines 290–300.

Additional System Commands

The system commands that we have illustrated are a small subset of the many commands available for a typical system. For example, commands exist for displaying the names and other characteristics of files within our library, for deleting files from the library, for copying files, for renaming files, for resequencing the line numbers within programs, and for altering or editing programs. Ask your instructor about other useful commands on your system (and check your system's *User Manual*).

Editors

Editors are powerful tools that enable a user to enter, alter, and store programs. There are two types of editors: line-oriented and screen-oriented.

A line-oriented editor[2] has a set of commands that typically operate on one line at a time (or a range of lines) within the program in the workspace. For example, suppose the program in Example A.1 had a typographical error within the keyword INPUT in line 255.

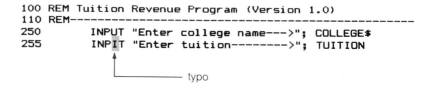

```
100 REM Tuition Revenue Program (Version 1.0)
110 REM-------------------------------------------------------
250        INPUT "Enter college name--->"; COLLEGE$
255        INPIT "Enter tuition-------->"; TUITION
                    ↑
                    |_____ typo
```

The following general description indicates one approach (of many) to correcting line 255 with a typical line editor.

Step 1.   Invoke the line editor by typing a system command that puts us under control of the line editor. The line editor conceptually points to the first line in the program (line 100), and offers an edit prompt as it waits for us to type an edit command.

Step 2.   We type a special edit command that moves the pointer to line 255.

Step 3.   We type a special edit command that substitutes the string INPUT for the string INPIT.

---

[2]The VAX-11 EDT editor in line mode and the **IBM-PC EDLIN** editor are examples of line editors.

Step 4. We end the editing session by typing a special edit command that files or stores the revised program in our library.

A screen-oriented editor[3] allows movement of the cursor to any point on a screen that shows a listing of the program. Text is then altered through straightforward typing, including the use of any special keys for insertions, deletions, and other tasks. For example, suppose we wish to correct line 255 as before, and lines 100–255 are listed on the screen. The following describes an approach using the **IBM PC BASIC** editor. The cursor initially resides at the 1 in line 100.

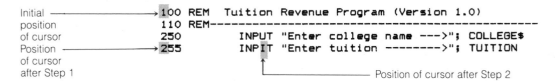

```
Initial ──────────────────→ 100 REM    Tuition Revenue Program (Version 1.0)
position                    110 REM──────────────────────────────────────────
of cursor                   250           INPUT "Enter college name --->"; COLLEGE$
Position ─────────────────→ 255           INPIT "Enter tuition -------->"; TUITION
of cursor
after Step 1                                    └────────────── Position of cursor after Step 2
```

Step 1. Move the cursor straight down to line 255 by striking the appropriate cursor control key three times.

Step 2. Move the cursor to the right along line 255 until it reaches the second I in INPIT.

Step 3. Type the letter U.

Step 4. Strike the "Enter" key. This enters our changed line into the program in the workspace.[4]

As you can see, the process of editing with a screen-oriented editor is much simpler than with a line-oriented editor.

By the way, the ultimate screen-oriented editors are the wordprocessors commonly available for microcomputers. These allow not only the full-screen movements illustrated above but also the use of powerful commands for copying, moving, searching, and replacing text. You might want to try a word-processor if one is available to you, especially if you're developing long programs.

You will be doing a lot of editing in this course, *so check out the editor on your system and invest some time in learning how to use it.* Of course, you could just "brute force" your editing by simply retyping entire lines (we could easily have retyped line 255 entirely in our sample illustration); for extensive editing, however, this approach doesn't help your productivity (unless you have nothing better to do!).

NOTE On many systems it's possible to work strictly within the OS environment, thereby bypassing the BASIC environment. In this case, programs are developed and modified using the OS editor, and OS commands are used for housekeeping tasks. *Is this possible on your system?*

---

[3]The VAX-11 EDT editor in keypad mode and the IBM-PC BASIC editor are examples of screen-oriented editors.

[4]The listing shown on the screen actually resides in a special storage area called the screen buffer. Thus, changing a line on the screen changes the corresponding line within the screen buffer, not the corresponding line within the workspace. The act of striking the "Enter" key copies the line from the screen buffer to the workspace.

FOLLOW-UP EXERCISES

1. Try the following on your system.
   a. Duplicate our illustrative run on your system. If you make a mistake typing a line, simply retype the line. The newly typed line will replace the old, incorrect line in your workspace. Better yet, learn to use your system's editor.
   b. Experiment. Try different things. Be bold. For example, it's OK to type lines out of numeric sequence, since the BASIC system rearranges lines numerically in your workspace. In other words, we could have typed lines 250, 255, 100, 110, 260, . . . , 999, and they would be stored in the correct numeric sequence. Try it, and then list the program. Try some system commands we haven't illustrated, such as the command that lists your library directory.

   Note 1: Make sure that the syntax in the INPUT statements (lines 250–260) is appropriate for your system. If not, make any necessary changes. (The Minimal BASIC approach in Table 2.3 will work on any system.)

   Note 2: Does your system allow multicharacter variable names such as COLLEGE$, TUITION, ENROLLMENT, and REVENUE? If not, change these to C$, T, E, and R.

2. Try separate runs of the tuition revenue program in the preceding exercise to answer the following questions.
   a. What revenue will be generated if the tuition is increased to $875?
   b. What revenue will be generated if the tuition is increased to $875, and enrollment drops to 850?
   c. Validate each of your computer results by hand calculation. Validation is an important part of testing programs.

3. Make any necessary changes to the system commands table (Table C) inside the back cover and/or add other system commands of interest.

Debugging Programs

B *

Debugging is the process of detecting and correcting errors.[1] Much of your time, in fact, will be spent on this process. To help you along, we now define types of errors, illustrate them in actual computer runs, and indicate how you go about debugging such errors.

B.1 ERROR DETECTION AND CORRECTION

The process of uncovering and correcting errors requires an understanding of the possible types of errors and some classic techniques for their debugging.

Types of Errors

Any programming error will be one of the following:

1. Syntax error
2. Execution error
3. Logic error

A **syntax error** occurs when a BASIC statement violates a rule of the BASIC language. When we make this type of error, our program will fail to run, and the translator (compiler/interpreter) will identify the incorrect statement by an appropriate diagnostic message. Thus syntax errors are detected by the translator during the translation of the program.

An error that aborts execution of the program is said to be a **fatal error**. Virtually all syntax errors are fatal; that is, the program never enters the execution phase of a run.

Some syntax errors that are common when one is learning to program include the following.

---

*This module is best assigned immediately after Module A is assigned.

[1]According to computer lore, the term *bug* was born when the Mark I computer at Harvard University stopped working one day in 1945. It seems that a moth got crushed between a set of relay contacts, thereby causing the malfunction. The computer was "debugged" by removing the moth with tweezers.

1. **Typographical errors.**   Take care with typos; the computer isn't very permissive. For example, typing PRONT instead of PRINT yields a fatal error.

2. **Inattention to syntax.**   BASIC lives by the rules, and so must you. Pay attention to the rules that govern a particular statement. For example, note the correct spelling of keywords (such as READ) and special punctuation (such as the commas that separate items in a read list).

3. **Key confusion.**   Don't confuse the letter O key and the zero key. To help with this issue, many computer systems slash the zero. Also, those of you who are accustomed to using typewriters may have a tendency to substitute lowercase L for the digit 1, since these often look the same. This kind of mistake can be very difficult to debug and can cause any of the three types of errors (syntax, execution, or logic).

Once we determine the exact nature of our syntax error (with the help of error messages printed by the system), we simply replace the incorrect statement with a syntactically correct statement. This can be done either by entirely retyping the line that contains the error (the brute-force approach) or by using an editor (as described in Module A).

Our program executes completely only after it is free of syntax errors. Unfortunately, a second type of error can occur after the translation phase: An **execution error** is one that takes place during the execution of the program. Typically, when an execution error is encountered, an error message or code is printed, and the computer terminates execution (the error proves fatal). Common execution errors relating to the material in Chapter 2 include the following.

1. **Improper numeric condition during the evaluation of a numeric expression.**   For example, we might attempt to divide by a variable that has the value *zero* in its storage location, or we might attempt to raise a negative number to a noninteger power, or the evaluation might exceed the range of values allowed. If a computed value is larger than that allowed by the system, then an overflow error occurs; if smaller, then an underflow error message is printed. Many systems continue execution by assigning machine infinity (largest possible value) to the value that overflows and machine zero to the value that underflows.

2. **Initialization of variables.**   The act of giving a variable an initial value is called **initialization**. Just before execution most systems initialize all *numeric* variables to zero, but others don't. To illustrate the possible difficulties we might encounter, consider the following statement:

200 LET K = K + 1

Now, suppose that earlier in the program we did not *explicitly* assign a value to K. Usually one of two things will happen when the system executes this statement.

a. A value of zero is used for the K to the right of the equal sign. Thus the system itself initialized K to zero. This works fine if we want K to have an initial value of zero; otherwise, we have committed a logic error. In general, it's best to assign explicitly the initial values we want by LET, READ, or INPUT statements.

b. The system treats the initial contents of K as undefined and aborts execution due to a fatal execution error. Thus a variable used in a numeric expression must have been previously defined (assigned an explicit value) either through a LET statement or through input/read statements. For example, if we want *K* to have an initial value of zero before the execution of line 200, then earlier in the program we could write

10 LET K = 0

Systems that access the contents of an uninitialized *string* variable usually behave in a manner similar to uninitialized numeric variables; that is, either the system initializes the variable to a blank (instead of zero) or the system treats the contents as undefined. The former is more common.

3. Input/read errors.   See items 5 and 6 in Section 2.8 on page 34.

Generally, it's more difficult to determine the exact location and nature of an execution error than of a syntax error, for several reasons: execution errors tend to be system-dependent; execution-error messages may be more ambiguous than syntax-error messages in locating and diagnosing errors; and the cause of an execution error may be due to faulty program logic, which is related to the third category of errors.

If our program runs but gives us unexpected, unwanted, or erroneous output, then we may assume that a **logic error** exists. Common logic errors include the following:

1. No output.   Did you forget to include PRINT statements?

2. Wrong numeric results.

    a. Are the provided data correct?

    b. Are the numeric expressions and LET statements correct? In particular, check the sequence of arithmetic calculations in numeric expressions based on hierarchy rules.

    c. Is the program logic correct? For example, are the statements in proper sequence.

    d. Have any statements been omitted?

3. Wrong sequence of statements.   Sometimes an execution action is attempted before the appropriate value has been stored in a memory location. For example,

```
10 PRINT A  ←— PRINT precedes READ
20 READ A
30 DATA 50
99 END
```

either yields a logic error when a system initializes all variables to zero (the output will be 0 instead of 50) or yields an execution error because the value in A is undefined when line 10 is executed.

ADVICE   *Just because your program runs (that is, you get results) does not mean your program is correct—check your results for logic errors against a set of known results.* We cannot overemphasize the importance of this advice. In Step 4 of the four-step procedure, *always* validate your program under varying conditions using a set of test data for which you already know the correct results.

Classic Debugging Techniques

In your efforts to debug execution and logic errors, you might try the following classic debugging techniques.

1. **Roleplaying the computer.** Pretend that you're the computer and begin "executing" your program line by line. As you do this, enter data into boxes that represent storage locations. You will be surprised at how many errors you can find this way. Really. You should do this with every program you write. In practice, roleplaying is carried out by small groups of programmers and is called the **group walkthrough**, or **structured walkthrough**.

2. **Data validation techniques.** To check your data for read/input errors, place a PRINT statement immediately after each READ statement. The paired statements must have identical variable lists. Once you have confirmed that the data are correct, remove these statements. This technique is called **mirror**, or **echo**, **printing**. Other data validation techniques include **error routines** that trap user input errors and otherwise check for incorrect data types and values. We take a look at these approaches in Chapters 4 and 5.

3. **Diagnostic PRINT (trace) statements.** Place temporary PRINT statements at strategic points in your program. These should print the values of important variables as the calculating sequence evolves. In other words, these PRINT statements provide intermediate results that may be helpful in tracing what, where, and when something went wrong. When the error is corrected, remove these PRINT statements. Alternatively, we can halt or break program execution at strategic points either through a "break" key at the keyboard or by using **STOP statements** within the program. Then we can type

   PRINT list of important variables

   in **immediate mode**; that is, use a PRINT statement without a line number. The computer thus prints the current values of these variables. Finally, we can resume execution by typing the BASIC command **CONT**, which continues execution from the point at which the break occurred. *Will this approach work in your BASIC environment?*

4. **BASIC error-handling routines.** Special segments of code can be written that trap execution and syntax errors and follow with a programmer-specified action. These BASIC error-handling routines utilize the ON ERROR/GO TO statement, which we illustrate in Module E.

5. **Programming technique.** You will avoid many errors if you carefully practice the first three steps of our four-step program development cycle. Get in the habit now.

6. **Experience.** Learn by your mistakes. Experience is the classic teacher.

7. **Attitude.** Time and again we have seen students become frustrated and upset during the process of correcting errors. This is a good time to practice detachment. Actually, debugging can be fun. Finding and correcting errors can be a very satisfying experience. Perhaps you will become the greatest debugging sleuth in computer history.

Once we realize the exact nature of our errors, we can correct them either by typing new lines to replace old lines, by deleting certain lines, by adding new lines, or by changing lines using the system's editing capabilities. We illustrate this process next.

B.2 ILLUSTRATIONS

In this section we run the tuition revenue program once more, with syntax, execution, and logic errors purposely included. *Keep in mind that the specifics in these illustrations relate to the VAX-11 system (Example B.1) or the IBM PC system (Example B.2). If your system is different, pay attention to the general procedures and concepts, and then duplicate our run on your system.*

In these illustrations we shade the error messages printed by the computer. *To distinguish clearly what the computer prints from what the user types,* all user-typed text is in color.

E X A M P L E B . 1   VAX-11 Debugging Illustration

1.
```
100 REM   Tuition Revenue Program (Version 1.0)
110 REM-----------------------------------------------
250         INPUT "Enter college name --->"; COLLEGE$
255         INPIT "Enter tuition -------->"; TUITION
260         INPUT "Enter enrollment ----->"; ENROLLMENT
265 REM-----------------------------------------------
280         LET TUITION*ENROLLMENT = REVENUE
285 REM-----------------------------------------------
290         PRINT
300         PRINT "Revenue ..............$"; REVENUE
325 REM-----------------------------------------------
999         END
```

This program was entered with syntax errors in lines 255 and 280.

2.
```
RUN
NONAME          6-MAR-1984   14:24


Error on line 255

        255            INPIT "Enter tuition -------->"; TUITION



Error on line 280

        280            LET TUITION*ENROLLMENT = REVENUE

Ready
```

The BASIC compiler in the VAX-11 first compiles the entire source program. Execution is aborted because fatal **syntax errors** are encountered. These are listed one by one. We realize that INPIT should be INPUT in line 255 and that REVENUE must appear to the left of = in line 280.

3.
```
255            INPUT "Enter tuition -------->"; TUITION
280            LET REVENUE = TUITION^ENROLLMENT
```

The syntax errors are corrected by retyping the incorrect lines. Sometimes it's easier to retype lines entirely (if they're short), but usually it's best to use the system's editor (the screen-oriented one, ideally).

4.
```
RUN
NONAME          6-MAR-1984   14:30

Enter college name --->? Micro U
Enter tuition -------->? 750
Enter enrollment ----->? 1000
%BAS-F-FLOPOIERR, Floating point error or overflow
-BAS-I-USEPC_PSL,   at user PC=00074B00, PSL=03C00000
-BAS-I-FROLINMOD,   from line 280 in module NONAME
-MTH-F-FLOOVEMAT, floating overflow in math library
    user PC 0013BFED
Ready
```

The program is executed again. This time no syntax errors exist, since the program begins execution by prompting for input data; however, we use exponentiation (^) instead of multiplication (*) in line 280. This causes an **execution error** called overflow (result of calculation is larger than 10^{38}, the maximum for this system). On the VAX-11, this error is fatal, and execution terminates.

5.
```
280      LET REVENUE = TUITION*ENROLLMENT
```

Correction of line 280 by retyping the line.

6.
```
RUN
NONAME          6-MAR-1984   14:34


Enter college name --->? Micro U
Enter tuition -------->? 750
Enter enrollment ----->? 2000

Revenue ..............$ .15E+07
Ready
```

The program is run again. Previously calculated test data gave us revenue of $750,000, not the .15E+07 ($1,500,000) that the computer prints. Thus a **logic error** exists. The reason for the logic error is incorrect entry of enrollment data. It should be 1000, not 2000. To correct, we run the program again and enter the correct data.

7.
```
RUN
NONAME          6-MAR-1984   14:36

Enter college name --->?  Micro U
Enter tuition  -------->?  750
Enter enrollment ----->?  1000

Revenue ...............$
Ready
```
The program is executed again. Finally, we get the correct results.

E X A M P L E   B . 2   IBM PC Debugging Illustration

1.
```
100 REM   Tuition Revenue Program (Version 1.0)
110 REM---------------------------------------------------
250         INPUT "Enter college name --->"; COLLEGE$
255         INPIT "Enter tuition -------->"; TUITION
260         INPUT "Enter enrollment ----->"; ENROLLMENT
265 REM---------------------------------------------------
280         LET TUITION*ENROLLMENT = REVENUE
285 REM---------------------------------------------------
290         PRINT
300         PRINT "Revenue ...............$"; REVENUE
325 REM---------------------------------------------------
999         END
```
This program was entered with syntax errors in lines 255 and 280.

2.
```
RUN
Enter college name --->?  Micro U
Syntax error in 255
Ok
255         INPIT "Enter tuition -------->"; TUITION
```
The IBM PC interpreter first interprets a line and then executes it. Line 250 interprets without errors and then executes, so we enter the college name following the conversational prompt; however, a **syntax error** is encountered in line 255. The system aborts execution at this point and displays line 255 for review and full-screen editing.

3.
```
255         INPUT "Enter tuition -------->"; TUITION

LIST 255
255         INPUT "Enter tuition -------->"; TUITION
Ok
```
The syntax error is corrected by simply moving the cursor to the second I in INPIT and typing U. Next we press the "Enter" key and list the line to show that it stands corrected. *Note:* A corrected line on the screen is not corrected in the workspace until the "Enter" key is pressed while the cursor is on that line.

4.
```
RUN
Enter college name --->?  Micro U
Enter tuition  -------->?  750
Enter enrollment ----->?  1000
Syntax error in 280
Ok
280         LET TUITION*ENROLLMENT = REVENUE
```
The program is again executed, and another syntax error is detected, this time in line 280. We realize that REVENUE must be to the left of the = sign.

5.
```
280         LET REVENUE = TUITION^ENROLLMENT
```
The syntax error is corrected by retyping line 280.

6.
```
RUN
Enter college name --->?  Micro U
Enter tuition  -------->?  750
Enter enrollment ----->?  1000
Overflow

Revenue ...............$ 1.701412E+38
Ok
```
The program is executed again. This time no syntax errors exist; however, we used exponentiation (^) instead of multiplication (*) in line 280. This causes an **execution error** called overflow (result of calculation is greater than 1.7E + 38, the maximum value for this system). The error is not fatal on this system. Thus REVENUE is set to the maximum value in line 280, the overflow message is printed, and an incorrect value for REVENUE gets printed as part of the output.

7.
```
280         LET REVENUE = TUITION*ENROLLMENT
```
Correction of line 280 by retyping the line.

8.

```
RUN
Enter college name --->? Micro U
Enter tuition -------->? 750
Enter enrollment ----->? 2000

Revenue ...............$ 1500000
Ok
```

The program is executed again. Previously calculated test data gave us revenue of $750,000, not the $1,500,000 that the computer prints. Thus a **logic error** exists.

The reason for the logic error is incorrect entry of enrollment data. It should be 1000, not 2000. To correct, we run the program again and enter the correct data.

9.

```
RUN
Enter college name --->? Micro U
Enter tuition -------->? 750
Enter enrollment ----->? 1000

Revenue ...............$ 750000
Ok
```

The program is executed again. Finally, we get the correct results.

NOTE 1 BASIC compilers (as in Example B.1) print all syntax error messages in one place following the RUN command. BASIC interpreters print only one syntax error at a time (as in Example B.2). *Are you using a compiler or an interpreter?*

NOTE 2 The compiler or interpreter will identify syntax errors, and the operating system will print execution error messages; but *we* must identify any logic errors by validating the output.

NOTE 3 *Any time we edit a line, replace an old line with a new line, delete a line, or insert a line, the change is made in the workspace, not in the library.* So if we want to use the corrected program at a later date, we must type the system command that replaces the incorrect program in the library with the correct program in the workspace.

FOLLOW-UP EXERCISES

1. With respect to our debugging illustration:
  a. Duplicate it on your system, noting any differences. Practice line changes using your system's editor.
  b. Once your program is error-free, try deleting line 255 and see what happens. Do you get an execution error in line 280 (undefined variable TUITION) or do you get a logic error (as shown by the output value for REVENUE) because TUITION is initialized to zero?

2. Practice some of the classic debugging techniques discussed on pages 147–148.

Built-In Functions

C *

BASIC includes numeric functions to handle common mathematical calculations and string functions for manipulating letters, phrases, and words. This module defines built-in functions and illustrates their use.

C.1 BUILT-IN NUMERIC FUNCTIONS

Suppose we wish to determine the square root of the arithmetic expression

$$b^2 - 4ac$$

and to store it in the address labeled Y. As you know, we could simply use the statement

    LET Y = (B^2 − 4*A*C)^0.5

An alternative approach is to use the following SQR (SQuare Root) function:

    LET Y = SQR(B^2 − 4*A*C)

The right-hand side of this statement is called a **built-in function**,[1] which can be generalized as follows:

Built-in Function

    function name (argument)
                    └──────┘
                        ↑   ── Not always required,
                                          depending on the function
    SQR (B^2 − 4*A*C)

---

*This module can be covered anytime after Chapter 3, except for Example C.3, which uses the WHILE statement found in Chapter 5.

[1]Other commonly used terms for built-in functions are **BASIC-supplied function, implementation-supplied function**, and **library function**.

The **function name** is a keyword of three letters. In our example, SQR is the function name. The **argument** is any valid numeric expression in the case of numeric functions and any valid string expression in the case of string functions. In our example, the numeric argument is B^2 − 4*A*C. The purpose of the SQR function, of course, is to determine the square root of the argument. For example, if A stores 10, B stores 7, and C stores 1, then the argument is evaluated as 9, and the SQR function returns the value 3.

Built-in functions in BASIC can be grouped into the four categories shown in Table C.1.[2] We might note that Table C.1 just shows some of the more popular built-in functions. Any BASIC dialect includes additional functions as well, which you should check out in your system's BASIC manual. The algebraic, arithmetic, and utility functions are broadly used across disciplines like business, the social and physical sciences, and engineering. The string functions are popular in business, social science, and the arts. The built-in string functions comprise a numerous and important class of specialized functions, which are best treated in a separate table (see Table C.2).

Study the examples in Table C.1 and note the following points.

1. **Function call.** The built-in function is implemented, referenced, or called by using its function name followed by the parenthetically enclosed argument, if required.

2. **Whence came the function?** The machine-language instructions for evaluating the function are provided by the translator (interpreter or compiler). For example, to find the natural logarithm of a number, we would use the LOG function. When the translator processes the LOG function, it provides a set of prewritten instructions that calculates the natural logarithm of the argument.

3. **Motivation for use.** The use of built-in functions within our programs has several advantages.

    a. For certain standardized tasks, as in calculating logarithms, it saves us programming effort by not having to "reinvent the wheel" (write these instructions ourselves) each time we wish to perform the same task.

    b. Prewritten systems instructions for evaluating functions are more computationally efficient than those that might be written by the programmer in a high-level language such as BASIC. For example, an SQR function requires less processing time than raising an expression to the 0.5 power.

    c. The use of a built-in function is stylistically preferred, since the task suggested by the function name is well understood by any programmer that might read a listing of the program.

In the next example, we illustrate common uses of the INT and RND functions.

---

[2]For simplicity we omit a fifth category, trigonometric functions. These are primarily used in engineering and the physical sciences.

Table C.1 Selected Built-in Functions

Category	Function[a]	Dialects[b]	Purpose	Argument	Algebraic Example	BASIC Example	Result
Algebraic	1. **EXP(X)**	1, 2, 3	Exponential of X, or antilog of X, or base e raised to Xth power	Numeric value	$y = ae^{2t}$	LET Y = A*EXP(−2*T)	A 10 T 0.5 Y 3.678795
	2. **LOG(X)**	1, 2, 3	Natural (base e) logarithm of X	Positive numeric value	$p = q \ln 5$	LET P = Q*LOG(5)	Q 1 P 1.609438
	3. **SQR(X)**	1, 2, 3	Square root of X	Positive numeric value	$r = (\sqrt{s})(t + 1)^2$	LET R = SQR(S)*(T + 1)^2	S 9 T 4 R 75
Arithmetic	4. **ABS(X)**	1, 2, 3	Absolute value of X	Numeric value	$z = |x - y|$	LET Z = ABS(X − Y)	X 4 Y 10 Z 6
	5. **INT(X)**	1, 2, 3	Greatest integer less than or equal to X	Numeric value	$k = [a/b]$	LET K = INT(A/B)	A −8 B 3 K −3
	6. **IP(X)** 1 or **FIX(X)** 2, 3		Integer part of X	Numeric value	$k = [a/b]$	LET K = IP(A/B) or LET K = FIX(A/B)	A −8 B 3 K −2
	7. **SGN(X)**	1, 2, 3	Algebraic sign of X	Numeric value	$y = \begin{cases} -1 & \text{if } X < 0 \\ 0 & \text{if } X = 0 \\ +1 & \text{if } X > 0 \end{cases}$	LET Y = SGN(X)	X −10 Y −1
Utility	8. **RND**	1, 2, 3	Uniformly distributed random real number between 0.0 and 1.0	Not required	$y = 0 \le m < 1$	LET Y = RND	Y 6291626
	9. **DATE$** or (1)(2)		Returns current date in form of: yyyymmdd / mm-dd-yyyy	Not required / Not required		PRINT DATE$	19860727 / 07-27-1986
	DATE$(0) 3		dd-Mmm-yy	Integer value		PRINT DATE$(0)	27-Jul-86
	10. **TIME$** 1, 2 or **TIME$(0)** 3		Returns current time in form of: hh:mm:ss / hh:mm AM or PM	Not required / Integer value		PRINT TIME$ / PRINT TIME$(0)	13:55:31 / 01:56 PM
Strings	See Table C.2.						

[a]The symbol X refers to any expression, including a single numeric variable or single numeric constant.

[b]1 = ANS BASIC and True BASIC   2 = IBM PC (Microsoft) BASIC   3 = VAX-11 BASIC   4 = your system (if different)

Table C.2 Selected Built-In String Functions

Function	Dialects[a]	Meaning	Examples	Results
LEN(e$)	1,2,3	Returns the number of characters in the string expression e$	LEN ("I LOVE BASIC") LEN (" ") LEN("")	12 1 0
LEFT$(e$,n)	2,3	Returns the first n characters of the string expression e$	LEFT$("I LOVE BASIC",5) LEFT$("I LOVE BASIC",1) LEFT$("I LOVE BASIC",0)	I LOVE I null or empty value
RIGHT$(e$,n)	2	Returns the last n characters of the string expression e$	RIGHT$("I LOVE BASIC",5) RIGHT$("I LOVE BASIC",12)	BASIC I LOVE BASIC
	or			
	3	Returns the characters starting in position n of the string expression e$ and ending in the rightmost character	RIGHT$("I LOVE BASIC",5) RIGHT$("I LOVE BASIC",12)	VE BASIC C
MID$(e$,p,n)	2,3	Returns n characters starting at position p in the string expression e$	MID$("I LOVE BASIC",3,4) LEFT$(MID$("I LOVE BASIC",8,5),2)	LOVE BA
INSTR(e$,s$)	2,3	Searches the string expression e$ for the occurrence of a substring s$ and returns the beginning position of the substring. A zero is returned if no match occurs	INSTR("I LOVE BASIC","BASIC") INSTR("I LOVE BASIC","basic")	8 0
or				
POS(e$,s$)	1		POS("I LOVE BASIC","BASIC") POS("I LOVE BASIC","basic")	8 0

Concatenation Operator	Dialects[a]	Meaning	Examples	Results
+	2 3	Act of joining two or more strings to form one larger string	PRINT "Mrs. " + "Calabash" FIRST$ = "Frank"	Mrs. Calabash
&	1		LAST$ = "Newman" PRINT LAST$ + ", " + FIRST$	Newman, Frank

(Use this space for describing other string functions that are of interest on your system.)

[a]Dialects: 1 = ANS BASIC and True BASIC; 2 = IBM PC (Microsoft) BASIC; 3 = VAX-11 BASIC; 4 = your system (if different)

E X A M P L E   C . 1   **State Lottery Numbers Using the RND Function**

The RND function is used to generate a uniform real number between 0.0 and 1.0 (including 0.0 but less than 1.0). By *uniform* we mean that every decimal value between 0.0 and 1.0 has an equal chance of occurring. This function is particularly useful in computer simulation models.

To illustrate the RND function, we consider a program for simulating a state lottery that generates a three-digit winning number each day. To select the winning number, many states use a machine with 10 "whirling" balls numbered 0, 1, 2, 3, 4, 5, 6, 7, 8, 9. These balls are randomly whirled by air streams, so that the machine selection of any one ball is as likely as the selection of any other ball. Thus, digits between 0 and 9 have an equal chance of occurring. To generate a three-digit random number, the lottery commission simply uses three different machines of the type described.

We simulate the lottery drawing with the following program:

```
100 REM  State lottery drawing
110 REM
120      INPUT "Enter number of digits in lottery"; N
130      PRINT
140      PRINT "The winning number for tonight is ";
150 REM
160      FOR J = 1 TO N
170        LET DIGIT = INT(10*RND)
180        PRINT DIGIT;
190      NEXT J
200 REM
999      END

RUN
Enter number of digits in lottery? 3

The winning number for tonight is  6  1  6
```

The variable DIGIT stores an integer number between 0 and 9 inclusive. We guarantee that each number (0 to 9) has an equal chance of being generated by using the random number function RND. Several steps are needed to produce each random digit, as illustrated in line 170. First, a random number between 0 and 1, but less than 1, is generated using the function RND. Then the random number is scaled into the range 0 to 10, but less than 10, using the expression 10*RND. Finally, the INT function is used to create a random digit between 0 and 9. Thus, for the given run we obtain the sequence:

RND	10*RND	INT(10*RND)	
.6291626	6.291626	6	← first random digit
.1948297	1.948297	1	← second random digit
.6305799	6.305799	6	← third random digit

which gives 616, the winning lottery number.

On most systems, this program will generate the same lottery number, or sequence of random digits, each time the lottery program is run. This undesirable result occurs in systems that generate random numbers from the same internal value called a seed. Unless the seed is changed for each run, the sequence of random numbers is the same. The following program illustrates this behavior.

```
100 REM  Sequence of 5 random numbers
110 REM
120      FOR J = 1 TO 5
130        PRINT RND;
140      NEXT J
150 REM
999      END

RUN
  .6291626  .1948297  .6305799  .8625749  .736353


RUN
  .6291626  .1948297  .6305799  .8625749  .736353
```

Same sequence of 5 random numbers

The ability to generate identical sequences of random numbers is useful for debugging simulation models and for other statistical purposes, but for some situations such as the lottery example, it's undesirable. The RANDOMIZE statement can be used to generate different sequences of random numbers each time the program is run. The general form of this statement is

RANDOMIZE Statement

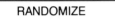

For example, the program

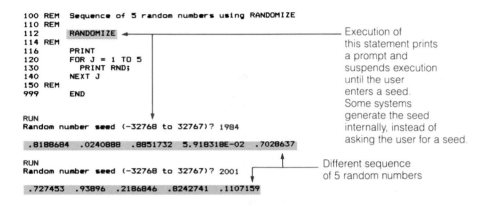

```
100 REM   Sequence of 5 random numbers using RANDOMIZE
110 REM
112       RANDOMIZE
114 REM
116       PRINT
120       FOR J = 1 TO 5
130          PRINT RND;
140       NEXT J
150 REM
999       END

RUN
Random number seed (-32768 to 32767)? 1984

 .8188684  .0240888  .8851732  5.918318E-02  .7028637

RUN
Random number seed (-32768 to 32767)? 2001

 .727453  .93896  .2186846  .8242741  .1107159
```

Execution of this statement prints a prompt and suspends execution until the user enters a seed. Some systems generate the seed internally, instead of asking the user for a seed.

Different sequence of 5 random numbers

generates a different sequence of random numbers each time the user enters a different seed. This particular example illustrates the approach taken in Microsoft BASIC on the IBM PC. Other systems, however, may internally generate their own unpredictable seed each time the RANDOMIZE statement is executed (as on the VAX-11, for example). *How does your system implement the RANDOMIZE statement?*

C.2 BUILT-IN STRING FUNCTIONS

BASIC also includes **built-in string functions** that specifically process and manipulate string data, as summarized in Table C.2 for selected string functions.

E X A M P L E   C . 2   **Line Centering with the LEN Function**

We can use the following formula to center a title or heading on a report line:

$$\text{Starting print position} = \frac{\text{total length of line} - \text{length of heading}}{2}$$

In line 130 of the program below, the LEN function is used to find the length or number of characters in the title PAYROLL REPORT. This number is used in the formula on line 140 to determine the starting print position for the title. Finally, the starting print position is used as the argument of the TAB function in line 150.

```
100 REM   Line centering using the LEN function
105 REM
110       LET HEAD$        = "PAYROLL REPORT"
120       LET LINE.LENGTH = 80
130       LET HEAD.LENGTH = LEN(HEAD$)
140       LET START       = INT( (LINE.LENGTH - HEAD.LENGTH)/2 )
145 REM
150       PRINT TAB(START); HEAD$
155 REM
999       END

RUN
```

Length function (line 120)

Start column = 33 (see lines 140–150)

PAYROLL REPORT

Head length = 14 (see line 130)

Line length = 80 (see line 120)

E X A M P L E   C . 3   User Entry Stripping with the LEFT$ Function

In an interactive program it's best to anticipate various entries a user may give in response to a prompt. In the following program responses like *yes*, *ye*, and *y* are treated as acceptable responses by a user to continue execution of the program.

```
100 REM   Stripping using the LEFT$ function
105 REM
110       LET ANSWER$ = "yes"
115 REM
120       WHILE LEFT$(ANSWER$,1) = "y"
130         PRINT "Hello"
140         PRINT
150         INPUT "Do you want another run (y/n) "; ANSWER$
160       WEND
165 REM
170       PRINT
180       PRINT "End of run."
185 REM
999       END
```

LEFT$ function strips all characters but the leftmost or first

```
RUN
Hello

Do you want another run (y/n) ? yes
Hello

Do you want another run (y/n) ? ye
Hello

Do you want another run (y/n) ? n

End of run.
```

Line 120 uses the LEFT$ function to strip off or ignore all but the first character of the user's response.

E X A M P L E   C . 4   Date Substrings with the MID$ and RIGHT$ Functions

In the United States the date is often expressed as a string in the form

mm/dd/yy

where *mm* is a two-digit month, *dd* is a two-digit day of the month, and *yy* is the last two digits of the year. Sometimes we need to extract the year, month, or day to use separately in some other part of the program, as the following illustrates.

```
100 REM    Date substrings using the RIGHT$ and MID$ functions
105 REM
110        INPUT "Date of sale"; SALES.DATE$
115 REM
120        LET YEAR$ = RIGHT$(SALES.DATE$,2) ←— RIGHT$ function finds the year substring
130        PRINT "  Year of sale: "; YEAR$
135 REM
140        LET DAY$  = MID$(SALES.DATE$,4,2) ←— MID$ function finds the day substring
150        PRINT "  Day  of sale: "; DAY$
155 REM
999        END

RUN
Date of sale? 08/03/85
  Year of sale: 85
  Day  of sale: 03
```

In line 120 the RIGHT$ function is used to find the year substring by assigning the last two digits of the variable SALES.DATE$ to the variable YEAR$. In line 140 the MID$ function is used to extract the day of the sale. The MID$ function extracts two characters beginning with the fourth position in SALES.DATE$ and stores the day substring in the variable DAY$.

C.3 POINTERS

1. **Use built-in functions.**   Don't write your own code to accomplish what a built-in function can accomplish. It's more efficient and stylistically preferred to use built-in functions.

2. **Transportability.**   String built-in functions are more dialect-specific than their numeric counterparts. If a program is to be used on more than one system or is to be ported to another system at a later date, then particular attention must be given to any differences in the built-in string functions.

3. **Logic errors.**   These are the most common errors in string processing, so it pays to devote special attention to test data selection and output validation during the testing phase. It's especially important to roleplay difficult logic.

4. **Returned numeric versus string values.**   Pay attention to whether a built-in string function returns a numeric value or a string value. *If the name of the function ends in a $ sign, then we can be sure the function returns a string value.* For example, LEN(A$) returns a numeric value, and LEFT$(A$,N) returns a string value.

FOLLOW-UP EXERCISES

1. In Table C.1 look at the column labeled *BASIC Example* and answer the following:
   a. Example 1. What is stored in Y if 2 is stored in A and 4 is in T?
   b. Example 2. What is stored in P if 10 is stored in Q?
   c. Example 3. What is stored in R if 25 is in S and 3 is in T?
   d. Example 4. What is stored in Z if 5.4 is in X and 2.1 is in Y? If 5.4 is in X and 7.4 is in Y?
   e. Example 5. What is stored in K if 7 is in A and 2 is in B? If 7.6 is in A and 2 is in B? If 6 is in A and 2 is in B? If −7.6 is in A and 2 is in B?

   f. Example 6. Answer the same questions as in part e.
   g. Example 7. What is stored in Y if −73.2 is stored in X? If 105 is in X? If 0 is in X?

*2. With respect to the first program in Example C.1:
   a. Modify the program to generate seven three-digit lottery numbers, one for each day of the week. Print the three digits of a lottery number on the same line as its corresponding day. Each lottery number is to appear on a separate line. This program is to be used week after week by a lottery commission, so make sure you don't generate the same numbers each week.

b. Implement this program on your system.

*3. **Coin-Flip Simulation.**   Write and run a program that simulates *N* flips of a coin, where *N* is input by the user. Remember that a fair, or balanced, coin will theoretically result in 50% heads and 50% tails over the long run (which none of us is destined to witness). Consider a random number between 0 and less than 0.5 to be a head and one between 0.5 and less than 1.0 to be a tail.

a. Simulate 10, then 50, then 100, and finally 1000 flips of a coin. Visually count the number of heads and tails. Any interesting results?

b. Use the IF/THEN statement from Chapter 4 to count the number of heads and tails for you. Next to each random number that is printed, print whether it represents a head or a tail. Then print each count and the proportion of heads and tails that were simulated.

4. Specify exactly what is output for each PRINT statement.

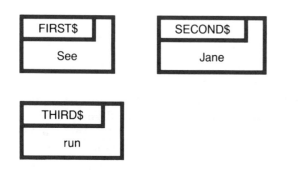

a. PRINT FIRST$ + SECOND$ + THIRD$
b. PRINT FIRST$ + " " + SECOND$ + " " + THIRD$
c. PRINT SECOND$ + " " + FIRST$
d. PRINT THIRD$ + THIRD$ + THIRD$

5. In Example C.2:
   a. In what column or print position is the *P* in PAY-ROLL? Show by hand how this is calculated.
   b. Modify the program so that dashed lines are centered under the report title.

6. In Example C.3:
   a. Is the response *yep* acceptable?
   b. Suppose the user were to mistakenly hit the *t* key instead of the *y* key. What happens?
   *c. Correct the problem in part **b** by modifying the program to trap any entries that don't begin with *y* or *n*.

7. Modify Example C.4 so:
   a. The month is extracted and printed.
   b. The year is printed in the form 19yy.

*8. Write a short program that enters product *id* as a four-digit string value. Then use the LEN function to verify that the product *id* is valid by not being more than four digits. If the product *id* is valid, then print the message *valid*; else print *invalid*. Use the following test data: 1234, 123, 12345.

*9. Write a short program that uses the DATE$ function on your system along with built-in string functions to print dates in the following formats:
   a. yymmdd   Example: 861225
   b. dd–mm–yyyy   Example: 25–12–1986
   c. Mmm dd, yyyy Example: Dec 25, 1986

*10. A person's name is stored in the string variable FULL.NAME$ in the format

   first name <space> last name

   Write a short program that manipulates the string and prints the name in the following format:

   last name, <space> first name

   Use the following test data: Harvey Core
                                            H. Core

PRINT USING Statement and Formatted Output

D*

Many computerized reports require more precise control and more features than PRINT statements can provide. The statements in this module allow us to implement **formatted output**, which means that the output line is printed precisely according to an image that we provide.

D.1 PRINT USING STATEMENT AND FORMAT STRINGS

Compare the two sets of output below. The first version uses PRINT statements, while the second version uses PRINT USING statements. Notice that version B is easier to read and more attractive than version A.

Version A: Based on PRINTs.

```
                    PAYROLL REPORT

     ---------------------------------------------------
       Name          Hours        Rate        Pay
     ---------------------------------------------------
     Phil Murray     15           6.35        95.25
     Hilda Snark     30.25        5.85        176.9625
     Margo Barker    32           6.8         217.6
     Ralph Kiner     20.75        6.25        129.6875
     Mark Fargo      35           6           210
     Anna AlDente    38           7.78        295.64
     ---------------------------------------------------
     Totals                                   1125.14
```

*This module can be covered anytime after Chapter 2, except for Section D.3, which requires Chapter 3.

Version B: Based on PRINT USINGs.

```
                       PAYROLL REPORT

     ---------------------------------------------------
         Name              Hours      Rate       Pay
     ---------------------------------------------------
     Phil Murray           15.00      6.35       95.25
     Hilda Snark           30.25      5.85      176.96
     Margo Barker          32.00      6.80      217.60
     Ralph Kiner           20.75      6.25      129.69
     Mark Fargo            35.00      6.00      210.00
     Anna AlDente          38.00      7.78      295.64
     ---------------------------------------------------
     Totals                                 $1,125.14
```

In general the **PRINT USING statement** allows us to conveniently implement the following features:

1. *Right-justify* (align on the right) rather than left-justify numeric output
2. Round numbers to a specified number of decimal places
3. Align a column of numbers so that decimal points appear one below the other
4. Insert commas into a number
5. Assign a fixed or floating dollar sign to a number
6. Output numeric values in exponential notation
7. Insert blanks and other characters at any location

As usual in life, we pay a price for our benefits: the PRINT USING statement includes demanding detail, and BASIC dialects vary in their implementation. The general form of this statement for several systems is illustrated in Table D.1.

For either version of the PRINT USING statement an image of the output
line is written using a format string that describes how the items in the output
line are to be printed. The **format string** is a string expression containing one
or more **format fields (format items)**. A format field controls the output of a
single value. There are three types of format fields: **numeric format fields** for
printing numeric values, **string format fields** for printing string values, and
literal format fields for printing unquoted string constants as labels, headings, and so on. Numeric and string format fields contain one or more consecutive **format characters (format symbols)**. In Table D.1,

- ###.#   is a numeric format field or item
- #   is the format character or symbol for printing digits
- .   is the format character or symbol for locating the decimal point

Table D.1 Variations of the PRINT USING Statement

Dialect	Structure	Examples *Note:* Assume VALUE stores 50.76. All three examples print the output value 50.8 in columns 2–5.
VAX-11 BASIC Microsoft BASIC	**PRINT USING** *format string; output list* where *format string* is a string expression that provides an image of how the items in the output list are to be printed. The format string can be either a string constant (Example 1) or a string variable (Example 2). *output list* is a list of constants, variables, and/or expressions whose values are to be printed according to the format string.	1. PRINT USING "###.#"; VALUE 2. LET F$ = "###.#" PRINT USING F$; VALUE ———— Format string
ANS BASIC True BASIC	*Version 1:* The same as VAX-11 and Microsoft, except use a colon (:) instead of a semicolon (;) to separate the format string from the output list. *Version 2:* **PRINT USING** *image line no: output list* *image line no.* **IMAGE:** *format string* where *image line number* is a numeric constant that identifies the IMAGE statement with the format string *output list* is defined above *format string* is an unquoted string constant beginning immediately to the right of the colon (:) that provides an image of how the items in the output list are to be printed. (See Example 3.)	Image line number 3. 40 PRINT USING 50: VALUE 50 IMAGE:###.# ———— Format string

Your system
(if different)

Table D.2 Selected Format Characters or Symbols

Format Symbol	Description (Note any differences between this table and your system)
#	Each pound sign (#) represents a digit position within a numeric format field.
.	The decimal point (.) represents an actual decimal point inserted into the printed output.
,	The comma (,) prints a comma between every third digit to the left of the decimal point.
$	A single dollar sign as the first character in a numeric format field prints a dollar sign in that position.
$$	A double dollar sign at the beginning of a numeric format field prints a dollar sign to the immediate left of the most significant digit.
\ \	Two back-slash symbols separating n spaces indicate the starting and ending positions of a string format field for printing string values (the field width or length is $n+2$ character positions).[a]

---

[a]ANS BASIC uses the pound symbol (#) instead of back-slashes to print string values.

Table D.2 identifies a popular subset of format symbols that are used in ANS, VAX, and Microsoft versions of BASIC.

D.2 FORMAT FIELDS AND SYMBOLS

This section illustrates how we can design some common format fields.

Printing Numeric Values

Numeric values are printed by using the pound symbol (#) as a format symbol. The symbol is repeated for each numeric digit of the field. For example, study the following program and its output.

E X A M P L E D . 1 Numeric Values

Program	Output	Comments

```
100 REM   Numeric values
105 REM
110       LET X = 10
120       LET Y = -3
125 REM
130       PRINT USING "##" ; X          10      Printed in columns 1 and 2
140       PRINT USING "###"; X          10      Printed in columns 2 and 3 (see note 1)
150       PRINT USING "#"  ; X          %10     Insufficient field width (see note 2)
160       PRINT USING "###"; Y          -3      Printed in columns 2 and 3 (see note 3)
170       PRINT USING "### ##"; X,Y     10  -3  X is printed in columns 2 and 3, and Y is printed in columns 6 and 7 (see note 4)
180       PRINT USING "### ##"; X       10      X is printed in columns 2 and 3 (see note 5)
190       PRINT USING "##" ; X,Y        10-3    X is printed in columns 1 and 2, and Y is printed in columns 3 and 4 (see note 6)
998 REM
999       END
```

Consider the following points concerning the # symbol:

1. If the number of # symbols is greater than the number of digits stored in the variable, then the numeric value is right-justified within the format field. See line 140 in Example D.1.

2. If the value stored in the variable is larger than the number of digits in the format field, then the value is displayed with a percent sign (%) before the value to indicate an insufficient field width. See line 150 in Example D.1.

3. A # symbol reserves space for a digit or a minus sign (if the number is negative). See line 160 in Example D.1.

4. Two or more items in the output list imply the use of multiple format fields within the format string. Multiple format fields are separated by spaces, as follows:

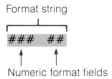

See line 170 in Example D.1.

5. *If the number of items in the output list is less than the number of format fields within the format string, then the extra format fields are ignored.* See the output for line 180 in Example D.1. In this case, the single output-list item X is printed based on the first numeric field ###. The second numeric field ## is ignored.

6. *If more items are in the output list than in the format fields within the format string, then the format string is repeatedly used to output the remaining items.* See the output for line 190 in Example D.1. Here we have two items in the output list (X and Y), but only one numeric field within the format string (##). Thus, the 10 in X is printed in columns 1 and 2 using ##; then the −3 in Y is printed in columns 3 and 4 again using the same ##.

Printing Numeric Values with a Decimal Point

Decimal or real values are printed by using the # symbol and a single decimal point as a format symbol. The placement of the decimal point indicates its precise location, and the number of # symbols to the right of the decimal point specifies the number of decimal places to be output. For example, study the following program and its output.

E X A M P L E   D . 2   Numeric Values with a Decimal Point

Program	Output	Comments
100 REM Numeric values with decimal point		
105 REM		
110 LET X = 57.183		
115 REM		
120 PRINT USING "##.###" ; X	57.183	Printed as stored
130 PRINT USING "##.##" ; X	57.18	Rounded to 2 places (see note 1)
140 PRINT USING "##.#" ; X	57.2	Rounded to 1 place
150 PRINT USING "##.####"; X	57.1830	Unused position filled with zero (see note 2)
998 REM		
999 END		

Note the following concerning the decimal point symbol:

1. When the value stored in the variable contains more decimal positions than the width of the format field, then the printed value is rounded to the number of decimal places shown in the format field. See lines 130 and 140 in Example D.2.

2. When the fractional part to be output has fewer decimal positions than specified in the format field, then the unused symbols are filled with zeros. See line 150 in Example D.2.

Printing Numeric Values with a Comma

To make larger numbers more readable, a comma can be inserted in the format field. This symbol causes a comma to be printed between every third digit to the left of the decimal point.

E X A M P L E   D . 3   Numeric Values with a Comma

Program	Output	Comments

```
100 REM   Numeric values with comma
105 REM
110       LET X = 16032
120       LET Y = 478
125 REM
130       PRINT USING "##,###" ; X      16,032  ◄── Field width is 6 since comma takes up a space
140       PRINT USING "##,###" ; Y         478  ◄── A leading comma is not printed
998 REM
999       END
```

Printing Numeric Values with a Dollar Sign

To print the currency symbol in the output, the dollar sign($) format symbol is placed in the format field. There are two ways the $ symbol can be used: in either a fixed position or a floating position. When the format field begins with two dollars signs ($$), the $ sign is printed to the immediate left of the number. This is often called a floating dollar sign. If the format field begins with a single dollar sign ($), then the $ sign is printed in the exact position found in the format field. This is sometimes called a fixed dollar sign.

E X A M P L E   D . 4   Numeric Values with a Dollar Sign

Program	Output	Comments

```
100 REM   Numeric values with $
105 REM
110       LET X = 6.03
120       LET Y = .57
130       LET Z = 4327.52
135 REM
140       PRINT USING "$###.##"; X      $  6.03  ◄──── Fixed dollar sign
150       PRINT USING "$$##.##"; X        $6.03  ◄──── Floating dollar sign
160       PRINT USING "$$##.##"; Y        $0.57  ◄──── Floating dollar sign. Note zero before decimal point
170       PRINT USING "$$##.##"; Z      %$4327.52 ◄─── Field width is not large enough
998 REM
999       END
```

Printing String Variables

Data stored in string variables can be output with a string field. A pair of backslash (\) symbols are used to specify the beginning and end of the string format field. Blank spaces are included between the backslashes to determine the width of the field.

E X A M P L E D . 5 String Variables

Program	Output	Comments
100 REM String variables 105 REM 110 LET N$ = "HELP" 115 REM ------ 120 PRINT USING "\ \"; N$	HELP	Field width is 6. Value printed in columns 1–4 (see note 2).
130 PRINT USING "\ \" ; N$	HELP	Field width is 4. Value printed in columns 1–4.
140 PRINT USING "\ \" ; N$	HEL	Field width is 3. Lose rightmost character (see note 3).
998 REM 999 END		

Consider the following points concerning the backslash (\) symbol.

1. The two backslashes define the beginning and end of the string format field. If n spaces appear between the two backslashes, then the field width is $n + 2$. In our example, field widths of 6, 4, and 3 were used.

2. When the number of characters in the string value is fewer than the field width, then the characters are printed left-justified in the field, and the remaining positions are filled with blanks. See line 120 in Example D.5.

3. When the number of characters in the string value is greater than the field width, then the rightmost characters are truncated. See line 140 in Example D.5.

Printing String Constants (Literals)

Messages, titles, and labeled output can also be printed with the PRINT USING statement. A **literal format field** is a set of characters other than format characters that is to be printed exactly (literally) as it appears in the format string. The following example illustrates the labeling of output with literal fields.

E X A M P L E D . 6 String Constants (Literals)

Program	Output	Comments
100 REM Literal fields 105 REM 110 LET FMT1$ = "REVENUES: $###.##" 120 LET FMT2$ = "COSTS : $###.##" 130 LET FMT3$ = "PROFITS : $###.##" 135 REM 140 READ REVENUE,COST 150 DATA 40.05,45.20 155 REM 160 LET PROFIT = REVENUE - COST 165 REM		Note how each format string has a literal field that labels the numeric field to its right. Also note how format strings are stored within the string variables FMT1$, FMT2$, and FMT3$ in lines 110–130. These string variables are then referenced in lines 170–190.
170 PRINT USING FMT1$; REVENUE	REVENUES: $ 40.05	
180 PRINT USING FMT2$; COST	COSTS : $ 45.20	
190 PRINT USING FMT3$; PROFIT	PROFITS : $ -5.15	
998 REM 999 END		

The following points are illustrated in Example D.6.

1. Each format string is stored in a special string variable which is referenced by the appropriate PRINT USING statement. For example, the string variable FMT1$ stores the first format string in line 110. Then this variable is used in line 170 to print the revenue. Note that the format string in line 110 contains two fields: the literal field REVENUES: and the numeric field $###.##.

2. All format strings are placed in a group to facilitate the alignment of output. (See lines 110–130.)

D.3 BUILDING A COMPLETE REPORT

The real value of the PRINT USING statement becomes evident when we format an entire report. To illustrate this point, let's consider a payroll program that calculates gross pay and prints the employee name, hours worked, rate of pay, and gross pay.

Before we encode format strings for a report, it's best to design the actual layout of the report on a sheet of paper. Ideally, the paper should have column and row markings, such as quadrille paper or special computer forms called print charts.

A sample payroll report layout is illustrated by the print chart in Figure D.1. In the report layout, report headings such as titles and column labels are aligned above the detail lines that appear within the body of the output table. Numeric values using the # symbol (including any decimal points) and string values using the x (or some other) symbol are placed exactly where they would appear on the printed line. Spacing between fields is designated by blank spaces on the layout sheet. Finally, the report footing, or ending, is designated by appropriate labels and field values.

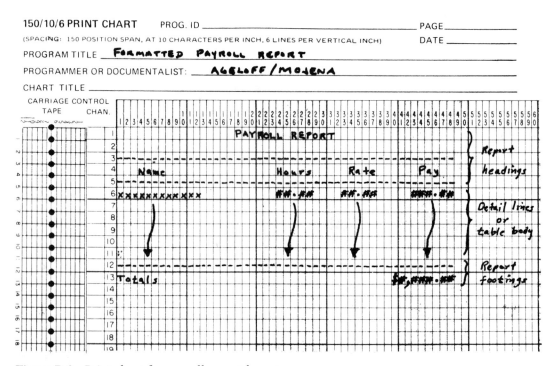

Figure D.1 Print chart for payroll report layout

The following program demonstrates the use of PRINT USING statements for building the formatted report described in Figure D.1.

E X A M P L E   D . 7   Formatted Payroll Report

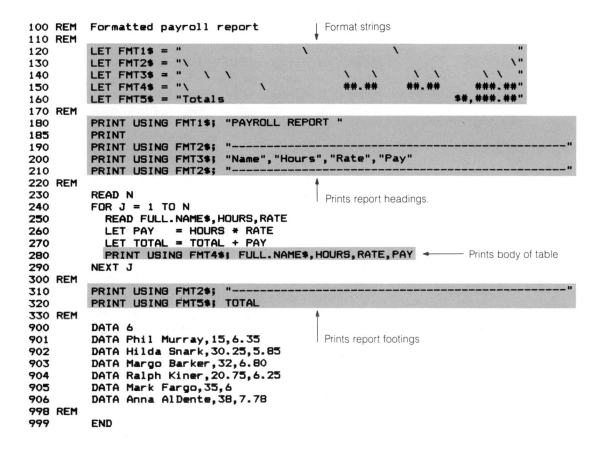

```
100 REM   Formatted payroll report                    | Format strings
110 REM
120       LET FMT1$ = "                    \                    \                    "
130       LET FMT2$ = "\                                                            \"
140       LET FMT3$ = "   \   \                      \   \        \   \        \   \ "
150       LET FMT4$ = "\              \              ##.##    ##.##    ###.##"
160       LET FMT5$ = "Totals                                          $#,###.##"
170 REM
180       PRINT USING FMT1$; "PAYROLL REPORT "
185       PRINT
190       PRINT USING FMT2$; "------------------------------------------------"
200       PRINT USING FMT3$; "Name","Hours","Rate","Pay"
210       PRINT USING FMT2$; "------------------------------------------------"
220 REM                                               ↑
230       READ N                                      | Prints report headings.
240       FOR J = 1 TO N
250          READ FULL.NAME$,HOURS,RATE
260          LET PAY   = HOURS * RATE
270          LET TOTAL = TOTAL + PAY
280          PRINT USING FMT4$; FULL.NAME$,HOURS,RATE,PAY  ←────── Prints body of table
290       NEXT J
300 REM
310       PRINT USING FMT2$; "------------------------------------------------"
320       PRINT USING FMT5$; TOTAL
330 REM                                               ↑
900       DATA 6                                      | Prints report footings
901       DATA Phil Murray,15,6.35
902       DATA Hilda Snark,30.25,5.85
903       DATA Margo Barker,32,6.80
904       DATA Ralph Kiner,20.75,6.25
905       DATA Mark Fargo,35,6
906       DATA Anna AlDente,38,7.78
998 REM
999       END
```

```
RUN
                    PAYROLL REPORT

------------------------------------------------
    Name              Hours     Rate      Pay
------------------------------------------------
Phil Murray           15.00     6.35       95.25
Hilda Snark           30.25     5.85      176.96
Margo Barker          32.00     6.80      217.60
Ralph Kiner           20.75     6.25      129.69
Mark Fargo            35.00     6.00      210.00
Anna AlDente          38.00     7.78      295.64
------------------------------------------------
Totals                                 $1,125.14
```

Let's note the following points.

1. The format strings are stored within special string variables and grouped together in lines 120–160. This design is consistent with the print chart in Figure D.1.
2. The same format string can be referenced more than once. See lines 190, 210, and 310.

D.4 POINTERS

Design and Style

1. **Report design.**   Use a sheet of paper or (preferably) print chart to design the output report. This report layout facilitates the coding of format strings.
2. **Format strings within string variables.**   For output other than simple output, use string variables to store format strings rather than including the format strings in PRINT USING statements. Place these format strings together at the beginning or end of the program, as done in Examples D.6 and D.7. The use and grouping of these special string variables aid in the alignment of output and make programs more readable.

Common Errors

1. **Unaligned or unintended output.**   This logic error is often the result of spending insufficient time in designing output reports. Use a report layout to design the output and then encode the format strings according to this design.
2. **Field overflow.**   Make sure field widths are sufficiently large to handle the output data. If the width of the format field is not large enough for a numeric field to print properly, then the system usually widens the field to accommodate the value and prints a leading % sign. *Is this the way your system handles field overflow?* (See Example D.1.) Field overflow for *string* fields results in a truncated string value. (See Note 3 on page 167.)
3. **Format string inconsistencies.**   We may get unintended output results if the number of items in an output list is different from the number of numeric and string fields in a format string. Also, make sure that output list items and fields match with respect to *type;* that is, match string values with string fields and numeric values with numeric fields.

FOLLOW-UP EXERCISES

1. Indicate the output if

    X   stores 4645.8184
    Y   stores   3.2

    a.   PRINT USING "####.#"   ; X
    b.   PRINT USING "#,###.##"   ; X
    c.   PRINT USING "#,###.##"   ; Y
    d.   PRINT USING "$$,###.##"   ; Y
    e.   PRINT USING "###   #####" ; X
    f.   PRINT USING "###   #####" ; Y,X
    g.   PRINT USING "#######"   ; Y,X

    Try these on your system.

2. Assume 500 is stored in B and 25.75 in C. Indicate the PRINT USING statements necessary to output the following:

Column
```
      1 2 3 4 5 6 7 8 9
a.                5 0 0
b.  B =       5 0 0
c.  5 0 0     2 5 . 7 5
```

3. Assume 3.283 is stored in X. Write code and make the following successive changes to output X right-justified in column 8. First output X to zero decimal places without printing a decimal point; then output X to zero decimal places, printing the decimal point; then to one decimal place; then to three decimal places; and finally to five decimal places.

4. Assume "GOOFUS" is stored in A$. Develop PRINT USING statements that output GOOFUS, GOOF, and GO, beginning in output column 5.

*5. Assume the following values are stored:

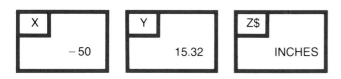

Given the following format strings:

LET FMT1$ = "###⌐⌐##.#" ←—— Two spaces

LET FMT2$ = "Number⌐=⌐####" ←—— One space

LET FMT3$ = "###.###⌐\⌐⌐⌐⌐⌐⌐⌐\"
One space ——— ⌐⌐⌐⌐⌐⌐ Field width = 10

LET FMT4$ = "⌐\⌐⌐⌐⌐⌐\⌐\⌐⌐⌐⌐⌐⌐\"
One space ——— ⌐⌐⌐⌐ Field width = 8 / Field width = 10

Indicate on Figure 1 the exact output for each of the following:

a. PRINT USING FMT1$; X,Y
b. PRINT USING FMT2$; X
c. PRINT USING FMT3$; Y,Z$
d. PRINT USING FMT4$; "scale in",Z$
e. PRINT USING FMT3$; Z$,Y

*6. Specify PRINT USING and format strings as string variables to output:
   a. The label and the value of the variable *B*, whose value ranges from 0.00 to 999.99. (See Figure 2.)
   b. The column headings and the values of variables N$ (14 characters or less), S$ (11 characters), R (positive real numbers less than 10 to two decimal places with dollar sign), and P (positive real numbers less than 1000 to two decimal places with floating dollar sign). (See Figure 3.)

7. Run Examples D.1 through D.6 on your system. Any differences in the output?

8. Make the following changes in Example D.7.
   a. Insert two dashed lines (equal sign) after the totals line is printed.
   b. Use floating dollar signs in the Rate and Pay columns.
   c. Allow up to 20 characters in an employee's name, without affecting the positions of the other fields.

9. Implement Example D.7 on your system. Try making improvements in the (almost perfect!) output design.

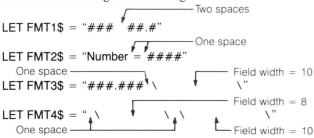

Figure 1

Figure 2

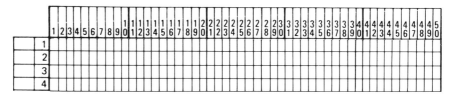

Figure 3

External Data Files

Many applications, particularly those with large amounts of data, require the processing of data files that reside within secondary storage media. For example, customer files are typically stored on either magnetic tape or magnetic disk in mainframe and minicomputer environments, and within either diskettes or hard disks in microcomputer environments. This module motivates and illustrates the storage of data within external media.

E.1 MOTIVATION

Until now we have entered data into storage locations in three ways:

1. **LET statements.** This approach works for data that change infrequently from run to run (parameters); however, it's far too inefficient for large amounts of data, it's cumbersome to change values when necessary, it does not make the data available to other programs, and it's inappropriate for data values that change during a computer run.

2. **INPUT statements.** This approach is needed for entering choices and data values interactively, but it's inefficient for large amounts of data. Moreover, the data have to be reentered if they are needed by another program.

3. **READ/DATA statements.** This approach is good for storing parameters and data values that change during a computer run (especially the *internal data files* described in Chapter 3). For large internal data files, however, the maintenance of data (changing, adding, or deleting lines) is tedious. Also, it's cumbersome to merge or append the internal data file should another program require the same data.

An **external data file** stores data within a secondary storage medium such as magnetic disk, diskette, or magnetic tape. External data files are uniquely referenced by names (as are the program files we have been working with),

---

*This module can be covered anytime after Chapter 5.

which means that programs can either write data to the files or retrieve data from them for processing and viewing.

The advantages of external data files include the following.

1. **Multiprogram access.**   A file is easily accessible by different programs that require its data. For example, an employee file might be processed weekly by a payroll program and daily by a personnel query program. The savings in storage and maintenance costs by avoiding use of identical multiple files are obvious.

2. **Multifile access.**   A program can process more than one file within a computer run. For example, a bank checking-statement program might process the following three files: a file that contains monthly transactions such as deposits, cleared checks, and withdrawals; a file that shows customer data such as name, address, and last month's balance; and a file that updates the customer's account with the new balance. Try doing this with an internal data file!

3. **Cheaper maintenance.**   The task of adding, deleting, or changing records (lines of data within the data file) in large files is less costly than for the three storage approaches discussed above.

4. **Output storage.**   Programs can store the results of processing within an external data file that is subsequently used by the same or other programs. For example, a sales program might output a monthly sales report to a data file. At a later time the report can be viewed on a screen or printed. Moreover, the same report file might be processed by another specialized program that prints graphs on color slides for a sales presentation. These procedures were not possible with our earlier data storage methods.

Before going on to the next section, let's take a look at two very simple programs that use the same external data file.

E X A M P L E   E . 1   **Creating and Viewing a Simple Grade File**

Suppose we wish to store the exam scores 90, 75, 85, 95, and 70 within an external data file called "grades" for later viewing. Table E.1 shows two typical programs for these purposes. (Your instructor will provide the necessary changes if your system's implementation differs.) The programs and their brief explanations should give you a good idea of the following fundamental steps for using external data files:

1. **Open the data file.**   This step uses the OPEN statement to tell the operating system the name of the file, its intended use (we plan either to output *to* the file or input *from* the file), and relates the *file name* ("grades" in our example) to a *file number* (#1 in our example) for subsequent use within the PRINT # and INPUT # statements.

2. **Output to the file or input from the file.**   In the first program, the PRINT # statement is used to output the number of scores and the individual scores to the file. In the second program, the INPUT # statement is used to retrieve the same data for viewing on the screen.

3. **Close the data file when finished.**   This step uses the CLOSE statement.

At this time, don't worry about the details of using the OPEN, PRINT #, INPUT #, and CLOSE statements. We shall discuss these shortly. For now, all you need to understand is that we have placed data on an external file called "grades" with one program and subsequently have viewed that file with another program. And both tasks were accomplished by the same three fundamental steps.

Table E.1   Creation/Display of Grade File (Example E.1)

Implementation	Program/Execution	Comments
IBM PC VAX-11	*File creation program:*	This program takes the number of grades and the five grades within the internal data file in lines 90–95 and places them within the external data file called "grades." File "grades" resides within the diskette in drive A (IBM PC) or within your private library (VAX-11). The OPEN statement ties in the file name "grades" to the file #1 and opens the file for output (since we plan to output data from primary memory storage locations to the external file). The PRINT # statement is used to output data to file #1 (i.e., file grades). The CLOSE statement completes the process by closing the file.

```
10        OPEN "grades" FOR OUTPUT AS #1
15 REM
20        READ N
25        PRINT #1, N
30 REM
35        FOR J = 1 TO N
40           READ SCORE
45           PRINT #1, SCORE
50        NEXT J
55 REM
60        CLOSE #1
65 REM
70        PRINT "File grades has been created"
75 REM
90        DATA 5
95        DATA 90,75,85,95,70
98 REM
99        END


RUN
File grades has been created
```

File display program:

This program accesses the grades within the file named "grades" and displays them on the screen. Note that line 10 now opens this file as an input file; i.e., we plan to input the data into primary memory from the external file. The INPUT # statement is used for this purpose.

```
10        OPEN "grades" FOR INPUT AS #1
15 REM
20        PRINT "Scores: ";
25 REM
30        INPUT #1, N
35        FOR J = 1 TO N
40           INPUT #1, SCORE
45           PRINT SCORE;
50        NEXT J
55 REM
60        CLOSE #1
65 REM
70        PRINT
75        PRINT "File grades has been displayed"
98 REM
99        END


RUN
Scores:  90  75  85  95  70
File grades has been displayed
```

Your system
(if different)

E.2 FIELDS, RECORDS, AND FILES

There are many variations on the uses and types of external files. This section covers the necessary foundation material for our work with external files.

Let's review some definitions from our work with internal data files.

Field. A fact or attribute (data item) about some entity such as a person, place, thing, or event. For example, an employer might maintain data on employees' attributes such as name, identification number, salary, and sex. Each of these attributes is considered a field. The variables that appear within the lists of input and output statements are used to process fields; i.e., each variable in the list corresponds to a field.

Record. A group of related fields, retrievable as a unit. For example, all of the data items relating to one employee are a record. Typically, the execution of a file input or output statement processes a single record. The fields that make up a record are usually described by a **record layout**. For example, the record layout for an employee record might appear as follows.

Record Layout for Employee Record

Field	Type	Length (Bytes)
Full name	String	20
ID number	Numeric	4
Salary	Numeric	4
Sex	String	1

File. A collection of related records. Each record is a logical part of the file, because it contains the same data items (fields, not data values) as all the other records in the file. For example, an *employee file* contains all employee records.

Figure E.1 illustrates this relationship among fields, records, and a file. This file contains three records, and each record contains four fields.

Internal and External Files. An **internal file** is a collection of records stored within the program's DATA statements. Chapters 2–7 use this type of data file.

An **external file** is a collection of records stored separately from the program on a medium external to primary memory. For example, files stored on an I/O medium such as magnetic tape (reel or cassette) or magnetic disk (hard or floppy) are called external files. The typical storage medium within BASIC environments is magnetic disk. For example, diskettes ("floppies") and hard disks are used in microcomputers; hard disks are used in minicomputers and mainframes. In the latter case, we usually don't see the hard disk since it

		Fields			
		Name	Employee ID	Salary	Sex
	Record 1	Abatar Jane A.	1	20000	f
File	Record 2	Bomberg Bo B.	3	15800	m
	Record 3	Drury David D.	6	18000	m

Figure E.1 Relationship among fields, records, and file

resides at the computer center; however, we have used it all along to store program files (and soon data files) within our library.

Sequential and Relative Files.   The records in a **sequential file** are processed only sequentially; that is, the records cannot be processed any way except in the order of storage, one after the other. For example, if a sequential personnel file contains 1000 records (employees), then sequential processing means that we can process the 900th record if and only if we first process the first 899 records.

A record in a **relative file** (also called **random file** or **direct access file**) can be processed (input or written) without the need to process any other record in the file. For example, in a 1000-record relative file, we can directly input the 900th record without having to input the preceding 899 records.

Figure E.2 conceptually illustrates sequential and relative files for our personnel illustration. In part (a), note that sequential files always terminate with an **end-of-file (eof)** mark. When this mark is read the end of the file has been reached. In part (b), note that records in a relative file are numbered 1 to 6. These **record numbers** uniquely identify records for storage and retrieval. Also note that a record location either stores a record or is empty. For example, a relative employee file with 1000 record locations (numbered 1–1000) and 850 employees would contain 150 empty records.

Sequential files can be stored on media such as magnetic tape and disk, but relative files can be stored only within a direct access medium such as magnetic disk (but not a sequential medium such as tape). The "grades" file used in Example E.1 illustrates a sequential file with six records on a magnetic disk medium, as conceptually shown in Figure E.3. Note that the execution of each PRINT # statement within the first program in Table E.1 places

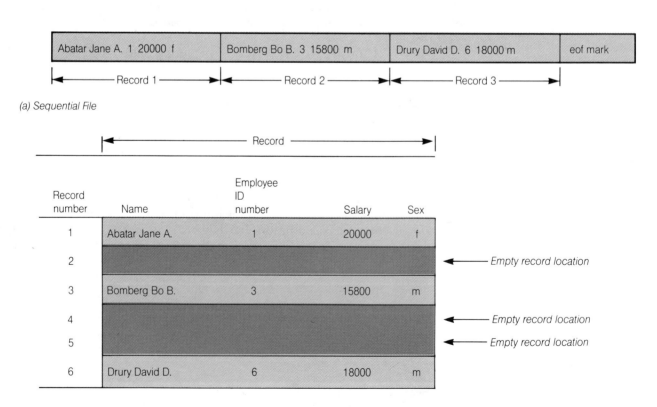

(a) Sequential File

(b) Relative File

Figure E.2   Conceptual representation of sequential and relative files

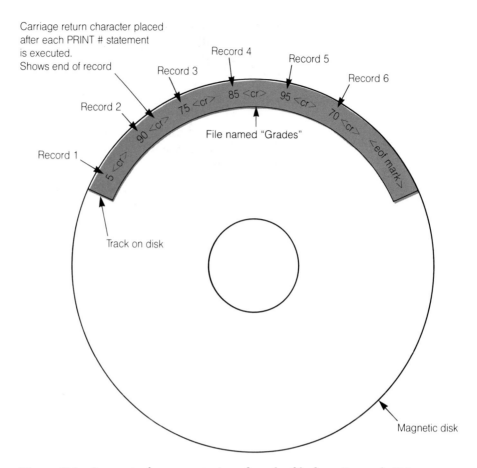

Carriage return character placed
after each PRINT # statement
is executed.
Shows end of record

Record 1

Record 2

Record 3

Record 4

Record 5

Record 6

5 <cr>   90 <cr>   75 <cr>   85 <cr>   95 <cr>   70 <cr>   <eof mark>

File named "Grades"

Track on disk

Magnetic disk

Figure E.3   Conceptual representation of grades file from Example E.1

a carriage return or <cr> mark after each data item, which effectively terminates a record. In other words, each PRINT # statement generates a single
record by placing a <cr> mark on the disk.

We strictly work with sequential files in this module, as relative files are
an advanced programming topic.

E.3 SEQUENTIAL FILES

We now turn to the details of processing sequential files. As indicated earlier
in Example E.1, the general operations for processing sequential files include
the following: opening, output to or input from, and closing the file. Additionally, there are some specialized operations.

Not surprisingly, the statements for accomplishing these operations vary
from system to system. We shall focus on the IBM PC (Microsoft) and VAX-11
implementations, with emphasis on the former. *If your system is not illustrated,
then you should focus on the general principles of file processing as discussed in
the text and illustrated in the examples. Then make any necessary changes within
the tables and examples according to your system's manual or your instructor.*

Opening a File

A program must first inform the computer that a certain external data file is
to be used in a particular manner. The **OPEN statement** is typically used to
communicate the following information:

1. The sequential data file to be processed is identified by name.

2. One of the following purposes is indicated: write (output) records to the file, append records at the end of the file, or read (input) records from the file.

3. A file number is indicated for subsequent use by other file-related statements like PRINT # and INPUT #.

4. The system sets the file pointer to either the beginning of the file (if the purpose is input or output) or the end of the file (if the purpose is to append new records).

The OPEN statement and some examples are illustrated in Table E.2. Study this table and make any necessary changes for your system.

NOTE 1   The OPEN statement must precede any other statements in the program that use the file.

NOTE 2   If more than one file is open at once, make sure that the same file number is not assigned to more than one file.

NOTE 3   Opening a file for input implies that we want to read from an *existing* file; opening a file for output implies that we want to *create* a new file; opening a file for append implies that we want to add, or append, new records to an existing file.

WARNING   If a file is opened for output, and it already exists, then its previous contents are deleted. If we had really meant to open for input but instead opened for output, then we have inadvertently erased an existing file.

Output to a File

The creation of a file implies that we wish to output or print data to the file. Up to now we have used the PRINT statement to output data to a screen. Similarly, we can use a PRINT # statement to output data to a sequential file. A second approach, the WRITE # statement, is also available on some systems. The first program in Example E.1 illustrates the creation of a complete sequential file using the PRINT # statement. Take a look at this program once more to get the overall picture.

The syntax and examples of the PRINT # and WRITE # statements are shown in Table E.3. Study these, make any necessary modifications for your system, and be aware of the following notes.

NOTE 1   The first use of a PRINT # or WRITE # statement must be preceded by an OPEN statement that opens the file for *output*.

NOTE 2   The file number used in the output statement must correspond to the file number used in the OPEN statement. For example, if #2 is used in the OPEN statement, then #2 must be used in the PRINT # or related statement.

NOTE 3   Remember that the field values within records placed on a file must be delimited as if we were entering data values in response to the execution of an INPUT statement. This means that we must make sure that at least one space or a comma follows each field value (except for the carriage return/line feed that follows the last value). Especially, see Examples 7 and 8 in Table E.3.

Table E.2 Opening a Sequential File

Implementation	Statement Syntax	Examples

Microsoft BASIC on IBM PC	**OPEN** *filespec* **FOR** *mode* **AS** #*filenum*
	
	 where
	
	 filespec is the following file specification
	
	 device:filename
	
	 such as B:F$ or "grades"
	
	 where
	 device indicates where to look for the file
	
	 such as A for disk drive A
	 B for disk drive B
	
	 Note: Drive A is assumed if "device:" is omitted.
	
	 filename is the name of the file to look for on that particular device. Filename can be either a string constant such as "grades" or "employee.dat" or a string variable such as F$ or FILE.NAME$
	
	 mode is one of the following
	
	 OUTPUT to output data onto the file
	 INPUT to input data from the file
	 APPEND to position the file pointer at the end of the file
	
	 filenum is an integer expression whose value is 1 to 3.
	 This value is used to associate the file number with the filespec, so that **PRINT #**, **WRITE #**, **INPUT #**, and **CLOSE** statements can use the file number in place of the file specification.
		1. OPEN "grades" FOR INPUT AS #1
		
		      — Identical
		
		 2. OPEN "A:GRADES" FOR INPUT AS #1
		
		 3. OPEN FILE.NAME$ FOR OUTPUT AS #2
		
		      Identical if FILE.NAME$
		      stores employee
		
		 4. OPEN "employee" FOR OUTPUT AS #2
		
		 5. OPEN FOLDER$ FOR APPEND AS #3

VAX-11 BASIC	The same as the IBM PC in its most simple form, except for the following: 1. The "device:" portion within the filespec is omitted. 2. APPEND is handled as an access clause rather than a mode. Thus, **the fifth example** above would be rewritten as 5. OPEN FOLDER$ FOR OUTPUT AS #1,ACCESS APPEND The complete form is rather involved, as it includes various file type, record, security, and other parameters. See the **VAX-11 BASIC USER'S GUIDE** (if you dare).	

(continued)

Table E.2   (continued)

Your system
(if different)

Table E.3   Output to a Sequential File

Implementation	Statement Syntax	Examples

Microsoft BASIC on IBM PC

PRINT #*filenum, list*

where
filenum is the corresponding file number used in the OPEN statement
list is the list of numeric and/or string expressions whose values will be written to the file. As usual, items in the list are separated by commas and/or semicolons.

Note 1: This statement writes a record image to the data file just as it would be displayed on the screen with a PRINT statement. Thus, it's best to use semicolon rather than comma delimiters in the list of items, so as to avoid unnecessary blank spaces between data values in the file.

Note 2: Items in a record within the file must be separated or *delimited* by at least one blank space or comma. For this reason, it's necessary to place a comma after the output of a string value by printing the string constant ",". This is not necessary for numeric values since these are printed with trailing spaces. Remember that items within the file must be delimited properly for successful processing by the INPUT # statement. A carriage return/line feed mark (which we show as <cr>) is placed on the file following the last item in the list, which effectively terminates a record. See Examples 1–4 to the right.

1. PRINT #1, SCORE

This places the record

b90b<cr>

on file #1 when SCORE stores 90 in primary memory. (b is our way of showing a blank space.)

2. PRINT #2, X;Y;Z

This places the record

b5b − 10bb15b<cr>

on file #2 when X,Y,Z store 5, − 10,15. Note the trailing space after the 5, which serves to delimit the 5 from the − 10 on input. The two spaces between − 10 and 15 are due to the trailing space for − 10 and the suppressed + sign for + 15.

3. PRINT #1, A$;",";B$

This places the record

Captain,Kirk<cr>

on file #1 when A$ and B$ store Captain and Kirk. Note the need for "," to delimit the two values in the file; otherwise, they would appear as the one value.

CaptainKirk<cr>

which could not be input as two separate string values.

4. PRINT #1, A$;",";B$;",";Y;X

This places the record

Captain,Kirk, − 10bb5b<cr>

on file #1. *Note the need to place a comma after each string value* Captain and Kirk. A comma could be used to delimit − 10 from 5, but the trailing space following the numeric value − 10 makes this unnecessary.

WRITE #*filenum, list*

where
filenum and *list* are defined above.

Note: This statement is more convenient to use than the PRINT # statement because it automatically inserts commas between data items in the file. It also encloses string values within quotation marks and eliminates spaces around numeric values. The visual look of records done by this method is the same as the usual way we prepare records within DATA statements. See Examples 5–8 to the right.

5. WRITE #1, SCORE

This places the record

90<cr>

on file #1. Compare with Example 1 above.

6. WRITE #2, X,Y,Z

This places the record

5, − 10,15<cr>

on file #2. Compare with Example 2.

7. WRITE #1, A$,B$

This places the record

"Captain","Kirk"<cr>

on file #1. Compare with Example 3.

8. WRITE #1, A$,B$,Y,X

This places the record

"Captain","Kirk", − 10,5<cr>

on file #1. Compare with Example 4.

VAX-11 BASIC	This is the same as the IBM PC except for the following. 1. The WRITE # statement is not available. 2. A PUT statement (which we don't cover here) is available for sequential output.
Your system (if different)	

Input from a File

In our earlier work we entered data from the keyboard to primary memory by using the INPUT statement, or we entered data from the data block to primary memory by using the READ statement. Similarly, we can read data from a sequential file to primary memory by using the INPUT # statement.

The syntax and examples of the INPUT # statement are shown in Table E.4. Study these, make any necessary modifications for your system, and be aware of the following notes.

NOTE 1 Do we really need to say this? We can't input from a file that has not been created earlier by one of the methods described in the preceding section. By the way, data files also can be created using editors and wordprocessors.

Table E.4 Input from a Sequential File

Implementation	Statement Syntax	Examples

Microsoft BASIC on IBM PC	**INPUT #**_filenum, list_
	
	where
	filenum is the corresponding file number used in the OPEN statement
	list is the list of variables whose values are to be input from the file. As usual, variables in the input list are separated by commas.
		Note: Assume the file pointer is at the beginning of each record.
		
		Record / INPUT # Statement — **Contents in Primary Memory**
		
		1. b90b\<cr>
		   INPUT #1, SCORE
		   See Example 1
		   in Table E.3.
		   — SCORE = 90
		
		2. b5b – 10bb15b\<cr>
		   INPUT #2, X, Y, Z
		   See Example 2
		   in Table E.3.
		   — X = 5, Y = –10, Z = 15
		
		3. Captain,Kirk\<cr>
		   INPUT #1, A\$,B\$
		   See Example 3
		   in Table E.3.
		   — A\$ = Captain, B\$ = Kirk
		
		4. Captain,Kirk, – 10bb5b\<cr>
		   INPUT #1, A\$,B\$,Y,X
		   See Example 4
		   in Table E.3.
		   — X = 5, Y = –10
		   — A\$ = Captain, B\$ = Kirk
		
		5. "Captain","Kirk", – 10,5\<cr>
		   INPUT #1, A\$,B\$,Y,X
		   See also Example 4
		   above and
		   Example 8 in
		   Table E.3.
		   — X = 5, Y = –10
		   — A\$ = Captain, B\$ = Kirk

VAX-11 BASIC	This is the same as the IBM PC.	
Your system (if different)		

NOTE 2   The first use of an INPUT # statement must be preceded by an OPEN statement that opens the file for input.

NOTE 3   The file number used in the input statement must correspond to the file number used in the OPEN statement. For example, if #1 is used in the OPEN statement, then #1 must be used in the INPUT # statement.

NOTE 4   Each pair of items within the file must be delimited properly by one or more spaces, a comma, or a <cr> mark. In other words, data items within the file must be delimited, just as we need to delimit data items within DATA statements or in responses to INPUT statements. Otherwise, the data items cannot be processed (input) by the INPUT # statement.

NOTE 5   As in our earlier understanding of the relationship between READ operations and the data block, the concept of a *pointer* is useful. Whenever a file is opened for input, the file pointer is placed at the first data item in the file. Thereafter, it advances according to the number of variables processed within the input lists of INPUT # statements. For example, if the pointer currently resides at data item 50, and the next INPUT # statement executed has five variables within the input list, then items 50–54 are processed and the pointer ends up at item 55. *Note that each execution of an INPUT # statement reads an entire record from the file.*

NOTE 6   As usual we need to make sure that variables within the input list correspond to data items within the file with respect to type and number. Thus, the input of a string variable requires a matching string value within the file; the input of a numeric variable requires a corresponding numeric value within the file; and the total number of individual input operations must not exceed the total number of data items within the file.

Closing a File

All files that have been opened during the execution of a program should be explicitly closed through a CLOSE statement, for any of the following reasons.

1.   If a file is left open, the system may not print the last record to the file.
2.   Systems allow a maximum number of files to be opened at one time. If we need new files after reaching this maximum during any computer run, then we must close some files.
3.   If a particular file is to be used first as an input file and then as an output file (or vice versa) within the same program, then the file must be closed before it is reopened.

   The syntax and examples of the CLOSE statement are shown in Table E.5. Study these, make any necessary modifications for your system, and be aware of the following note.

NOTE   The CLOSE statement is often overlooked, because execution of an END statement automatically closes all open files. If execution terminates through a run-time error or a STOP statement, however, then the sequential file may end up missing the last record and an eof mark. So, as a matter of safety (not to mention good programming style), we should explicitly close any opened files when we are finished with them.

Table E.5 Closing a Sequential File

Implementation	Statement Syntax	Examples
Microsoft BASIC on IBM PC	**CLOSE** *list of filenums* *Note:* This statement concludes I/O to a file as follows. 1. It terminates the association between a named file and its file number (as defined in the OPEN statement). 2. It writes any remaining record to the file (from an area of primary memory called the *buffer*). 3. It places an eof mark at the end of the file. The list of file numbers is optional. If omitted, then all previously opened files are closed.	CLOSE #1 CLOSE #1,#2,#3 CLOSE 1,2,3 CLOSE
VAX-11 BASIC	This is the same as the IBM PC, except that the list of file numbers is not optional.	
Your system (if different)		

Other File Operations

All systems include special statements and functions for implementing specialized sequential file operations. For example, specific statements, functions, or procedures exist, depending on the system, for detecting end-of-file conditions. Table E.6 illustrates three approaches to testing for an end-of-file (eof) condition

Table E.6 Sequential File Eof Procedures

Implementation	General Procedures	Examples
Microsoft BASIC on IBM PC	*Procedure 1:* **EOF function** Open file for input . . . WHILE NOT **EOF(filenum)** . : .] Body of loop, including INPUT # statement . : WEND	100 REM　　EOF function 110 REM 120　　OPEN "file.dat" FOR INPUT AS #1 130 REM 140　　WHILE NOT EOF(1) 150　　　INPUT #1, A,B,C　　Note 160　　　PRINT A;B;C　　filenum 170　　WEND　　consistency 180 REM 190　　CLOSE #1 998 REM 999　　END RUN 　10　20　30 　15　25　35 　20　25　30

Note: If an eof mark is encountered for the indicated file number, then the EOF function returns a true value. Thus, NOT EOF(filenum) would be false, and exit from the while loop would be achieved; however, if the end-of-file mark hasn't been reached, then the EOF function returns a false value, the logical operator NOT changes this to true, and the body of the loop is executed again.

Procedure 2: **ON ERROR statement**

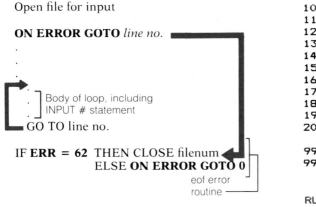

Open file for input	100 REM	ON ERROR statement
	110 REM	
ON ERROR GOTO *line no.*	120	OPEN "file.dat" FOR INPUT AS #1
	130 REM	
	140	ON ERROR GOTO 200
	150 REM	
Body of loop, including INPUT # statement	160	INPUT #1, A,B,C
	170	PRINT A;B;C
GO TO line no.	180	GOTO 160
	190 REM	
IF **ERR = 62** THEN CLOSE filenum ELSE **ON ERROR GOTO 0**	200	IF ERR = 62 THEN CLOSE #1 ELSE ON ERROR GOTO 0
eof error routine	998 REM	
	999	END

```
RUN
   10   20   30
   15   25   35
   20   25   30
```

Notes: 1. The ON ERROR statement traps run-time errors by transferring control to a special error routine. The ON ERROR statement must precede the point where an error might occur. Most programmers place the statement in the first part of the program, as we did in the above example (line 140). If a run-time error occurs any time after the ON ERROR statement is executed, control is automatically transferred to the error routine (line 200).

2. A special system variable called **ERR** is assigned an error number code when a run-time error occurs. (See Appendix A in the IBM PC BASIC User Manual for the more than 70 errors that can disrupt program execution. Note that the error code for an eof error is 62.)

3. Within the program, a loop is created (lines 160–180) to read data from the file. When the INPUT statement (line 160) attempts to read from the file after all the data in the file have been read, a run-time error (end-of-file) is committed and the system assigns a value of 62 to ERR. As soon as the error occurs, control is transferred to the error routine (line 200).

4. Within the error routine (line 200), if the end-of-file error has occurred (ERR = 62 is true), the file is closed and execution resumes with the first statement following the error routine; however, if the run-time error is not 62, the **ON ERROR GOTO 0 statement** is executed, which instructs the system to stop execution and print the error message corresponding to the error that caused the trap.

(continued)

Table E.6   (continued)

Procedure 3: eof record/sentinel

```
100 REM     Eof record with sentinel
110 REM
120     OPEN "file2.dat" FOR INPUT AS #1
130 REM
140     INPUT #1, A,B,C
150     WHILE A <> -99    ←——— Test for eof record
160       PRINT A;B;C
170       INPUT #1, A,B,C
180     WEND
190 REM
200     CLOSE #1
998 REM
999     END


RUN
  10   20   30
  15   25   35
  20   25   30
```

Note: Here we assume that the file was created with a special eof record that contains a sentinel, as first described for eof loops in Chapter 5. In effect, this procedure is the same as our earlier eof-loop procedure that processed internal data files. In this example, loop exit is achieved as soon as variable A stores the sentinel −99. When the file is created, the last record in the file, the eof record, might appear as follows:

−99,0,0<cr>

We recommend the more natural and straightforward procedure 1 over this procedure.

VAX-11 BASIC	The EOF function procedure is not available. The ON ERROR statement procedure is the same as the IBM PC, except that the eof condition error code is 11. The eof condition/sentinel procedure is the same as the IBM PC, except for using NEXT in place of WEND.

Your system
(if different)

E X A M P L E   E . 2   Creation of Sequential Personnel File

Now that we have the necessary tools, let's put it all together and illustrate the creation of the sequential personnel file shown in Figure E.2.

Analysis

Let's develop an interactive program that conversationally inputs employee records and writes the records to a sequential file.

Data requirements include the following:

Output

Write records to a sequential file according to the record layout shown on page 175.

Input

1. Name of file entered from keyboard

2. Each record entered from keyboard

Design

The primary task of this program is to create a sequential file. The file-creation logic inputs a record into primary memory from the keyboard: then the record is copied or written to the file medium (tape or disk) from primary memory. After all records have been written to the file, the file is closed, which places an endfile mark at the end of the file. Figure E.4 illustrates these data flows for file creation through the use of a **system flowchart**. The pseudocode below describes the design in more detail.

```
Input file name
Open sequential file for output
Print reminders message to operator
Input employee name
While name not eof
    Input remaining fields in record
    Write record to file
    Input employee name
End while
Close file
Print file creation message to operator
End
```

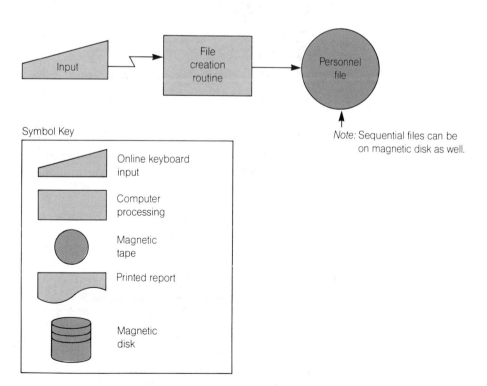

Figure E.4   System flowchart: Creation of sequential personnel file

Code and Test

The following program and run were implemented in Microsoft BASIC on an IBM PC. Note the following as you study the program and its I/O.

1. *The filename is treated as a string variable in lines 340 and 360 for greater generality.* For example, this program can be used unaltered for different personnel files, if the same record layout is used in each.

2. Keep in mind that primary memory always acts as a temporary intermediary medium for each record. Looking at Figure E.4, each record in the file-creation process is entered at the keyboard, resides temporarily in memory locations as the variables FULL.NAME$, ID, SALARY, and SEX$ (until the next record overwrites it), and finally stays permanently on tape or disk.

```
100 '-----------------------------------------------------------------------------
110 '
120 '   Personnel File Creation
130 '
140 '     Record Layout :
150 '     ---------------------------
160 '     Field                Type
170 '     ---------------------------
180 '     FULL.NAME$           String
190 '     ID                   Numeric
200 '     SALARY               Numeric
210 '     SEX$                 String
220 '     ---------------------------
230 '
240 '-----------------------------------------------------------------------------
320     PRINT TAB(10); "FILE CREATION ROUTINE"        Note use of string
330     PRINT                                         variable for file name
340     INPUT "Enter file name"; FILE.NAME$
350 '
360     OPEN FILE.NAME$ FOR OUTPUT AS #1              File opened as output file
370 '
380     PRINT
390     PRINT TAB(10); "Reminders:"
400     PRINT TAB(12); "Don't use commas"
410     PRINT TAB(12); "Enter last name first"
420     PRINT TAB(12); "Terminate input with eof for name"
430     PRINT
440     PRINT TAB(10); "Now enter data for each employee."
450     PRINT
460 '
470     INPUT "Full name ======>"; FULL.NAME$
480 '
490     WHILE FULL.NAME$ <> "eof"
500 '
510       INPUT "ID number ======>"; ID
520       INPUT "Salary ========>"; SALARY
530       INPUT "Sex (f or m) ===>"; SEX$
540 '
550       WRITE #1, FULL.NAME$,ID,SALARY,SEX$         Record written to file
560 '
570       PRINT
580       INPUT "Full name ======>"; FULL.NAME$
590 '
600     WEND
610 '
620     CLOSE #1                                      File closed
630 '
640     PRINT : PRINT TAB(10); "File "; FILE.NAME$; " has been created.": PRINT
998 '
999     END
```

```
RUN
            FILE CREATION ROUTINE

Enter file name? employee

            Reminders:
              Don't use commas
              Enter last name first
              Terminate input with eof for name

            Now enter data for each employee.

Full name ======>? Abatar    Jane A.
ID number ======>? 1
Salary ========>? 20000
Sex (f or m) ===>? f
```

```
Full name ======>? Bomberg  Bo B.
ID number ======>? 3
Salary =========>? 15800
Sex (f or m) ===>? m


Full name ======>? Drury     David D.
ID number ======>? 6
Salary =========>? 18000
Sex (f or m) ===>? m

Full name ======>? eof

        File employee has been created.
```

E X A M P L E   E . 3   Processing of Sequential Personnel File

Once a sequential file is created, different programs can process the data in the file for the purpose of providing reports.

Analysis

A federal agency is in the process of auditing the company's files for compliance with various laws. The company's salary history is under review by the agency and the personnel officer needs a report on the average employee salaries by sex.

Output

1. Employee records with designated sex.

2. Average salary.

Input

1. Entered from keyboard: name of file; sex code for report.

2. All employee records from the file.

Design

The primary purpose of this file-processing program is to access the data from the personnel file and display the average salary report. The file-processing logic first inputs a record from the file and stores the record in primary memory; if the record is of the desired sex, then the salary and count are accumulated and the record is copied from primary memory to the screen.

The procedure for processing records from a sequential file is described in the system flowchart illustrated in Figure E.5. The pseudocode below describes the design in more detail.

```
Input file name
Input desired sex
Open file for input
Print table headings
Initialize counters to zero
While not eof
    Input employee record from file
    If desired sex = sex of employee then
        Accumulate salary and count
        Print record to screen
    End if
End while
Print average salary
Close file
End
```

Code and Test

The following program and run were implemented in Microsoft BASIC on an IBM PC. Note the following as you study the program and its I/O.

1. The personnel file, having been created in Example E.2, is now opened for input.

2. The EOF function is used in line 250 to stop the while loop after all records have been read. This approach is cleaner than the alternatives described in Table E.6. Does your BASIC implementation have an EOF function?

3. Each record is read from the personnel file to primary memory, but only the records of male employees are displayed, along with their average salary.

```
100  ' -------------------------------------------------------
110  ' File Processing/Average Salary Report
120  '-------------------------------------------------------
130    INPUT "Enter file name"; FILE.NAME$
140    INPUT "Enter sex type for report (m/f)"; SEX.TYPE$
150  '
160    OPEN FILE.NAME$ FOR INPUT AS #1  ◄──────────── File opened for input
170  '
180    PRINT : PRINT TAB(10); "AVERAGE SALARY REPORT "
190    PRINT TAB(10); "----------------------------------------"
200    PRINT TAB(10); "Name";TAB(30);"Salary";TAB(45);"Sex"
210    PRINT TAB(10); "----------------------------------------"
220  '
230    LET COUNT = 0 :  LET SUMSAL = 0
240  '
250    WHILE NOT EOF(1)  ◄──────────── Note use of end-of-file function
260  '
270      INPUT #1, FULL.NAME$,ID,SALARY,SEX$  ◄──── Reads records from file
280  '
290      IF SEX.TYPE$ = SEX$ THEN
             LET SUMSAL = SUMSAL + SALARY   :   LET COUNT = COUNT + 1  :
             PRINT TAB(10); FULL.NAME$;TAB(30);SALARY;TAB(46);SEX$
300  '
310    WEND
320  '
330    PRINT TAB(10); "----------------------------------------"
340    PRINT TAB(10); "Average salary ....."; TAB(30); SUMSAL/COUNT
350  '
360    CLOSE #1
370  '
999    END
```

```
RUN
Enter file name? employee
Enter sex type for report (m/f)? m

     AVERAGE SALARY REPORT
     ----------------------------------------
     Name            Salary      Sex
     ----------------------------------------
     Bomberg   Bo B.    15800      m
     Drury     David D. 18000      m
     ----------------------------------------
     Average salary ..... 16900
```

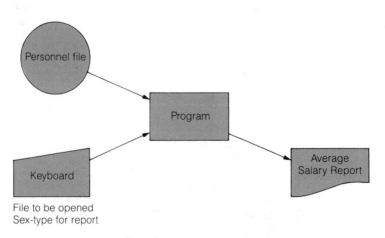

File to be opened
Sex-type for report

Figure E.5   System flowchart: Processing of sequential personnel file

E.4 POINTERS

Design and Style

1. **Record layout.** Don't forget to specify the record layout when you analyze the problem and to include this as part of the program's documentation.

2. **Backup files.** The greatest worry in computer installations is the complete loss of a database. The loss of a database through fire, theft, sabotage, or some other disaster is more damaging than the loss of the hardware system. Hardware is easily replaced, but a database is not easily reconstructed. An integral part of database protection is the backup (duplication) of all existing files. In large organizations, this is not a trivial task. For example, the TWA airline reservation system has 144 magnetic disk spindles for its more than one million customer records. Half of these are a backup of the other half. Moreover, on a daily basis, these files are dumped to magnetic tape and stored offsite.[1] For your purposes, it's best either to back up files using your system's copy or save command or to build backup file procedures in programs that manage files (as in Exercise 11) and to ensure that you have both backup *data* files and backup *program* files. If you have yet to lose any files, you may not be as nervous as those of us who have been around computers for a while.

Common Errors

1. **Mis-opening files.** Make sure that the OPEN statement precedes I/O statements, that file numbers are unique if more than one file is to be open at once, and that you don't inadvertently open an existing file for output (unless you like to see the destruction of file contents).

2. **Record mishaps.** Make sure that sequential I/O statements (PRINT # and INPUT #) reflect the record layout with respect to the type (numeric or string) and ordering of variables. In creating sequential files, take care that each field value is properly delimited from the next by blanks or a comma.

3. **Eof errors.** If we get an error message like "Input past end" or "Not enough data in record," then we have committed an eof error. These occur either when an INPUT # statement is executed that attempts to read beyond the last data item in a sequential file or when we attempt to input from a file that's been opened for output or append. This error is fatal to execution and is best avoided by the use of an eof function. If your system lacks this function, then use one of the other procedures described in Table E.6.

FOLLOW-UP EXERCISES

1. Try running the two programs in Table E.1 on your system.

2. Change the two programs in Table E.1 as follows:
   a. Use the file name mgs207.
   b. Use file #3. Do you think we could use #1 in the first program and #3 in the second program?
   c. Store the two additional scores 65 and 95.

3. Briefly describe the possible makeup of a student grade file for a large (say, 500 students) academic course. What kind of storage medium might be used? Suppose this file is to be used by a menu-driven interactive query program to answer questions such as "What are the current grades for Bob Meyer?" Which type of file would be best, sequential or rel-

[1] David Gifford and Alfred Spector, "The TWA Reservation System," *Communications of the acm,* July 1984, pp. 650–665.

ative? Suppose the application is a program that calculates and assigns final grades and prints a report at the end of each term. Which file type might be best?

4. Suppose we have to add the following record to the employee file:

   Clark G.W. 2 24000 m

   From the standpoint of processing efficiency, which file type do you think would be easier to update, sequential or relative? (Use Figure E.2 to help you.)

5. Go back to Example E.1.
   a. How would the file look if we were to use the following?

      45   PRINT #1, SCORE;

   b. Same as part **a**, except use (if available on your system)

      45   WRITE #1, SCORE

   c. Would the second program have to change to read the revised file?

*6. Consider the following program:

```
10 OPEN "SALES.DAT" FOR OUTPUT AS #1
20 READ N
30 PRINT #1, N
40 FOR J = 1 TO N
50    READ R$,S
60    PRINT #1, R$;S
70 NEXT J
80 CLOSE #1
90    DATA 2
91    DATA "East",5000
92    DATA "West",4000
99 END
```

   a. Write the exact appearance of each record in the file.
   b. Same as part **a** except use

      60 PRINT #1, R$;",";S

   c. Same as part **a** except use

      60 PRINT #1, S;R$

   d. Same as part **a** except use (if available on your system)

      60 WRITE #1, R$,S

   e. Run each of these variations on your system and display the files.

*7. Consider the files created in the preceding exercise. For each part, write a program that displays the following report:

   Number of regions = 2

Region	Sales
East	5000
West	4000

*8. Rewrite the programs in Example E.1 as follows:
   a. Use an eof loop within the create program, but don't place an eof record within the external file.
   b. Use an EOF function within the display program (if available on your system).
   c. Use an ON ERROR statement approach within the display program.
   d. Use an eof loop (eof/sentinel approach) within the display program. How would we have to change the program in part **a**?

9. Make any necessary changes to the program in Example E.2 and implement it on your system.

*10. In Example E.2:
   a. Modify the program to display all records from the file after the file has been created.
   b. Implement the revised program on your system.

*11. **Backup files.** In Example E.2:
   a. Modify the program to create a backup copy of the personnel file. Use the file name employee.bak and the following pseudocode.

      While not eof on file 1
        Input record from file 1
        Write record to file 2
      End while

   b. Implement this version on your system.

12. Implement Example E.3 on your system, after making any necessary changes.

*13. Modify Example E.3 to:
   a. Print the average salary only.
   b. Print the average salary for males and females, with a count of the number of employees in each category.
   c. Implement this version on your system.

ADDITIONAL EXERCISES

14. Revisits. Rework one of the following problems.

  a. Select a program that you have already written and revise it to give the option of output to the screen, line printer (if available), or a file. Make sure you output to the file. Then display this file as a report through another program.

  b. Payroll. (Exercise 20, Chapter 4.) Use a sequential file for the payroll file.

  c. Alumni File. (Exercise 21, Chapter 4.) Use a sequential file for the alumni file.

  d. Student Grades. (Exercise 12, Chapter 5.) Use a sequential file for the student file.

  e. Personnel Benefits Budget. (Exercise 16, Chapter 5.) Use a sequential file for the employee file.

  f. Property Tax Assessment. (Exercise 13, Chapter 5.) Use a sequential file to store the property owner's data.

  g. Population. (Exercise 11, Chapter 6.) Use a sequential file to store the county population data. Also see the suggestion in part **a** above. Apply this to the population change report.

  h. Exam Reports. (Exercise 12, Chapter 6.) Use a sequential file to store the student records. Add a menu item that displays the grades for a particular student.

  i. Depreciation. (Exercise 14, Chapter 6.) Use a sequential file for the asset file.

  j. Electric Bill. (Exercise 15, Chapter 6.) Use a sequential file for the customer file.

  k. Crime Data Summary. (Exercise 24, Chapter 7.) Use a sequential file to store the arrest data. Also see part **a** above.

  l. SAT Scores. (Exercise 25, Chapter 7.) Use a sequential file to store the student file. Also see part **a** above.

  m. Stock Portfolio Valuation. (Exercise 27, Chapter 7.) Use a sequential file to store the stock portfolio.

  n. State Taxes. (Exercise 28, Chapter 7.) Use a sequential file to store the tax-dollars-collected data.

15. Bond Issue. Write a program that offers the following menu:

  C   Create file
  D   Display file
  S   Stop processing

  a. Create a sequential file called BOND with the following records:

County	Yes votes	No votes
Dade	300,000	400,000
Cuyahoga	100,000	75,000
Washington	50,000	30,000

  b. Include a menu option, append to file (A), and add the following records to the file:

Orange	250,000	100,000
Broward	150,000	75,000

  c. Display the revised file.

  d. Include a menu option to print a report. You decide what might be nice to include in this report.

16. Payroll. Each week a small firm processes its weekly payroll for hourly employees. The following file is used to process the payroll.

Employee File Record Description
Employee ID
Name
Hourly rate of pay
Number of dependents
Number of hours worked

  a. Write a program that creates the employee file and then lists the contents of the file.

  b. Develop a program that generates a "wage summary report" consisting of a line for each employee: the line contains employee name, employee number, hourly rate, hours worked, gross pay, FICA, income tax, group health, and net pay. After individual figures are printed, the program is to print totals for gross pay, each deduction, and net pay. Include appropriate report and column headings.

    To determine the pay for each employee, the following facts must be included in your program:

  1. Gross pay is defined as pay for regular time plus pay for overtime. Overtime pay is 1.5 times the regular rate for each hour above 40.

  2. Social Security tax (FICA) is 6.65% of gross pay.

  3. Deduction for withholding tax and group health plan are tied to the number of dependents as follows.

Dependents	Income Tax (% of gross pay)	Group Health ($ per week)
1	22	2.50
2	20	3.60
3	18	5.10
4	16	6.00
5 or more	13	6.50

4. Net pay is defined as gross pay less FICA deduction less income tax deduction less group health deduction. Use the data below to test your program.

Payroll File

1	Bella Bitta, Al	2.50	4	60
2	Budget, Frank	8.25	5	40
61	Manicotti, Diane	6.00	1	45
92	Saintvi, Arun	8.00	3	35

c. Design a routine that edits the data for errors. Specifically it ensures that the

1. Number of dependents is greater than zero and less than 15.
2. Rate of pay is greater than $3.30 and less than $10.00.
3. Number of hours worked is greater than zero and less than 65.

If an error is detected, print an appropriate error message that includes the employee's name and number, bypass the calculations and printout for this employee, and go on to the next employee. Add new data to test each of these three possible input errors.

Answers to Selected Follow-up Exercises

Chapter 1

1–7. Don't get lazy. Look up the answers in the chapter.

8. You're in trouble if you need to look this one up!

Chapter 2

1. **(a)** Incorrect. No commas permitted. **(b)** Normally the plus sign is not printed with a positive number. **(c)** Incorrect. Minus sign is misplaced. **(d)** Correct. **(e)** Incorrect. Asterisk doesn't belong. This describes multiplication of 5 and 7. **(f)** Incorrect. Exponent is too large. **(g)** Incorrect. Exponent should be an integer. **(h)** Incorrect. Quote after T is missing. **(i)** Incorrect. $ is not allowed. **(j)** Incorrect. Number is too large in this format. Use 6.57890E10.

2. **(a)** $-6.142E15$ **(b)** $7E-5$

3. **(a)** 123000000000 **(b)** 0.0456

4. **(a)** Incorrect. First character must be a letter. **(b)** Numeric. **(c)** Incorrect. No space permitted. **(d)** Correct string on some systems. **(e)** Correct string on some systems. **(f)** Correct numeric on most systems. **(g)** Incorrect. First character must be a letter. **(h)** Incorrect. First character must be a letter.

5. **(a)** I'm not sure   I love BASIC
   (b) I love BASIC   I love BASIC

6. **(a)** 5000   5000   2500
   (b) 5000   5000   10000
   (c) 5000   5000   2.5E+07

7. A=7.4 B=9 C=6 D=81

8. C=85.77779

9. P=20 R=.002

10. **(a)** 116 **(b)** 28 **(c)** 8.5 **(d)** 10.5

11. **(a)** X^(I+1) **(b)** S^2/(P−1) **(c)** (Y−3^(X−1) + 2)^5

12. **(a)** Only one variable to left of equal symbol. Use 5 LET A = B + C. **(b)** Two arithmetic operation symbols cannot be together. **(c)** Variable must appear on left side of equal symbol. Use 15 LET A = 5. **(d)** Many systems allow omission of LET, but it's not stylistically recommended.

13. Unique to each system.

14. Unique to each system.

16. The input prompt (?) would appear on a separate line if we were to omit the trailing semicolon.

17. **(a)** INPUT "Enter name, SS number and age (separated by commas)"; N$,S,A
(b) INPUT "Do you wish to print output (Y/N)"; R$

19. **(a)** Syntax error, extra comma. **(b)** No effect on the IBM PC. **(c)** Execution error in line 30—data type mismatch when numeric variable ZIP is matched with data item "Miami,   ". Some systems, like the IBM PC, indicate a syntax error in line 60. **(d)** Kingston, RI 2881—make zip code a string variable to avoid missing leading zeros. **(e)** Execution error: Out of data in line 30.

20. **(a)** July 21 **(b)** July 21, 2001

21. A = 100   B = 150   C = 100   D = 150

Chapter 3

1.

(a)	(b)	(c)	(d)
1	9		6
2			4
3	8 iterations	0 iterations	2
4			0
5			
6			4 iterations
7			
8			

8 iterations

(e)	(f)	(g)
2	5.1	10
5	5.2	12.5
8	5.3	15
	5.4	17.5
3 iterations	5.5	
	5	4 iterations

5 iterations

2. Change line 900 to

900 DATA 15

Add 12 additional data lines following line 903.

3. A dashed line would precede the output line for each college.

4. **(a)** No change. **(b)** Yes. SUM does not include last college (SUM = 3250000).
(c) Not likely, but it's best to initialize summers for reasons of style and safety.
(d) The label Total and a running sum are printed after each college's line.

7. **(a)**

1	5
2	10
3	15
4	15

8. **(a)** The sums and averages for all students but the first are incorrectly calculated.

```
Name               Average
----------------------
Smith              90
Jones              160
Ellie              235
Budzirk            317
----------------------
```

(b) The output is unchanged, but the extra (and meaningless) calculations of AVE are inefficient.

9. (a) 16 iterations   (b) 12 iterations

1	1	1	1
1	2	1	1.5
1	3	1	2
1	4	2	1
2	1	2	1.5
2	2	2	2
2	3	3	1
2	4	3	1.5
3	1	3	2
3	2	4	1
3	3	4	1.5
3	4	4	2
4	1		
4	2		
4	3		
4	4		

10. Specific to system.

Chapter 4

1. (a) T (b) T (c) F (d) F (e) T (f) Invalid

2. (a) SALES > 10000 (b) LNAME$ = "Smith" (c) LNAME$ <> "Smith"
   (d) B^2 > 4*A*C

3. (a) 123 (b) O.K.
   BY ME

4. (a)
```
10   READ N
15   FOR J = 1 TO N
20     READ S
25     IF E > 32400 THEN 40
30       LET F = S * .067
35       GO TO 45
40       LET F = 0
45     PRINT F
50   NEXT J
90   DATA . . .
     .
     .
     .
99   END
```

(b) As in part **a** except:
```
25   LET F = 0
30   IF E < = 32400 THEN LET F = S * .067
(Delete lines 35 – 40)
```

(c) As in part **b** except:
```
(Delete line 25)
30   IF E > 32400 THEN LET F = 0 ELSE LET F = S * .067
```

(d) As in part **a** except:
```
25   IF E > 32400 THEN
30     LET F = 0
35   ELSE
40     LET F = S * .067
42   END IF
```

The approaches in parts **c** and **d** are preferable since they visually reproduce the if-then-else control structure, and unlike the approach in part **a** they avoid explicit line number transfers.

5. (a) IF SALES > 10000 THEN LET PAY = PAY + 150
    (b) IF CREDITS >= 12 THEN LET TUITION = 1200 ELSE LET TUITION = CREDITS*100
    (c) IF PART.NAME$ = "WRENCH" THEN PRINT QUANTITY
    (d) 20   IF FIXED + VARIABLE < SALES THEN
         30   LET PROFIT = SALES − (FIXED + VARIABLE)
         40   PRINT "Profit ="; PROFIT
         50   ELSE
         60   LET LOSS = (FIXED + VARIABLE) − SALES
         70   PRINT "Loss ="; LOSS
         80   END IF
    (e) IF M=N THEN LET I = I + 3 : LET J = J + 2 : LET K = K + 1

8. (a) No (b) Yes (c) No

9. (a) IF GRADE > 0 AND GRADE < 100 THEN PRINT GRADE ELSE PRINT "Grade
                                                                out of range"
    (b) IF NOT (GENDER$ = "F" OR GENDER$ = "M") THEN PRINT "Error
                                                                in gender data"

10. 240   LET BONUS1   = 150
                  TRAVEL.CUT1 = 300
     285   LET TRAVEL.CUT2 = 600
     370   IF SALES > SALES.CUT AND TRAVEL <   TRAVEL.CUT1 THEN
                  LET BONUS = BONUS1
     380   IF SALES > SALES.CUT AND TRAVEL >= TRAVEL.CUT1
                                     AND TRAVEL <   TRAVEL.CUT2 THEN
                  LET BONUS = BONUS2
     390   IF SALES <= SALES.CUT THEN
                  LET BONUS = BONUS3
     395   IF TRAVEL >= TRAVEL.CUT2 THEN   Note: Color
                  LET BONUS = BONUS3   indicates changes

Alternatively, lines 390 and 395 can be combined:

     390   IF SALES <= SALES.CUT OR TRAVEL >= TRAVEL.CUT2 THEN
                  LET BONUS = BONUS3

(b) Unique to system.

11. IF SCORE >= 90   THEN LET GRADE$ = "A"
     IF SCORE >= 80   AND   SCORE < 90   THEN LET GRADE$ = "B"
     IF SCORE >= 70   AND   SCORE < 80   THEN LET GRADE$ = "C"
     IF SCORE >= 60   AND   SCORE < 70   THEN LET GRADE$ = "D"
     IF SCORE < 60   THEN LET GRADE$ = "F"

12. Unique to system.

13. Unique to system.

Chapter 5

1. Unique to system.

2. Unique to system.

3.

CCOST	PIRATE	Year	FCOST
90000	.10		
	10		90000
		1	99000
		2	108900
		3	119790
		4	131769
		5	144945
		6	159440
		7	175384
		8	192923

4. **(a)** Infinite loop. FCOST is zero and is always less than

MULTIPLE * CCOST.

(b) Infinite loop. FCOST is always 99000 and always less than

MULTIPLE * CCOST.

(c) Output values for YEAR would be one higher than they should be. Move line 430 to line 455.

(d) 20% (interactively forced to enter value between 1 and 100)

(e) Place the constant expression

(1 + PIRATE/100)

in the initialization section as follows:

405   LET FACTOR = (1 + PIRATE/100)

Modify line 440 as follows:

440   LET FCOST = FCOST * FACTOR

(f) Chance of these two expressions being equal is very unlikely. Thus, an infinite loop would occur.

8. Unique to system.

9. **(a)** The sentinel eof and an age of zero get printed following Crammer's output line.

10. **(a)** Same results.

(b) The last line in the table gets printed

.

.

.

Crammer 40

and then we get the error message

Out of data in 60

(c) A fourth line gets printed

end   0

and then the error message

Out of data in 60

(d) Replace "eof" with "end" in line 40.

Chapter 6

1. Line executed   Action

.   .
.   .
.   .

290   Read in B for LABEL$ and 15 for LENGTH
300   Call subroutine
420   Print label B
430   Set FOR/NEXT parameters
440   ⌐
450   │
440   │ Print 15 = signs
450   │
.   │
.   │
.   ⌐
460   Print length 15
470   Return
310   Next bar

2. Yes and no. The only problem would be large frequencies that wrap the bars around the screen or paper. For example, 300 Cs in a large class would give a bar that wraps around to a fourth line in an 80-column display. The program could be modified to scale down all frequencies whenever any one frequency exceeds the maximum screen display.

(a) 905 DATA "Age Distribution of Employees"
910 DATA 6
911 DATA "Under 20",5
912 DATA "20 – 29",30
913 DATA "30 – 39",50
914 DATA "40 – 49",70
915 DATA "50 – 59",40
916 DATA "Over 59",10

3. The message "Break in 330" is printed. *Alternative 1:* Use GOTO 999 at line 330 instead of STOP. Our preference is to avoid GOTOs. *Alternative 2:* Use END instead of STOP at line 330. This is fine if the system allows it, since no break message is printed. Try it on your system.

4. (a) No problem for the first menu choice. Thereafter, however, any menu choice other than 4 yields an "end of data" error message, since the pointer is at the end of the internal data file.

(b) Insert the following line in the menu module:

308   CLS

Unfortunately, the screen is faster than the eye here. A report gets printed and the screen is cleared (almost) immediately as the menu module is called. In short, we don't get to read the reports. The best solution is to pause output to the screen immediately after each report is printed. In Microsoft BASIC on the IBM PC we would insert a GOSUB 700 just before the RETURN statement in modules 3–5. The following subroutine freezes the screen until the user strikes a key:

```
700 '                   Module 6:   Subroutine Pause
705 '
710         PRINT
715         PRINT "Strike any key to continue ..."
720 '
725         WHILE INKEY$ = ""
730 '          This keeps looping while no key is pressed
735         WEND
740 '
745         RETURN
```

Alternatively, we can momentarily pause on any system by using the following FOR/NEXT loop:

```
FOR J = 1 TO 10000
NEXT J
```

where the value of the limit parameter (10000 above) determines the length of the pause.

Find out what you can do on your system and try it.

(c) Specific to system.

Chapter 7

1. (a) Invalid (b) Valid (c) Invalid (d) Valid

2. (a) Variable number of locations reserved for X in line 20; the DIM statement must precede the READ statement. (b) A has not been dimensioned; the subscript in line 50 ($M - 2*N$) has a value of -11, which is not permitted; the subscript 0 in line 30 may not be permitted on some systems.

3. (a) Change lines 130 and 900 to

    130 DIM DEPOSITS(100)
    900 DATA 100

In version B we would need 97 more READs, 97 more LETs, and 97 more PRINTs. The expression in line 170 would contain 100 variables. Brutal, huh?

4.
    110 READ N
    120 FOR J = 1 TO N
    130   INPUT B(J)
    140 NEXT J
    900 DATA   50

6. FOR J = 1 TO 100
        ARRAY(J) = 50
    NEXT J

7. (a) Yes. The original approach is preferable because it is easier to locate and modify departmental data. This is because each data line corresponds to a specific department. For example, the 3rd department's data is found in line 903.

(b)

Line	Action/Result
210	3 stored in DEPT
230	False
250	PROFIT = SALES(3) − COSTS(3)
	$\quad = \quad 175 \quad - \quad 140$
	$\quad = 35$
270−290	Report printed
210	5 stored in DEPT
230	True; error message is printed and processing stops.

8.
```
RUN
Name       :? Rip Van Winkle
Age        :? 99
Uninsurable-- over 65


Another quotation (y/n)? Y


Name       :? Rip Van Winkle
Age        :? 55
Premium is:$ 327


Another quotation (y/n)? Y


Name       :? Rip Van Winkle
Age        :? 63
Premium is:$ 357


Another quotation (y/n)? Y


Name       :? Rip Van Winkle
Age        :? 20
Premium is:$ 277


Another quotation (y/n)? n


See you tomorrow at 8 sharp!
```

9. Change line 900, move line 906 to 907 and add new line 906:

```
900   DATA 7
906   DATA 75,500
```

The use of ROWS has two advantages, both relating to less program maintenance whenever the number of rows in the table changes: we need not change the upper limit in the FOR statement (line 520); we don't tie the uninsurable message (line 810) to a constant such as "Uninsurable—over 65," as this constant can change in the data section.

10. This logic works as long as age is 65 or under. For an age above 65 a premium of zero, or PREMIUM(6), is output instead of an error message. This error problem can be corrected by an if-then-else structure at line 810 that checks for a J-value of 6. In fact, this approach to the table look-up problem is the traditional approach. We don't recommend it because it's unstructured (the loop has two exit points at lines 720 and 730), and the GOTO statement increases the likelihood of error.

12. X is dimensioned to 5 elements in line 10. When J is 6 in line 30, a "subscript out of bounds" error would occur.

15. (a)
```
DIM DAY$(7)
   FOR J = 1 TO 7
      READ DAY$(J)
   NEXT J
   DATA Monday, Tuesday, Wednesday, Thursday
   DATA Friday, Saturday, Sunday
```

(b)
```
INPUT "Enter jth day of week"; J
   PRINT DAY$(J)
```

16. (a)

1000	800	500	1200	500	2000	2000	500	1500	300	700	1500

(b)

1000	500	1500
800	2000	300
500	2000	700
1200	500	1500

(c) As in the original version. The arrangement of data in the original version is preferable because it's visually consistent with the data table or array.

17. Add TOTAL(4) to the DIM statement in line 130 and insert between lines 270 and 280:

```
271   FOR COL = 1 TO QUARTERS
272      LET TOTAL(COL) = 0
273      FOR ROW = 1 TO BANKS
274         LET TOTAL(COL) = TOTAL(COL) + DEPOSITS(ROW,COL)
275      NEXT ROW
276   NEXT COL
```

After line 340 insert:

```
341   FOR COL = 1 TO QUARTERS
342      PRINT TOTAL(COL);
343   NEXT COL
```

19.
```
FOR  I = 1 TO 100
   FOR J = 1 TO 50
      LET WEIGHT(I,J) = 100
   NEXT J
NEXT I
```

22. Specific to system.

Module A

1. Specific to system.
2. **(a)** $875,000
   (b) $743,750
   (c) Get in the habit now!
3. What are you doing looking here?!

Module B

1. Specific to system.
2. Specific to system.

Module C

1. **(a)** 6.70925E-04   **(f)**   3
   (b) 16.0944   3
   (c) 80   3
   (d) 3.3   −3
       2   **(g)** −1
   (e) 3   1
        3   0
        3
       −4

4. **(a)** SeeJanerun **(b)** See Jane run **(c)** Jane See **(d)** runrunrun

5. **(a)** 33
   ```
   START = INT((LINE.LENGTH − HEAD.LENGTH)/2)
         = INT((    80    −    14    )/2)
         = INT( 33 )
         = 33
   ```
   (b) 115 LET DASH$ = "------- ------"
   155 PRINT TAB(START); DASH$

6. **(a)** Yep.
   (b) Line 120 would test false, the "End of run" message would be printed, and processing would end.

7. **(a)** 160 LET MONTH$ = LEFT$(SALES.DATE$,2)
   165 PRINT "Month of sale:"; MONTH$
   (b) 120 LET YEAR$ = "19" + RIGHT$(SALES.DATE$,2)
   or
   125 LET YEAR$ = "19" + YEAR$
   or
   130 PRINT "Year of sale: 19" + YEAR$

Module D

1. **(a)** 4645.8
   (b) 4,645.82
   (c)   3.20
   (d) $3.20
   (e) %4646
   (f) 3   4646
   (g)   3   4646

2. **(a)** PRINT USING "   ###"; B
   (b) PRINT USING "B= ###"; B
   (c) PRINT USING "### ##.##"; B,C

```
3.    1  PRINT "12345678"
     10  LET X = 3.283
     20  PRINT USING "        #";X
     30  PRINT USING "        #.";X
     40  PRINT USING "        #.#";X
     50  PRINT USING "    #.###";X
     60  PRINT USING " #.#####";X
     99  END


     run
     12345678
            3
            3
          3.3
        3.283
        3.28300
```

```
4.   10  LET FM1$ = "      \      \"
     20  LET FM2$ = "      \   \"
     30  LET FM3$ = "      \\"
     40  LET A$ = "GOOFUS"
     50  PRINT USING FM1$; A$
     60  PRINT USING FM2$; A$
     70  PRINT USING FM3$; A$
     99  END


     RUN
         GOOFUS
         GOOF
         GO
```

7. Specific to system.

8. (a)
```
170  LET FMT6$ = "                              \           \"

325  PRINT USING FMT6$;  "========"
```

   (b)
```
150  LET FMT4$ ="\          \          ##.##   $$##.##    $$###.##"
```

   (c)
```
150  LET FMT4$ ="\          \    ##.##    ##.##     ###.##"
```

9. Specific to system.

Module E

1. Unique to system.

2. **(a)** In line 10 of each program, replace "grades" with "mgs207." **(b)** Replace #1 with #3 in all OPEN, CLOSE, PRINT, and INPUT statements. Yes, the file names must be the same for both programs, but the file numbers need not be the same for different programs. Within the same program, however, there must be consistency in the file number. **(c)** In the first program, change the 5 to a 7 in line 90, and add 65 and 95 to the data list in line 95.

3. Possible record layout:

Field	Type	Bytes
Student ID	String	11
Student name	String	30
Course number	String	6
Section	Numeric	2
Date enrolled	String	8
Grade	String	1

The likely storage medium is hard magnetic disk.

A relative file is best for query programs, since the few records required can be accessed directly.

A sequential file is best when a high percentage of records in the file are processed, as in an end-of-term grade report.

4. The relative file is more efficiently updated than the sequential file. The new record is simply placed in an available (empty) record space. If the file were sequential, then the entire file would have to be processed to append a record. If the record had to be inserted alphabetically by name, then the sequential file approach requires the creation of a new file that places Clark's record between Bomberg's and Drury's.

5. **(a)**   `5 <cr>`
      `90  75  85  95  70 <cr><eof mark>`

   (b)   `5<cr>`
      `90<cr>`
      `75<cr>`
      `85<cr>`
      `95<cr>`
      `70<cr><eof mark>`

   (c)   No.

9. Specific to system.

12. Specific to system.

Index

T A B L E B BASIC Built-in Functions Used in This Book[a]

Function Name	Dialects[b]	Your System[c]	Pages
ABS	1 2 3 4		154
DATE$	2 3 4		155
EOF	4		184
ERR	3 4		185
EXP	1 2 3 4		154
FIX	3 4		154
INSTR	3 4		155
INT	1 2 3 4		154, 156
IP	2		154
LEFT$	3 4		155, 158
LEN	2 3 4		155, 157
LOG	1 2 3 4		154
MID$	3 4		155, 158
POS	2		155
RIGHT$	3 4		155, 158
RND	1 2 3 4		154, 156
SGN	1 2 3 4		154
SQR	1 2 3 4		154
TAB	2 3 4		26
TIME$	2 3 4		154

(Use this space to add additional functions of interest for your system)

[a]Function names may not be used as variable names.

[b]1 = Minimal BASIC
2 = ANS BASIC or True BASIC
3 = VAX-11 BASIC
4 = Microsoft BASIC on the IBM PC

[c]Try to get a listing of the function names that apply to your system. Then place a check in this column for each name that's the same on your system.